THE STORY OF
CHESS RECORDS

JOHN COLLIS

BLOOMSBURY

THE STORY OF
CHESS RECORDS

JOHN COLLIS

Published by Bloomsbury Publishing, New York and London
Distributed in the book trade by St Martin's Press

Picture sources
Marshall Chess: pages 1, 8, 11, 45
Decca Records, supplied by A. Lauder: pages 64, 65, 82, 83
Hulton Deutsch: page 16
Rae Fleurlage: pages 23, 176, 187
Jazz Index: pages 169, 171, 173, 185
M.C.A. supplied by A. Lauder: pages 56, 123, 132, 135, 151,
152, 154, 162, 170, 174
Michael Ochs Archives: pages 166, 172, 179, 180
Pictorial: pages 36, 51, 69, 72, 85, 88, 89, 104, 107, 111,
119, 124, 125, 127, 131, 136 *left*, 137, 138, 140, 141, 143,
144, 145, 162, 164, 165 *top*
Sylvia Pitcher: pages 3, 12, 13, 14, 15, 19, 28, 33, 34,
36 *bottom right*, 42, 74, 80, 86, 87, 93, 94, 97, 100, 102,
103, 105, 147, 151 *top*, 159, 160, 161
Redferns: pages 20, 63, 90, 113, 128, 129, 163, 165 *bottom*
Val Wilmer: pages 39, 70, 98, 101

Every reasonable effort has been made to ascertain and
acknowledge the ownership of copyrighted photographs
and illustrations included in this volume. Any errors that
have inadvertently occurred will be corrected in subsequent
editions provided notification is sent to the publisher.

A CIP catalogue record for this book
is available from the Library of Congress

ISBN 1-58234-005-6

First U.S. Edition
10 9 8 7 6 5 4 3 2 1

Designed by Bradbury and Williams
Graphic Reproduction by Radstock Reproductions Ltd, Bath
Printed in Italy by Artegrafica S.p.A., Verona

FOREWORD
BY BUDDY GUY
PAGE 7

INTRODUCTION
PAGE 9

CHAPTER 1
OPENING
GAMBITS
PAGE 10

CHAPTER 2
BROADENING
THE ATTACK
PAGE 36

CHAPTER 3
IN COMMAND OF THE
GAME
PAGE 68

CHAPTER 4
THE TWO KINGS
PAGE 110

CHAPTER 5
ACROSS THE
BOARD
PAGE 146

CHAPTER 6
TOWARDS THE
ENDGAME
PAGE 168

POSTSCRIPT BY
BUDDY GUY
PAGE 190

BIBLIOGRAPHY AND
ACKNOWLEDGEMENTS
PAGE 192

FOREWORD

The blues is at the heart of popular music, and Chess Records was at the very heart of the blues. Although I recorded for the label I can be objective about this, since Chess turned me down first time around, I saw very little money from my records, and Leonard Chess thought I played too loud!

But any label that can bring together Muddy Waters, Jimmy Rogers, Little Walter, Howlin' Wolf, Sonny Boy Williamson, Bo Diddley, Chuck Berry, Willie Mabon, Eddie Boyd, Etta James – the list goes on and on – has got to be one of the most significant in the whole record business, not just in the blues field.

It is a remarkable story.

Buddy Guy
1998

Another day at the office
Behind Leonard Chess, from left to right, are shipping clerk Peaches, Esmond Edwards, Marshall and Phil Chess, Max Cooperstein and Dick LaPalm, circa 1964.

INTRODUCTION

The brief for this book was to celebrate the music of Chess Records, undoubtedly one of the very few record companies without which the history of popular music would have taken a significantly different course. It is not, therefore, primarily a music-business story of scams and scandals, though this element is present throughout. Leonard Chess, the company's driving force, was clearly too complex to be characterized either as heroic blues patron or white entrepreneur ripping off black musicians, and so a variety of views for prosecution and defence are aired. But the music is the real story.

I have been a Chess fan since the day in the late 1950s when a school friend sold me his import copy of Chuck Berry's 'Beautiful Delilah' for sixpence, because he didn't much care for it. What an extraordinary chap! Ever since then my floorboards have groaned more and more under the weight of Chess, from early Muddy Waters to late Dells.

In Britain, the leasing deal between Chess and Pye Records was surely the single most significant element in the 'blues revival' of the 1960s – on Pye's budget label Marble Arch just 14s 6d would secure an album's worth of prime Chicago blues.

If the emphasis of the book is on blues and r&b rather than, say, Chess's successful diversions into jazz, gospel or 1960s soul – though all these avenues are of course explored – this is partly personal enthusiasm, but more because it is here, between Muddy Waters in the late 1940s and Chuck and Bo a decade later, that the label's unique contribution to postwar music lay. From the Mississippi Delta to Chicago, from the blues to rock 'n' roll, from 'Can't Be Satisfied' to 'Sweet Little Rock 'n' Roller', this is the heart of the Chess story.

CHAPTER 1

OPENING GAMBITS

I CAN'T BE SATISFIED

In April 1948, five years after making the trip from the Mississippi Delta to Chicago, Muddy Waters went into the recording studio for the second time in a month. Indeed some discographies suggest that both sessions took place on the same day. But whereas the previous cuts had involved pianist Sunnyland Slim, alto saxophonist Alex Atkins and bassist Big Crawford, producing high-quality but unsurprising Chicago blues, Muddy returned with Crawford alone. The results, 'I Can't Be Satisfied' and 'I Feel Like Going Home', brought the Delta passion of Robert Johnson and Son House to postwar Chicago, and changed the course of the blues.

The interplay between Waters's whining, rattling, amplified bottleneck guitar and Crawford's stand-up slap bass was electrifying, an urgent, syncopated duel fought out beneath the rich Mississippi drawl of Waters's voice. The record established him as the new star of Chicago blues, and gave the year-old record label Aristocrat its first hit, selling some 60,000 copies. When in 1950 the Polish immigrant brothers Leonard and Phil Chess became sole owners of the label and changed its name to Chess Records, Waters was still on hand to provide another success, 'Rollin' Stone'.

'What the hell's he singing?' a mystified Leonard Chess had allegedly wanted to know when Muddy Waters first abandoned the formalities of citified blues and gave vent to the vengeful 'I Can't Be Satisfied'. However, by now, as the success of his label grew, Chess was getting used to it, and the indelible link between the Delta, the breeding ground of southern blues, and Chicago, its northern branch office, was confirmed once more.

The Chess story came about because Chicago was the chosen destination for two distinct migrations, of rural blacks from the South and of European Jews. Muddy Waters took the train from the Delta, while the Chess brothers, their surname Westernized from Chez, joined the transatlantic influx from Eastern Europe, in their case the region known as White Russia. Chicago had long been such a refuge – successive censuses in 1890 and 1900 showed that more than three-quarters of the city's population were either foreign-born or their first-generation

Family business
Leonard, Marshall and
Phil Chess, circa 1965.

**Muddy Waters grew up in
a wooden shack near
Clarksdale, Mississippi.**

Chicagoan offspring. The meeting between the
Polish entrepreneurs and the young bluesman
from Rolling Fork, Mississippi, prompted an
unparalleled flowering of Chicago blues that
lasted into the 1960s.

RAMBLIN ON MY MIND

The blues is a wandering music, always moving
on in search of a night-time paying crowd, and
usually a necessary reward for daytime sweat. As
the 20th century progressed, this non-musical
labour became less and less southern and
agricultural, more and more northern and
industrial. Blues musicians most typically
travelled by rail, and the vehicle for the most
significant of all the blues migrations, from the
Mississippi Delta to Chicago, was the Illinois
Central Railroad, running a thousand miles
almost due north from New Orleans to Chicago's
Illinois Central Station.

It was hardly the 'Sweet Home Chicago' that
the greatest of the pre-war Delta singers, Robert
Johnson fantasized about in a song that has
become a blues anthem. 'Sweet ghetto' maybe,
sung with irony, because though the more

liberated North denied that racial segregation existed in matters of public housing, of course it did. And anyway, when you made that decisive move from some no-future dusty Delta settlement, as a free man working like a slave, you would naturally seek out your own kind, and preferably your own kin.

In the 15 years from 1935 America built 11 million homes for public housing projects, under guidelines laid down in the manual of the Federal Housing Administration. 'If a neighborhood is to retain stability,' this stated, 'it is necessary that properties shall continue to be occupied by the same social and racial classes.' This ingrained belief was strong enough to withstand testing by law, and was often – as in Chicago – in direct contradiction of officially stated policy. So the migrants were inevitably heading for the ghetto, deprived of the degree of public funding awarded to white neighbourhoods.

The drift from the rural South to the industrial North, particularly to Chicago, began

Another dusty day down south: a street in Bentonia, deep in the Mississippi Delta.

Detached dwellings:
poverty in Yazoo City, on
the river that marks the
western boundary of the
Delta.

loans at interest to buy seed and food, purchasing a share of the harvest at a rate that never allowed the farmer to prosper, to build for an independent future. Faced with such servitude, no wonder so many blacks had rambling on their mind.

This alarming dispersal of ready labour left white landowners with two options. One was to offer humane conditions, a sense of partnership, generous rewards for hard and productive work. Not surprisingly, this remedy appealed only to a minority.

Others exploited laws governing such matters as vagrancy and labour contracts, and lobbied for legislation forbidding the enticement of workers with promises of better conditions. And if blacks broke such laws, they could be forced to work for the local authority, which once again curtailed movement.

By 1900 there were some nine million blacks in the USA, and almost 90 per cent were still in the South – but this is already evidence of a growing diaspora, since with few exceptions they all started there. Of that huge southern majority 80 per cent lived outside the cities and large towns with citified ambitions, in settlements and villages. In 1920 the proportion of blacks remaining in the South had diminished, but only slightly. More significantly, a third of all American blacks were now urbanized. Move on another two decades, just before the huge population shuffle caused by the USA's entry into the Second World War, and half the nation's blacks were now in the cities – though the proportion in the South had only been nibbled away by a few more percentage points. The flight to the North was striking, but the flight from the

soon after the Civil War of 1861–5 and the subsequent emancipation of the slaves. Emancipation into what? The war had ruined the economy of the defeated South and so everyone there suffered, most of all the blacks at the foot of the social and economic ladder. In any case there was a growing distaste for plantation life, with its still-fresh association with the indignity, toil, poverty and often brutality of slavery. Therefore the impulse to move was probably more a rejection of the immediate past than a confidence in the industrial future, which would have been an unknown quantity to most rural blacks.

Former Confederates, the oppressors, gradually resumed power in a 'free' nation, their racial opinions intact. Landlords imposed harsh conditions designed to ensure that sharecropping farmers were for ever in their debt, advancing land – as cotton-picking became mechanized – was even more so.

However, during the war years another half a million blacks moved to the North – and stayed there. By 1970 80 per cent of black Americans lived in cities, and more than half of them were now in the North. So in a hundred years most blacks had moved northwards and almost all, even those who remained in the South, had moved from country to city. In terms of numbers today, Chicago is second only to New York City as far as the size of the black population is concerned, an increase of over a million from the quarter of a million in 1940.

The flight to the cities, whether or not to the industrial North, had been prompted by a series of triggers. To those already mentioned could be added the growing sense of economic depression in the 1920s, which was felt by those at the bottom of the economic scale long before the period was officially baptized 'The Depression'. Add to poverty, racism and exploitation such devils as the boll weevil, soil erosion and increasing foreign competition in the staple products of the South, cotton, tobacco and sugar cane – a global shift that the average southern landlord, let alone his tenants, could have little control over – and the dirt farm, which had long ago lost its charm, was less and less viable.

As the Depression continued, statistics

Movin' on:
Greenville, on the Mississippi, is a short hop from the rail line to Chicago, the Illinois Central Railroad.

Sweet home Chicago?
transport links made the
Windy City an industrial
boom town, but for most
black immigrants it still
meant slums, poverty and
racism.

produced in 1934 suggested that 17 per cent of
whites and 38 per cent of blacks were incapable
of supporting themselves. A year later a survey
in Atlanta, Georgia, one of the nearby urban
escape routes from the rural South, found that 65
per cent of those blacks capable of earning a
living actually needed public assistance to
survive, and in Norfolk, Virginia, the figure was
80 per cent. Worse, starving black people found
that even religious and other charitable
institutions often extended their benevolence only
to starving whites, turning away blacks.

So the reasons for the flight from the land are
clear. But why did so many blacks choose
Chicago? The city's story could be said to have

begun in 1673, when the explorers Louis Joliet, a French-Canadian, and Jacques Marquette, a Frenchman, traced a Y-shaped river inland from what is now Lake Michigan and discovered that its arms almost reached the Mississippi – so that it was just a short canal's length away from a mighty watercourse running through the heart of the continent.

For a further century, however, the residents of the mud-flat land where Chicago now stands remained the local native Americans, supplemented by a floating population of trappers and traders. In the 1770s the first known foreign – and black – settler arrived, Jean Baptiste Point Sable, the son of a French trader who had settled in Haiti and married a local black woman. In 1795 the United States obtained a six-mile-square area around the mouth of the river – as with most dealings with the indigenous population, 'obtained' may well be a euphemism.

Illinois became part of the Union in 1818, and with the opening of the Erie Canal in 1825, the final link with the Atlantic seaboard, the now-growing town of Chicago became a significant terminus at the western extremity. The Illinois and Michigan Canal was completed in 1848, forging that further vital link to the Mississippi, all the way down to New Orleans.

By now it was so strategically placed in the heart of the growing nation that Chicago became the centre of the developing rail network as well. With water and rail transport in place, industry inevitably flourished. Chicago was a significant contributor of labour and manufactured equipment to the Union side in the Civil War. Ironically, in rural Illinois many people held strong secessionist sentiments and argued for a link with the Confederacy – perhaps precisely because of those umbilical ties by water and rail.

A catastrophic fire in 1871 left 90,000 homeless, but with water supplies, sewage system and railways largely unaffected, there was an unsought opportunity to build a new city fit for the industrial revolution.

The industries that developed as a result of Chicago's geographical advantages were obviously another powerful magnet to disaffected rural southerners. At the railheads were the huge stockyards supplying the meat-processing factories, and the processing of other foodstuffs grew in their wake. The steel mills spawned factories producing all kinds of metal products, among them furniture, machine tools and railroad components. There were petrol refineries in the area, and Chicago also developed as a centre for 'the print', with industries ranging from paper manufacturing to publishing. By 1900 the city was established as an economic and industrial hub of inland North America.

Mike Rowe, in his celebrated *Chicago Blues: the City and the Music*, identifies a couple of more esoteric reasons why Chicago would have seemed familiar and attractive to blacks in the South. It was the home of the crusading black newspaper the *Defender*, which was widely circulated in the South and at one time actively encouraged migration to Chicago, and also the base of the huge mail-order firms Sears, Roebuck and Montgomery Ward, the chief suppliers of consumer durables to isolated farm workers, paid for at a few cents a week.

And as far as blues players were concerned, Chicago's magnet grew ever more powerful. Big Bill Broonzy in the 1930s, Muddy Waters in the years immediately following the Second World War, the explosion of Chicago blues clubs, record labels and stars in the 1950s – these were convincing endorsements.

IT'S JUST THE BLUES

One certainty about enacting Prohibition law is that it will do nothing to satisfy the public's thirst. A situation is simply created whereby the state renounces its right to liquor taxes and hands the exploitation over to gangsters instead. It is surely no coincidence that the cities where jazz and blues flourished in the years after Prohibition came into effect – New Orleans and Kansas City, for example – were those where the local authorities were sometimes inclined to take a relaxed, even an entrepreneurial, attitude towards this problem. It was good for the tourist trade and for the local economy, and it kept everybody happy.

Nowhere was this more marked than in Chicago – Al Capone's Chicago. The house parties – often called 'rent parties' as there was an entrance fee allegedly to help towards the host's housing costs, though it also provided a supply of moonshine liquor – and the illicit clubs and dives that sprang up to supply a demand for strong drink and hot music, were a ready-made platform for the blues singers attracted to the city, and these clubs survived the repeal of Prohibition law.

Many of the biggest names in pre-Second World War blues made Chicago their home, following the migratory routes we have already charted. Others, notably the great partnership from the early years of the blues, pianist Leroy Carr and guitarist Scrapper Blackwell, were frequent and influential visitors. Perhaps the most important resident figure in the early years was Big Bill Broonzy, a 'king of the clubs' who only renounced his title with the success of Muddy Waters in the late 1940s. Broonzy's reaction to the electric group sound that developed in Waters's wake in the early 1950s

was to reinvent himself as a folk-blues entertainer playing to white audiences. He made pioneering trips to Europe, including London, beginning in 1951. He would regale his audiences with folk tales like 'John Henry', sing work songs from the distant past, and bring a jazzy tinge to such blues-based standards as 'Careless Love' and 'Glory of Love'.

This was a deliberate career decision, an assumption that this was the version of black music that his newly found white audience wanted (and, judging by the poor reception given to Muddy Waters and his heavily amplified blues when he first played in Britain in 1958, Broonzy was probably right). His skill and versatility, his engaging manner as an entertainer, and the shrewdness with which he exploited this market help to protect him from charges of an 'Uncle Tom' attitude towards black culture, though his material was a long way from the racy blues of pre-war Chicago. So there were now, in effect, two Broonzys, the pre-war Chicago star and the postwar coffee-house hero.

Broonzy was born in Scott, Mississippi in 1893. He was one of the 17 children of parents who had been born as slaves. He grew up across the border in Arkansas, worked as a farm-hand from childhood and learned to play the violin. In his late teens and early twenties Broonzy combined work as a dance fiddler with that of the itinerant preacher. After moving to Chicago in

Big Bill's blues: whether singing in 1930s juke joints or on the European stage in the 1950s, Broonzy was a giant of Chicago blues.

Sonny and share: the 'first' Sonny Boy Williamson gave generous inspiration to those who followed him to Chicago.

1920, he was influenced into taking up the guitar by local performer Papa Charlie Jackson, and from 1924 was himself working in the clubs.

He recorded extensively, both as featured artist and accompanist, from 1927 onwards, though in commercial terms his career had a number of false starts before he really broke through in the 1930s. His appeal was strongest among those who, like him and a gathering tide of rural blacks, were migrating to the North, and many of his songs examined this phenomenon and its problems and frustrations. He did in fact cut one session for Chess, in 1953, and a single of 'Little City Woman'/'Lonesome' was released, but by this time he had moved into the coffee houses while the label was still catering for the black audience. Broonzy died of throat cancer in 1958, back home in Chicago.

Second in significance, and even more important in developing the postwar sound that, as we shall see, Chess above all represented, was John Lee 'Sonny Boy' Williamson. He was the original Sonny Boy – despite the protestations of the other 'Sonny Boy', who was born Aleck (or Alec) Miller and was in fact an older man who shrewdly delayed his move to Chicago until John Lee was dead. Williamson was the first virtuoso of the blues harmonica, and was thus the musical father of Chess's Little Walter and a whole generation of harmonica stylists. His forceful singing and an impressive catalogue of songs added to his influence on such younger men as Junior Wells and Billy Boy Arnold.

Clearly the harmonica had always been a natural instrument for adoption by blues musicians – it is cheap, portable and comparatively straightforward when it comes to coaxing a rudimentary sound to accompany the lyric. But Williamson showed that it could be

more, a pocket brass section that could punctuate the words with a riff, fill out the chords, spiral off into an inventive solo and take a worthy place at the front of the bandstand. Playing a harmonica tuned to the key of the second chord in a blues progression placed the emphasis more on sucking than blowing, and this enabled him to bend and slur to great effect the 'blue' notes – the term used to describe the occurrence of a minor interval when a major interval seems imminent. This style soon became the standard blues technique for the instrument.

Williamson was born in Jackson, Tennessee, in 1914, worked down South with Sleepy John Estes from a very young age and moved to Chicago when he was 20. Like his friend Broonzy, he recorded both as front-liner and accompanist, and with such songs as 'Good Morning Little Schoolgirl' he began to lay down the catalogue of distinctively postwar Chicago blues, the immediate forerunners of the Chess sound. Williamson was a heavy and gregarious drinker, universally liked among the blues fraternity for his generosity of both wallet and spirit. Tragically, when he left the Plantation Club on 1 June 1948 he was mugged and brutally beaten, and died of his injuries. His body was carried back home to Jackson for burial.

One of the great blues veterans who made Chicago his base – though he also spent many years in St Louis – was Lonnie Johnson, born in New Orleans in 1889. He was one of the most sophisticated of the early blues guitar stylists, and indeed by no means limited himself to the blues. On the one hand he could be employed to give structure and a touch of class to the field hollers of Texas Alexander; on the other he would be playing jazz with Louis Armstrong, as on a 1927 date in Chicago. By this time he was already well travelled, his excursions including, perhaps uniquely for a blues man of the time, a visit to England with a touring revue towards the end of the First World War.

He worked with Bessie Smith in the South and had his own radio show in New York, before returning to Chicago in 1937. His versatility and legendary reputation enabled him to return to music after the rude blast of 1950s Chicago r&b and rock 'n' roll had temporarily made him redundant, and indeed his last performance, before dying of a stroke in 1970, was a gig with Buddy Guy in his final home town, Toronto.

In the 1930s Washboard Sam, born in 1910 in Walnut Ridge, Arkansas and a Chicago resident from 1932, was almost as prolific a recording artist as Broonzy, with whom he often worked. Fittingly, his last great moment on record was a 1953 Chess recording of the double-entendre standard 'Diggin' My Potatoes', where his verve and good humour make up for the somewhat limited nature of his chosen musical instrument. This was cut at the same session as Broonzy's only Chess single, and Broonzy provided the accompaniment. Sam toured Europe in 1964 and died in Chicago in 1966.

John A 'James' Williamson, born in Somerville, Tennessee in 1910, was renamed Homesick James after his early-50s Chicago recording 'Homesick' – he had settled there at the age of 20. He was by many accounts, including his own, a cousin of Elmore James, who was himself the electric inheritor of Robert Johnson's passionate singing and piercing bottleneck-guitar style. Homesick perpetuated the Elmore sound after the latter's death of a heart attack in 1963 – at Homesick's Chicago house.

Two more legendary names from the early years of the blues helped to define the pre-war Chicago sound – Tampa Red and Memphis Minnie. The stage names of both identified their southern roots, but they were predominantly Chicago artists. Tampa Red links the days of the medicine shows with postwar Chicago blues. Born in Smithville, Georgia, in 1900 or 1904 and growing up in Tampa, Florida, the young redhead had developed a distinctive bottleneck style by the time of his arrival in Chicago in 1925, and was billed as 'The Guitar Wizard'.

He teamed up with pianist Thomas A Dorsey, and they scored one of the biggest hits of the first decade of the recorded blues with their 1928 version of 'It's Tight Like That', as much a double entendre as it sounds. They were the originators of so-called 'hokum' music – goodtime, rude and up-tempo, and Red often doubled on kazoo to stress the jug-band feel to their style. Dorsey soon went to the other extreme and turned to sacred music, but 20 years after that first hit Tampa Red was fronting a prototype Chicago blues band, playing an important role in defining the 'tough' r&b sound of the city, and recording with such later Chess sidemen as bassist 'Big' Crawford and drummer Odie Payne. In between times he had formed another significant partnership, with Atlanta-born pianist Big Maceo, and this proved to be one of the most popular acts in 1940s Chicago.

Tampa Red's career effectively finished with the death of his wife in the mid-50s, by which time Big Maceo was also dead, and he took to the bottle, although there were a couple of unsatisfactory 1960 comeback albums. He died in Chicago in 1981. His legacy is largely as a writer, above all for one of the greatest of all slow blues, 'It Hurts Me Too', best known in the impassioned, eerie version that gave Elmore James his last, posthumous, hit.

**Washboard Sam,
Broonzy's half-brother,
was one of the most
prolific recording artists
in 1930s Chicago.**

Memphis Minnie was born in the
New Orleans suburb of Algiers in
1897, established her career in the
city that gave her a stage name, and
died there in 1973. However, from
around 1930 until her retirement
from full-time music in the mid-50s,
she was based in Chicago. She
formed musical partnerships with
two of her husbands, Kansas Joe
McCoy and Little Son Joe, but
outshone both as a musician. Her
acoustic guitar style foreshadowed
the development of electric blues in
some of her techniques – dextrous
single-note runs and sustained, bent
notes among them, and she later
took to electricity with enthusiasm.
She cut the best-known version of
the double-entendre 'Me and My
Chauffeur Blues', and was a clear
influence on such white blues
revivalists as Bonnie Raitt and Jo
Ann Kelly.

These were the most notable
names that made pre-war Chicago
such a vibrant blues town. And this
was the milieu into which the
immigrant Chess brothers, moving
onwards from the liquor business to
clubs to recording, arrived and took
to like ducks to water.

Theirs was not, however, the first record
company to be established in the city. Two years
ahead of them, in 1945, came Mercury Records.
This label, which since 1972 has been part of the
vast PolyGram conglomerate, was never
exclusively a blues imprint, but it is significant
that its first release was 'It's Just the Blues' by

the Four Jumps of Jive. Driving the song along was the stand-up bass of Willie Dixon, soon to become the musical hub around which Chess Records – Chicago blues, indeed – would revolve. Mercury turned immediately to the blues, sensing that, with war just over and troops returning home, there would be a revived demand for ethnic styles of music.

Mercury had a firm foothold in the market since one of the founding partners, Irving Green, already owned pressing and manufacturing plants in Chicago and St Louis. The Four Jumps of Jive went into the studio on 12 September, and other 1945 Mercury sessions included ones with Sippie Wallace (Lonnie Johnson was her backing guitarist in Albert Ammons' group) and the Texan pioneer of electric blues guitar T-Bone Walker. By November Mercury was claiming to be pressing over a million discs a month.

Although based in Chicago, where early sessions featured such artists as Broonzy, Sunnyland Slim, Memphis Slim, Robert Jr Lockwood and the more sophisticated Dinah Washington, Mercury was truly national in its coverage of the blues. It cut, for example, Jay McShann's great 'jump blues' outfit in Texas, the founder of New Orleans r&b Professor Longhair in his home town, Lightnin' Hopkins in Houston, Johnny Otis and T-Bone Walker in Los Angeles, and later Eddie Vinson and Screamin' Jay Hawkins in New York. And so it remained not just the first but the most comprehensive of the postwar labels devoting a large part of their energies to the blues.

Until Leonard Chess imposed himself on the scene, the most important record man in Chicago was Lester Melrose, although Melrose's rival, J Mayo Williams, was particularly influential at Mercury, while Melrose's work defined the

'Bluebird sound' on the label of that name. These men were freelances with strong contacts and ties to particular record companies. They acted as talent scouts and producers, and were also managers to the extent that artists usually had a contract with them rather than the record label. But by the middle of the 1940s customer tastes were beginning to move away from the classic 30s-rooted blues styles that their work represented, towards more adventurous independent labels, towards the West-Coast jump blues, and – when Muddy Waters formed his alliance with Chess – towards his downhome Delta sound. What Chess was to provide in particular, therefore, was a more specific focus for the music, one in tune with changing moods, of the Delta blues in its new northern home.

In the process Leonard Chess became the new boss of Chicago music, displacing Melrose and Williams. Of all the major blues artists of the day the only one to have no contact whatsoever with Chess – outside his regular stable, and outside those like John Lee Hooker who would occasionally cut records for him – was Jimmy Reed, whom Chess turned down and who became the commercial mainstay of Chess's main local rival, Vee-Jay Records.

BACK IN THE USSR

In the early 1920s Josef Chez left his wife Cilia and three children in Motol, a small town in White Russia just east of the border with Poland, and travelled to the promised land of America in search of a better life. Like so many East European Jews at the time, he was leaving behind him poverty and anti-Semitism, gambling that he could establish a new family home in Chicago. Many hopefuls had already travelled there from Motol – hence the choice of destination – and had built a synagogue named for 'The People of Motol', Congregation Ansch Motele.

An earlier migrant from Motol, Chaim Weizmann, was to become the first President of the State of Israel in 1948, and once referred to the settlement he had left behind in the 1890s thus: 'Motol was situated in one of the darkest and most forlorn corners of the Pale Settlement, that prison house created by Tsarist Russia for its Jewish population.'

Chez adopted the Westernized version of his surname, Chess, and found work as a carpenter. By 1928 he had saved enough to send the fare back to Motol so that his wife and children, May, Leonard (born 1917) and Philip (born 1922), could also make the trip. Leonard, whose original name had been Lazer Shmuel, wore a calliper on one leg as a result of contracting polio as a child, and there were fears that this would scupper the entire adventure, since America was only interested in able-bodied immigrants. When the family arrived at Ellis Island on board the *Aquitania* his mother hid his leg in a quilt, and all was well as they passed through immigration control. In fact, Leonard found immediately that he could dispense with the splint.

The family had relatives in New York, who met them there and saw them off on the Chicago-bound train. Josef and Cilia made their home at 1425 South Karlov Avenue, and the children were enrolled in school. When Leonard left school he drifted through a number of jobs – selling newspapers, running a milk round and working as a shoe salesman – before going to work for his father, who by now had become a scrap dealer. Working in a junk yard was not to the taste of the entrepreneurial young man, though it did bring him into contact with the black community of the West Side, to whom he sold scrap metal.

When, in turn, Phil left school he and his older brother teamed up, a working relationship that was to last until Leonard's premature death in 1969. The progression of their early business career was a logical one, from operating liquor stores to running bars, and from there to hiring musicians as an additional attraction. They were working in Chicago's South Side, the main black section of the town, and so they began their relationship with black blues singers and black jazz performers.

The New Orleans musician Paul Gayten, who recorded for Chess in the second half of the 1950s with the cream of his home town's musicians, like saxophonist Lee Allen and drummer Earl Palmer, also worked for Chess Records as a southern talent scout and distributor. He recalled Leonard Chess in the early days in conversation with John Broven, for *Blues Unlimited* magazine (May–August 1978). 'Leonard really liked the blues. He was brought up around black people, he was brought up in the same neighbourhood, 35th and Jackson. He was a Polish Jew, and he didn't care what nationality you were, Leonard didn't have any hang up with that Jewish thing. He was a Jew, and he didn't care who knew it, everybody thought he was black before they met him because that's the way he talked. You talked to him on the phone, you didn't know he was white, because he was around black people all his life.' Muddy Waters, however, once expressed a different view: 'Leonard didn't know nothing about no blues.' Three negatives – a definite 'no'.

Their last and biggest club was the Macomba Lounge on 39th and Cottage Grove, where Albert Ammons's son Gene, a saxophone player, worked regularly. In black music terms the Macomba was clearly somewhat up-market, presenting Ella Fitzgerald and Billie Holiday, Lionel Hampton and Louis Armstrong, Billy Eckstine and Jump Jackson. But 'up-market' is of course only a comparative description – the club business at the time was notoriously rough and dangerous, the premises dingy and rudimentary. Musicians preferred the Macomba to other gigs, however, because the stage was behind the bar, which provided them with a degree of protection against assault from fists and knives, if not from bottles and bullets.

By 1946 Phil had returned from war service – Leonard's history of polio had excused him – and, with Mercury up and running, bluesmen were now being recorded in Chicago. Whether or not Leonard was beginning to formulate the obvious next step – instead of promoting artists in the unsavoury atmosphere of a club, why not record them on your own terms? – it was soon made clear to him.

Andrew Tibbs was resident vocalist with the band at the Macomba, and in 1946 was beginning to arouse the interest of talent scouts from out of town. As Leonard Chess recounted it to the *Chicago Tribune* shortly before his death: 'Tibbs told me they wanted him to cut a record and so I thought, if he's good enough for Hollywood, I'll put him on record myself. We bought some time at Universal, which was then in the Civic Opera building, and put out a record of "Union Man Blues" with a tune called "Bilbo's Dead" on the other side. Tibbs had the lyrics written on a brown shopping bag.'

It was not an auspicious start. Tibbs managed to offend the Teamsters trade union with the first song, which alleged racism in the unions, so they refused to handle it and smashed the records instead. And his celebration of the death of racist Mississippi governor Theodore Bilbo, who in running for re-election as a Democrat tried to

disenfranchise blacks, to whom he had been no friend in the previous term, ensured that the record was banned in the South. So it was cut off from its biggest potential market, and in any case it wasn't being delivered there!

This was Leonard Chess's early attempt at a&r. According to recent research by Robert L Campbell and Nadine Cohodas, his outlet the Aristocrat label was set up by record distributors Charles and Evelyn Aron early in 1947, and their financial partners were Fred and Mildred Blount, together with Art Spiegel. By June Chess was involved, and was lugging his tape recorder around Chicago looking for talent. Tibbs was an early signing.

Tibbs, as well as Chess, recovered from their début, with 'Married Man Blues' and 'I Feel Like Crying' proving the most successful of the singer's later sides for the label. But Aristocrat was underway, with a shop-front office on 71st and Phillips and distribution taken care of by the Arons. It remained a very personal business. 'I didn't know what I was doing,' Leonard Chess admitted, 'but I was doing it myself, working days on the record company and nights at the club. Pretty soon I had to get out of the club and I turned it over to Phil.'

Marshall Chess has recalled that a woman called Vivian was also involved, but it may be that he – only five years old, after all, when the label was born – was in fact recalling the name of Vivian Carter, whose first name gave the 'Vee' to Chess's competitor Vee-Jay Records, which was founded in 1953.

In Muddy Waters's view, it was Evelyn and not Leonard Chess who showed enthusiasm for the blues in the early days. Later she married Art Sheridan, the owner of a local pressing plant and distribution set-up, which Evelyn helped to run.

So there remained a business contact with Chess. In December 1950 Sheridan formed the rival Chance label. Early releases included some raw-sounding John Lee Hooker, cloaked in the impenetrable pseudonym John Lee Booker. Hooker's usual outlet at the time was Modern, but he was also happy to freelance at cash-in-hand sessions – sometimes adopting more convincing disguises such as Johnny Williams and Texas Slim. Sheridan re-released Little Walter's first, and unsuccessful, single, 'Ora Nelle Blues', which appeared on the short-lived Ora-Nelle label in 1947, and recorded JB Hutto and Homesick James, in addition to putting out both gospel and jazz sides.

In the earliest days of Aristocrat Leonard Chess became more and more centrally involved, and one by one he bought out the original investors. Releases seem to have commenced in the autumn of 1947. Precise details are hard to verify, because the label adopted an eccentric numbering system, seemingly giving a new 'hundred' designation to almost every artist, and even then leaving some gaps in the sequence. For example, the 101 series was jazz and pop novelties by Sherman Hayes, Aristocrat 201 and 202 were by the Five Blazes, 401 and 402 by Jump Jackson; 409, perversely, was assigned to the Dozier Boys, 501 to Lee Monti, 601 to Tom Archia, 701 to the Hollywood Tri-Tones, 801 to Jo Jo Adams, 901 to the Seven Melody Men, 1101 to Andrew Tibbs, 1201 to Prince Cooper and 1301 to Sunnyland Slim.

The Five Blazes' releases coupled 'Chicago Boogie' with 'Dedicated to You', 'All My Geets are Gone' with 'Every Little Dream'. The Dozier Boys' titles were 'All I Need Is You' and 'She's Gone', while Lee Monti's Tu Tones enjoyed a sequence of five singles, cut either side of the Sunnyland Slim

and Muddy Waters session that was to define the actual future for the label. Unfortunately, Monti's 'Gay Ranchero' remained on the shelf.

The Seven Melody Men added a gospel element to the roster with 'Rockin' Lord'/'Nobody Knows, Nobody Cares' and 'I'm On My Way'/'Mother Pray For Me'. Aristocrat tried a seasonal release with saxophonist Gene Ammons's 'Swinging for Christmas'/'It's the Talk of the Town', and he followed it with 'Stuffy' and 'Once in a While'. I have galloped through this somewhat dry discographical information to highlight the fact that, clearly, Leonard Chess did not join Aristocrat with the vision of a great Chicago

A true Aristocrat:
Sunnyland Slim served to bring together Muddy Waters and the Chess brothers.

blues label. It was a label, period, and he wasn't quite sure what to put on it. It took Sunnyland Slim and Muddy Waters to indicate that.

After the unsuccessful launch with Tibbs, the first actual release seems to have resulted from a session at Universal Studios held in early April, 1947, by the Sherman Hayes Orchestra, fronted by vocalists Wyoma and Paul Sherman Hayes. But confusion still clouded the venture. Aristocrat 1001 was the number given to the first release, 'Chi-Baba, Chi-Baba' coupled with 'Say No More'. But not only was the '1000' system almost immediately dropped in favour of three-figure

release numbers, with the Hayes single being instantly renumbered; it would seem that 'Chi-Baba, Chi-Baba' was also put out with 'Better To Love You Dear' on the flip side, and 'Say No More' as a separate release backed by 'Get on the Ball Paul'. This was hardly designed to give a crisp, clear identity to the fledgeling company. Around this time there is also a record of a session by vocalist Jackie Kane, producing four sides, none of which has ever surfaced.

Clearly Leonard Chess's fateful meeting with Muddy Waters could not come too soon. Of the above-mentioned names, only those of Jump Jackson and Sunnyland Slim mean much today, and the company could not have prospered for long by relying on the transient local celebrity of the others. Jackson (1917–85) was a drummer, a migrant from New Orleans who also acted as an agent and in 1959 went on to form his own label, La Salle, had already recorded for Columbia and Specialty, and typified the medium-sized combo jump blues of the era.

Jackson cut six sides for Aristocrat in 1947, comprising three singles – 'Sweet Thing' with 'Not Now Baby', 'Hey Pretty Mama' and 'My Greatest Mistake', 'Train Blues' and 'I'm Cutting Out On You'. His session band were trumpeter Johnny Morton, saxophonists Sax Mallard and Sugarman Pennigar, pianist Bill Owens, guitarist Hurley Ramey and bass player Dallas Bartley, with Melrose Colbert and Benny Kelly sharing the vocals. On three of the sides the brass section was replaced by solo saxophonist Tom Archia. Oett 'Sax' Mallard was later to cut several discs for Aristocrat and Chess offshoot Checker under his own name.

The Tom Archia All Stars were by and large the Jackson outfit, who were recorded at the same time, with Jackson billed simply as drummer. Four singles were also issued in this configuration, beginning with 'Mean and Evil Daddy'. And the All Stars were the backing group for vocalist Jo Jo Adams's two singles, 'Love Me' and 'Cabbage Head'.

The first two Tibbs singles – the ill-fated 'Union Man Blues' and 'Bilbo's Dead', followed by 'Toothless Woman Blues' and 'Drinking Ink Splint' – were recorded with the Macomba house band, the Dave Young Orchestra. Young was the tenor saxophonist, with Andrew 'Goon' Gardner on alto and Pee Wee Jackson on trumpet, pianist Rudy Martin, bass player Bill Settles and drummer Curtis 'Geronimo' Walker. However, for Tibbs's remaining releases (he survived the name change to Chess in 1950 for a final stab at stardom) Leonard Chess provided him with various permutations of the Tom Archia and Sax Mallard outfits.

The days were numbered for Jackson's swing style, as even the great Louis Jordan found when, in the early 50s, he tried to buck the trend towards smaller band units by increasing the size of his Tympany 'Five' (it was always Five, whatever the number). Sunnyland Slim (1907–95), a pianist who arrived in Chicago from Mississippi in 1942, and who played for a time in Jackson's band, was a far more significant figure than his former employer in the further development of Chicago blues into the new decade. He was one of the key musicians in ushering in the small-combo r&b of the 1950s, which was to supplant the Jackson style and of which Muddy Waters's band was to be the ultimate example. This prompted Jackson's move towards the business side of music.

Slim began recording in 1947 for Victor, billed as Doctor Clayton's Buddy, an example of the occasional habit adopted by record companies of trying to cash in on the name of a recently deceased performer. Clayton, an eccentric blues vaudevillian from Georgia, had died in Chicago in the January of that year. His former sideman Slim was on the earliest Muddy Waters sides for Aristocrat – indeed it was Slim who guided the comparative newcomer to the label – before forming a series of groups under his own name, recording in Chicago for a number of labels, including Aristocrat, JOB and Mercury.

Later in life Slim became a star of the growing 'blues festival' circuit and continued performing and recording into old age. This meant that he spanned the history of blues piano from the 'barrelhouse' circuit of the 1920s and 30s – playing in joints so makeshift that the bar was simply a plank supported by two barrels, for example to serve the workers of a logging camp or at a rent party – through the golden age of Chicago blues and on to the revival in the music prompted by newly awakened white interest during the 1960s.

That first Slim release on Aristocrat, designated 1301, was in fact double-billed to Sunnyland Slim and Muddy Water (*sic*) – 'Johnson Machine Gun' and 'Fly Right, Little Girl'. By the time of Aristocrat 1304, another collaboration, Muddy's surname had gained an 's'. The songs were 'She Ain't Nowhere' and 'My Baby, My Baby'. But it was a later record, the third issued as being by Muddy Waters alone, that was to change the course of the company and of Chicago blues.

I BE'S TROUBLED

McKinley Morganfield, nicknamed Muddy Waters as a child because of the time he spent playing and paddling in the creek, was born on 4 April 1915 in Rolling Fork, a settlement deep in the

Mississippi Delta, some 40 miles north of its southernmost point at Vicksburg. The boy's sharecropper parents, Ollie Morganfield and Berta Jones, were too poor to raise a family as they would have wished, although they would eventually have 12 children, and so he was immediately fostered by his maternal grandmother, Della Jones.

His natural mother died when he was three, and Della Jones moved due north up Highway 61 to settle on Stovall's Plantation near Clarksdale. John Lee Hooker had just been born nearby – or, if you believe Hooker's insistence that he's younger than the record books say, would *soon* be born there! 'I lied about my age to get in the army – the ladies love a uniform,' he once told me, though whether Muddy's main rival as the greatest bluesman of all time was born in 1917 or 1920 would surely not have affected his eligibility for the draft after Pearl Harbor. A little embellishment to the CV, no doubt.

The young Muddy Waters received little book learning. The economics of plantation life were such that, when it came to cotton-picking time, an extra pair of young hands out in the field was more important than a child sitting in school getting an education that wasn't going to be of much use for guiding a plough. Not that formal schooling was readily available, in any case, for a black plantation orphan. And so as soon as he had muscle enough Muddy went to work for Howard Stovall as a general farm labourer. The interest in music was planted early, though – from a two-cent Jew's harp as a child to the harmonica when he was seven. When he was 13 Muddy made the first moves towards semi-professional status as a musician, teaming up with a guitarist friend, Scott Bohanner, to busk on the corner.

Like fellow Delta man Howlin' Wolf, five years his senior, Muddy eventually escaped the more back-breaking duties on the plantation, and was employed as a driver of the field trucks and tractors. His horizons were never limited by the flat Delta skyline, though: 'I always felt that I could beat ploughing, chopping cotton or drawing water.'

Into this world, at the Saturday-night fish fries, town bar shacks and wedding dances, came the itinerant blues singers, playing for a few drinks and a few dollars. Sometimes, of course, they were the farm workers themselves in their weekend clothes. Howlin' Wolf was among them, and was once described as magically appearing on a Saturday night as if he was some great mythical beast who had spent the week slumbering in a cave, whereas in fact he had been just down the road apiece driving his tractor.

The young Muddy turned from his cheap harmonica to a second-hand guitar when he was 17. 'The first guitar I ever got cost me two dollars and fifty cents,' he told interviewer James Rooney, author of *Bossmen – Bill Monroe and Muddy Waters* (Da Capo, 1991). 'I saved nickels and dimes until I got two dollars and fifty cents, and I bought it from a young man named Ed Moore... The first time I played on it I made fifty cents at one of those all-night places, and then the man that run it raised me to two-fifty a night, and I knew I was doing right. Then I got one from Sears, Roebuck that cost eleven dollars. I had a beautiful box then...'

The musical magician that particularly impressed the young Muddy Waters was Son House, who, along with Charley Patton, Willie Brown and Robert Johnson, was one of the founding fathers of the Delta blues during Muddy's formative years. House 'played this same place for about four weeks in a row, and I was there every night,' Waters told *Down Beat* magazine in 1969. 'You couldn't get me out that corner, listening to him.' He was particularly intrigued by House's bottleneck technique, which made the strings moan and squeal behind the voice. In 1930 House had recorded for Paramount, one of the leading labels of the day to feature southern blues artists, though, unfortunately for later enthusiasts, one that used the cheapest possible materials to press their 'race' records. Among the House originals that Muddy Waters would have been aware of was his 'Walking Blues', though Muddy would of course have been influenced by the Robert Johnson version as well, and 'My Black Mama', which Muddy adapted first as 'Country Blues' on his historic Library of Congress recordings, and then for Aristocrat as 'I Feel Like Going Home'.

By the summer of 1941 the 26-year-old tractor driver Muddy Waters was also a proficient local entertainer, playing solo and as part of a quartet, the Son Simms Four, featuring Waters on guitar, Henry 'Son' Simms on violin, second guitarist Percy Thomas and mandolin player Louis Ford. But as with all such line-ups the roles were fluid: Simms occasionally switched to guitar, Thomas and Ford could handle vocals and a further guitarist, Charles Berry, was also featured on occasion. Waters was beginning to write songs, though that has perhaps too formal a ring: his work was usually expressed as improvised reworkings of existing Delta themes inherited, in particular, from Son House, as with the previously mentioned 'Country Blues'.

In July of that year there occurred the first fateful meeting between Muddy Waters and the folklorist Alan Lomax. By this time Waters was married, and to farm work and music had added a third source of income, running a roadside shack as a bar and gambling house.

Lomax's father, John A Lomax, was born in Goodman, Mississippi in 1875, and while still a child Lomax Senior developed an interest in the folk-song heritage of America. He began to 'collect' folk songs, initially white in origin, and identified their roots in the British, in particular the Celtic, song tradition. When the cylinder recorder was invented John Lomax was swift to make use of it, persuading the custodians of folk songs to preserve their performances by singing directly into a funnel, through a transmitting membrane and, via a needle, on to the revolving wax cylinder. The first substantial result was a collection called *Cowboy Songs and Other Frontier Ballads*, which he published in 1910. It was John Lomax who pinned down the sentimental buckskin classic 'Home on the Range', for example.

But all this was a labour of love – by profession, Lomax Senior was a college administrator. His son Alan was born in Austin, Texas in 1915, and by the time his father found himself out of work as a result of the Depression was ready to join him in his field studies. Eventually, in 1933, the Library of Congress supported John's work, identifying the need to catalogue and preserve the American heritage of folk song before it disappeared. The work of tracking down the southern bluesmen began, and at the age of 23 Alan became assistant director of the Archive of Folk Song.

There were other field researchers involved. Mary Katherine Aldin, in her revealing note to the historic CD release *Muddy Waters: The Complete Plantation Recordings*, identifies four in particular. 'John Work, Zora Neale Huirston, Harold Courlander and Elisabeth Barnicle criss-crossed the country, and American music benefited greatly from their careful forays through the South. They set up and took down their recording equipment hundreds of times in Alabama, Florida, Louisiana, Mississippi and Texas, at roadside markets, storefront churches and in the work camps connected to the prisons and penitentiaries.'

It was the penitentiaries that produced two of the Lomaxes' most celebrated 'finds' – Bukka White and Huddie 'Leadbelly' Ledbetter. The violent, truculent Leadbelly, convicted once for murder, once for murderous assault, famously 'sang his way out of prison' when the Lomaxes undertook to employ him as a chauffeur and promote him as a folk entertainer.

In conversation with Aldin, Alan Lomax stressed the breadth of their state-sponsored endeavour, which began in 1933. 'For the first time a national government published officially the field recordings of its own folk singers and folk musicians. This included Cajun, Mexican, Amerindian, Appalachian, sea shanties, it had everything. It was the first full-length portrait of a people that had ever been done with field recordings, this new step.'

As quoted in Paul Oliver's pioneering *The Story of the Blues*, the purpose was to capture 'the folk songs of the Negro – songs that, in musical phrasing and poetic content, are most unlike those of the white race, the least contaminated by white influences or by modern Negro jazz'.

By some accounts, including that of Muddy Waters himself, when the researchers happened upon Muddy and Son Simms on Stovall's Plantation in July 1941, they were in fact trying to track down the legendary Robert Johnson. Johnson had purportedly died of a jealous

husband's poisoned whisky in 1938, though the precise truth has never been established, and this was the second epoch-making gig that he had failed to fulfil owing to premature death: he was also intended to be part of the 'From Spirituals to Swing' concert at New York's Carnegie Hall in December 1938. This trip was a joint venture with Alan Lomax, who was employed by the Library of Congress and partnered by John Work of Fisk University.

As Muddy told James Rooney: 'Alan Lomax discovered me... Really what he was looking for was Robert Johnson, but Robert had got killed. And somebody pointed me out to him and he come out and found me. And he recorded me right in my house with my little group. I had a mandolin and a violin. That was a hot group. I was the youngest one in the thing but I could sing, you know. I was in my teens, see, and they was all older men.'

What is it about Clarksdale bluesmen that makes them so sensitive about their age? Muddy was 26 at the time. A year later Lomax conducted a further session with him. The 'plantation' tracks, first released on CD in 1993, reveal an artist already mature, firmly in the Delta tradition and with an original 'voice', though one that was to develop mightily once Muddy made the move to Chicago. Indeed it was hearing himself played back for the first time ever that resolved Muddy on his escape route from tractor driving. 'Man, this boy can sing the blues,' was his confident and totally justified opinion.

As with John Lee Hooker, who burst on to the blues scene in 1948, at about the same time as Muddy, with his Detroit recording of 'Boogie Chillen', it meant that the apprenticeship was well underway before the artist got near to a recording studio. From the 1941 sessions, 'I Be's

Troubled' is a working draft towards 'I Can't Be Satisfied', for example, but with the passion still reined in.

When Lomax and Work returned a year later for further field recordings they were coming specifically to see Muddy. Significantly, 'I Be's Troubled' and 'Country Blues' were chosen as the first Library of Congress sides to be released as a result of these field trips to Stovall's Plantation – the tunes which were to be reworked as Muddy's first Aristocrat hit.

Maybe it is indicative of the isolated, insular nature of the Delta that in 1943 Muddy Waters was planning a career as a Chicago bluesman rather than obeying the US Army's call-up. Perhaps the Draft Board simply didn't know where to send the letter to this fit 28-year-old. He was now an established musician on the Delta: apart from playing with the Son Simms musicians and any others who happened to pass through, he also played harmonica for a while with a travelling carnival.

One Friday in May, carrying his 'beautiful box' purchased from Sears, Roebuck, Muddy took the train to Memphis and hence to Chicago's Illinois Central Station, on a journey that continued overnight until Saturday morning. The train would have been crowded with similar hopefuls looking for a new life away from the plantations, but Muddy was luckier than some. Friends living at 3652 South Calumet met him and provided a roof for a while. He got a job at a paper factory as a labourer, moved briefly to a cousin's house at 1857 West 13th Street and then rented

his first apartment in Chicago, just three doors down at number 1851.

He also fitted fairly smoothly into the night-time music scene. Playing in a noisy South Side juke joint, however, was a different experience from back-porch picking back home. So whereas the country blues retains its roots as an acoustic music, the emerging rhythm and blues of the urban clubs was taking immediate advantage of the development of electric instruments, capable of making the wooden floor reverberate to the rhythm and carrying the solos over the noise of

That's all right:
Jimmy Rogers was the linchpin of the Muddy Waters ensemble sound.

Shopping for clothes?
Junior Walker (right)
visits Sunnyland Slim's
record store.

the crowd. Muddy Waters soon cottoned on to this change, and though he was a total unknown when he arrived, it wasn't long before he began to make the right musical contacts. In 1944 his cousin, Joe Brant, funded the purchase of his first electric guitar.

Most important of the newcomer's contacts was the reigning king of Chicago blues, Big Bill Broonzy. But Muddy also fell in with the other big names in the city during the 40s, notably the first Sonny Boy Williamson and pianist Sunnyland Slim. A warming thing about these men – and it was equally true of Muddy in turn when he was in a position to lend a helping hand – was their willingness to assist a promising

newcomer, employing him as a backing musician, guiding him towards the record producers.

In 1945 Muddy's grandmother Della Jones died, and he returned to Clarksdale for a short while to attend the funeral and help sort things out. In the meantime Jimmy Rogers, born in Ruleville, Mississippi in 1924, a harmonica player and guitarist who had arrived in Chicago via St Louis in 1939 and had been one of the Maxwell Street buskers since the early 40s, took a day job at the same factory as Muddy's cousin. So when Muddy returned to Chicago in the autumn of 1945 he was introduced to the man who was to become his most celebrated guitar partner.

Rogers recalled a familiar initiation into guitar playing in an interview with Willie Leiser: 'I'd take a bottle and go up and down the string till I'd get a sound. And so, that gave me the idea of wanting to play the guitar.' By the age of 12 he had got hold of a real instrument, and learned to play it while also practising on the harmonica. After arriving in Chicago and playing on the streets he was hired occasionally by Sunnyland Slim, and recorded behind Little Walter on unsuccessful sessions for Ora-Nelle, Apollo and Regal, local short-lived labels.

Waters and Rogers worked out a few tunes together, played at rent parties and moved on to the clubs, with Rogers on harmonica and Claude 'Blue Smitty' Smith on second guitar. Pianist Eddie Boyd, who in 1952 was to write and record one of the classics of the blues, 'Five Long Years', for the JOB label, was another musician often involved, and when he moved on to form his own band Sunnyland Slim replaced him. Muddy would also occasionally accompany the first Sonny Boy Williamson, as did Boyd, but the great harmonica stylist was soon to be brutally mugged, and pronounced dead on arrival at hospital.

In 1946 Muddy had his first opportunity to record in Chicago, and cut a song of his that he was to revive on Aristocrat, 'Mean Red Spider'. However, when the single was released it was done so surreptitiously that even Muddy was unaware of his début on a commercial record. The local label, 20th Century, put out a one-off single, 'Let Me Be Your Coal Man', credited to one James 'Sweet Lucy' Carter, and filled the b-side with Muddy's cut.

Broonzy introduced Muddy to Lester Melrose, as a result of which the next Chicago tracks by Muddy Waters – 'Jitterbug Blues', 'Hard Days Blues' and 'Buryin' Ground Blues' – were cut, on 27 September 1947. Melrose leased them to Columbia, but unfortunately they remained on the shelf. A change seemed to be taking place at this very time, with the major labels turning more and more to the sophisticated, uptown jump blues of the Louis Jordans and Jay McShanns, leaving mud-on-the-boots unknowns to the newly emerging independents. True, well into the 1950s Mercury, for example, was recording such names as Sunnyland Slim, Broonzy, Memphis Slim, Robert Jr Lockwood – even the old Aristocrat combination of Andrew Tibbs and Sax Mallard – but these were established names by that time, seen as less of a gamble than yet another Mississippi boy just starting out in Chicago.

Far more significant was Leonard Chess's teaming of Waters with Sunnyland Slim for those early Aristocrat sides. They led to the first cuts under Waters's name, 'Gypsy Woman' and 'Little Anna Mae'. By this time he had left the paper plant and was driving a delivery truck, but the record failed to sell.

Then, in April 1948, came the session that produced the new company's first hit, 'I Can't Be Satisfied' and 'I Feel Like Going Home', released as Aristocrat 1305. Although the records kept by Chess put the session at April 1948, this would seem also to be the release date, and the actual recording may well have happened before Christmas – at the time that the company was trying to deal with the problems arising from the controversial Andrew Tibbs release 'Union Man Blues' and 'Bilbo's Dead', which almost killed off +-Chess before it had even started. And, as we have already noted, Leonard Chess was far from convinced that this passionate, rural and, to him, incoherent singer had commercial appeal.

Although there were specialist record dealers in Chicago, the way of selling 'race' records in those days was much more informal than simple reliance on conventional channels. Straight from the pressing plant, one of the Chess brothers would deliver copies of the record to be played and, hopefully, sold at any place where black people gathered – at grocery stores, bars and barber shops as well as record stores.

Legend has it that supplies of 'I Can't Be Satisfied' were delivered in the morning and running out by the afternoon. Outlets immediately introduced a rationing system of one disc per customer, because railway stewards used to buy popular records in batches to sell on the trains, and in this case ready customers in the neighbourhood were finding it hard to track the disc down. Muddy Waters was one of them – he paid over the odds for a copy on the following morning, but had to send his wife into the shop to get a second one.

As record moguls, the Chess brothers were underway. 'Changed his tune,' said Muddy, referring to Leonard Chess's initial resistance to his biting bottleneck style and deep, southern singing, 'because I was selling so fast they couldn't press them fast enough.'

CHAPTER 2

BROADENING THE ATTACK

ROLLIN' AND TUMBLIN'

Aristocrat now had its all-important first hit, which in terms of the blues market meant selling around 60,000 copies, including making significant inroads into the southern market. The single, uncompromisingly rural in its Delta passion, simply borrowing a little citified electricity, was a revelation not only to Leonard Chess but to the business in general. Maybe there was a slight element of nostalgia involved in the record's impact – even the dirt fields and poverty of the South could have some charms when recalled from a gritty, steamy city ghetto – but it showed that the blues market hadn't turned completely to the slicker jump blues favoured by the uptown urbanites.

There was not yet an exclusively r&b chart for 'I Can't Be Satisfied' and 'I Feel Like Going Home' to feature in – *Billboard* magazine was to introduce its list on 17 June 1949. When Aristocrat started in business, *Billboard* was listing just 15 records, collated nationally and perhaps a little haphazardly, in its 'Race Records' chart, which was itself a progression from the 'Harlem Hit Parade' earlier in the decade, which had given prominence to just ten discs. 'I Feel Like Going Home' made the *Billboard* list in September 1948.

Muddy Waters was the new Chicago star, alongside Broonzy, the first Sonny Boy Williamson and Washboard Sam, who was now scoring heavily on the Victor label. In 1948 Leroy 'Baby Face' Foster was a new recruit to Muddy's stage band, joining Waters and Jimmy Rogers. He replaced 'Blue Smitty', who had become increasingly unreliable, often provoking drunken brawls. This could not be tolerated for long by the ambitious and professionally minded Muddy.

Foster, born in 1923 in Algoma, Mississippi, had arrived in Chicago in 1944 by the same inevitable railroad route as Muddy, and began, as so many did, by busking on Maxwell Street. Like his new partners, Foster was a guitarist, but was useful in that he could also play the drums, just as Rogers – until the recruitment of the great Little Walter – was as likely to be playing harmonica as guitar in the line-up.

The group was hot, and in demand at all the clubs – the Boogie Woogie Inn, the Ebony Lounge, the 708 Club, Club Zanzibar, the Du Drop

Ready to rock:
Muddy Waters was the biggest postwar Chicago star and the basis of Chess's success.

MUDDY WATERS - G

Chess Recorder

KING OF THE BLUES

4339 Lake Park Ave.   Chicago 15, Illinois

Inn and Romeo's Place among them. They also ventured as far east as Pittsburgh.

It was around this time that Muddy first ran into Willie Dixon, the bass player who was to become so central to the story of Chess Records and in 1954 was to figure in the greatest of the Muddy Waters line-ups. At the time, though, Dixon was working with the somewhat politer Big Three Trio, playing Top Ten tunes mainly to white audiences downtown.

As Rogers recalls it in Willie Dixon's autobiography *I Am the Blues*: 'I saw the Big Three Trio play at a couple of clubs... [but] ...after Muddy and I got pretty popular in the area, they didn't play the clubs that we was playing ... they were all hanging in the downtown area, the Old Town area. We were playing further south where places were swinging and the blues were big. We would get off at two – on Saturday it would be three – but Dixon and the downtown guys had short hours ... they'd come out in the neighbourhood where we were and get a chance to sit in...'

Although the Waters band was building a reputation in the South Side clubs, when it came to recording Leonard Chess stuck for some time with the winning formula, choosing to team him with Big Crawford alone (the formula, of course, that Chess only came to recognize as a winner when 'I Can't Be Satisfied' was disappearing from the shops as fast as he could press it). It may be, since he was still feeling his way as a record mogul, that he felt more comfortable with just two musicians, and it was certainly cheaper. Also, to be fair, Chess was already a perfectionist, and the smaller the group the easier it is to experiment until you hit on the sound you want.

Two tunes cut during a session on 10 November 1948, a 'Rollin' and Tumblin'' variation

called 'Down South Blues' and a song he'd have learned from Robert Johnson, 'Kind Hearted Woman Blues', stayed on the shelf at the time, but the session did produce his follow-up single, Aristocrat 1306, 'Train Fare Home' and 'Sittin' Here and Drinkin''. Crawford was billed on the label as 'Rythm [*sic*] Accompaniment'. Foster managed to sneak into the studio as second guitarist for a session three weeks later, though, and it produced the next single – a majestic, powerful coupling of 'You're Gonna Miss Me' and 'Mean Red Spider'.

The session was a doubly productive one, because Aristocrat also got a Leroy Foster single out of it – 'Locked Out Boogie' and 'Shady Grove Blues'. Foster went on to cut a single for the JOB label at this time, with Snooky Pryor on harmonica. In December 1948 the first Sonny Boy appeared in the charts for the last time.

Maybe it was the comparative weakness of the next Waters/Crawford collaboration that persuaded Chess to put his star into a band context at last. Waters, Rogers and Foster were present, augmented by pianist Little Johnny Jones at the 1949 session that produced the Waters hit 'Screaming and Crying' and 'Where's My Woman Been'. A Little Johnny single also resulted, teaming the first version of 'Big Town Playboy' (later a better-known hit for Jimmy Reed's guitarist Eddie Taylor) and 'Shelby County Blues'.

The move towards bands was encouraged further by a 'moonlighting' session for the new Parkway label in January 1950, where Foster and Waters were joined by Little Walter, who had been in Chicago since the mid-40s. Eight tracks were cut, which surfaced under various billings – Baby Face, the Baby Face Leroy Trio, Little Walter and the Little Walter Trio – while the presence of the more celebrated Waters remained surreptitious.

Walter was to be the next recruit to Muddy's great Chess band. Muddy may have been unbilled, but on the strongest single to result from this session, a two-sided workout on 'Rollin' and Tumblin'', there is no mistaking the bottleneck style that was by now his trademark. Leonard Chess, for one, didn't mistake it, and was not best pleased.

Although Aristocrat, during the brief life that gave Leonard Chess his invaluable 'learning curve' in the blues business, relied heavily on Muddy Waters and the spin-offs from his circle, there were a number of other signings, the most notable of whom was Robert Nighthawk.

Born Robert McCollum in Helena, Arkansas, in 1909, Nighthawk had left the South for St Louis, the next obvious stop north of Memphis, and was one of the first to adapt the bottleneck style of Robert Johnson and Son House into its new electric, urban setting. He was already established through recordings for the Bluebird label when Muddy Waters recommended him to Leonard Chess as another powerful exponent of this postwar updating of the southern blues.

An initial session in November 1948 did not produce a release, but it was significant in that Willie Dixon was present playing bass, the first step in his pivotal Chess career. Far more successful was a September 1949 essay of two Tampa Red songs, 'Sweet Black Angel' and 'Anna Lee Blues', with Dixon now as producer. After a further 1950 session for Aristocrat, just before its transformation into Chess, Nighthawk cut sides for a couple of other Chicago labels before heading back south – though there was a nostalgic return to Chess in 1964, backed by the younger generation of Chicago blues stars like Buddy Guy, pianist Lafayette Leake and harmonica player Walter 'Shakey' Horton.

Nighthawk, undoubtedly an influence on the younger slide-guitar men like Muddy and Elmore James, died in 1967 back home in Arkansas. Perhaps the best example of his later work is the Rounder CD *Live on Maxwell Street*. Jimmy Bell, a pianist and

Smooth slide: king of the clubs Muddy Waters.

singer who played at the Macomba with his trio, was another Aristocrat signing at this time. According to *Living Blues* he claimed to have secured a five-year contract, though only two singles – one each on Aristocrat and Chess – resulted, and five years after his deal with Leonard Chess he appears to have been cutting an unproductive session for rival label Chance. In his conversation with the magazine he was clearly less than content with this deal, though his estimates of his commercial value do seem to be exaggerated nonsense.

'Man, I lost a lot of money. I trusted him [Leonard Chess], I made $63,000. I should have made $263,000. The contract was all screwed up. I was so mad at the guy that if it hadn't been for my old lady, I probably would have shot him. It wasn't a matter of I didn't have no school or knowledge. I trusted him from the Macomba... We all helped this guy... At the time he didn't even have a studio to record. He had an office on Cottage Grove. "Easter Time" and "Me and My Baby" were made right [there]. He said, "Let's record them." He like tore my whole life apart. He cheated me out of a whole bunch of money... It didn't have to be a gold record but in five years I only got $63,000. You could hear it on the radio every day and every night. Actually, I was supposed to get a nickel on every record...

'Hey, man, he did it to people. Man's a crook, a thief. He's dead now, so why talk about him? He did it. He fucked a lot of guys to get rich... I said, "Man, you'd better get some money together or they'll find you in the mother-fucking river." He said, "Jimmy, I'm doing the best I can." I said, "Shit!" That was the last I seen him alive. I was on my way to Detroit and I stopped by his record outlet on Cottage Grove. He was the cause of me not recording.' This is bitter testimony, and

certainly after his two singles for Chess, a 1949 session in Shreveport, Louisiana that only appeared years later on a British album, a single on Royalty and the abortive Chance session,

Bell did indeed fade away from the session scene. His opinion contrasts sharply with Muddy Waters's evocation of the 'Chess family', and there can be no doubt that many Chess artists were unhappy with their financial treatment. On the other hand, bearing in mind inflation, $63,000 does not seem all that bad for a couple of long-forgotten singles, and the estimate that more than a quarter of a million was actually due to him is surely fantastic.

Aristocrat conducted a couple of sessions in 1949 and 1950 with a pick-up band called the Blues Rockers, notable in particular in that later Chess star Willie Mabon was present on piano. Another Arkansas man, Forest City Joe, was recorded in 1948 without producing a hit, and Chess also licensed one single by a Dallas artist, Charles Bradix, ('Numbered Days' and 'Wee Wee Hours'), which proved to be the last Aristocrat release. From his early uncertain start with Andrew Tibbs, Leonard Chess had stumbled upon the future of the blues with Muddy Waters, and was now, in 1950, ready to move on.

The next time that Muddy returned to the studio, in January 1950, it was once again as a duo with Big Crawford, for a session that was to be pivotal for the company – it produced the artist's last Aristocrat release and his first on Chess. He went back to the 'Rollin' and Tumblin'' theme, this time under its most familiar name, and there was a third party in the studio providing discreet, skiffling percussion – presumably it would have been either Foster or the next credited drummer on a Muddy Waters session, Elgar Edmonds (Elgin Evans). It was a spirited session, released as 'Parts 1 and 2' on Aristocrat 412. There can be no doubt that the choice of tune was prompted by Leonard Chess, and that he released the single to compete with the Parkway version.

Another return, this time to Robert Johnson's 'Walking Blues', gave Muddy his first Chess b-side. This is a respectful and somewhat subdued treatment of the 'woke up this morning' theme, effective nonetheless, with Crawford damping down the pyrotechnics in favour of a simple percussive throb. But it was the other cut of the day that produced the next landmark in the as yet parallel fortunes of the soon-to-be-reborn company and its major star – 'Rollin' Stone'.

As with all Muddy's compositions to date, this was another variation on a Delta theme, in this case 'Catfish Blues': 'I wish I was a catfish, swimming in the deep blue sea. I'd have all you good-looking women fishing after me.' He appears to be alone in the studio now, meditative, improvisatory, punctuating the lyric with that biting bottleneck guitar, providing his own percussion with a flatulent bass-string pulse, playfully complicating the rhythm in the instrumental fills. The title he gave to this virtuoso performance was, of course, to be picked up on, a decade or more later, by a group of south-east London blues enthusiasts who founded their early repertoire almost exclusively on Chicago blues.

ROLLIN' STONE

From 1948 onwards Aristocrat were based at 5249 South Cottage Grove, the building referred to by Jimmy Bell in the previous chapter. This was a more impressive office than the first premises, and in 1950 came an even more significant change in the company's structure.

Len and Phil came to a settlement with Evelyn and bought out her share of the company in January, the Muddy Waters 'Rollin' Stone' session took place in February, and they relaunched the label on 3 June as the Chess Record Corporation. The Aristocrat label itself had been largely a typographical design, with a little coronet the only motif. The new label was blue above, white below, with the 'horizon' between the two running through the spindle hole, and the upper half contained the company name and was decorated with three chessmen. For more than a decade it was a guarantee of the finest blues power.

The transition was a smooth one, with the first releases on Chess all by existing Aristocrat artists, and with pressings under the old logo continuing into 1951. The mercurial attitude towards record numbering lived on as well – the first Chess release, 'My Foolish Heart' by the Macomba Club tenor saxophonist Gene Ammons, was designated Chess 1425, after the address of the Chess family home on South Karlov Avenue. The Muddy Waters pairing of 'Rollin' Stone' and 'Walkin' Blues' came next. The Ammons single was remembered years later by Leonard as being 'such a hit that it gave me my distribution set-up. That was when Chess was really born.' Indeed the record crept into the r&b top ten, and the Waters single was equally instrumental in establishing the identity of the new venture.

The next Muddy Waters session, which took place in the summer of 1950, was also historic, in that it was the first time that Leonard Chess added Little Walter to the familiar studio line-up of Waters and Crawford. In matrix-number order, the day produced the next single, 'You're Gonna Need My Help I Said' and 'Sad Letter Blues', together with two later releases, 'Early Morning Blues' and 'Appealing Blues (Hello Little Girl)'.

From this time on, Walter was to be featured on almost all the Muddy Waters sides until 1960 – long after he had struck out on his own as a live act – as well as on many subsequent ones.

His given name was Marion Walter Jacobs, and he was born on 1 May 1930 in Marksville, Louisiana. Walter grew up on a farm, learned to play the harmonica at the age of eight, and before he was even in his teens had run away from home to New Orleans, where he worked as a busker. At the age of 14 he was featuring in the Helena, Arkansas sponsored radio show *King Biscuit Time*, which bumped him up against one of his defining musical influences and the show's most celebrated mainstay, Rice Miller, the 'second' Sonny Boy Williamson.

By 1945 Walter was in St Louis, and a year later he arrived in Chicago, where, like many other ambitious blues-playing arrivals, he worked as a Maxwell Street busker looking for a break. The boy's talent for the harmonica was instantly apparent to the city's seasoned bluesmen, and he was soon being hired as an accompanist to locally based musicians, before teaming up with Muddy Waters in 1948 – a remarkable two years before Leonard Chess was willing to use him in the studio. But Little Walter was already a recording artist at this stage, having cut 'Ora Nelle Blues (That's Alright)' and 'I Just Keep Loving Her' in 1947 for the Ora-Nelle label, with Jimmy Rogers on guitar.

The 'first' Sonny Boy, John Lee Williamson, was the next great influence on the teenager, during the two years between Walter's arrival in town and the older man's tragic death. If Sonny

Boy had indicated new potential for the humble blues harmonica, it was left to his student to develop and refine this legacy. In less skilled hands the mouth organ, cheap, portable and therefore attractive to impecunious bluesmen, was largely used as a wheezy punctuation mark. It could be mightily effective in this role, as exponents as different as Jimmy Reed and Bob Dylan have proved. Walter, though, took the diametrically opposite approach, and came to regard it not as a glorified Jew's harp but as a pocket brass instrument, even a whole stripped-down brass section, cupped in the palm of his hand. It is as if he was trying to distil the sound of an artist he much admired, Louis Jordan, into his harmonica.

Playing it through an amplifier increased the range of Little Walter's instrument, and there was the additional optional bonus of a basic echo effect in the studio, initially achieved by routeing the sound via the 'rest room'. From a gentle, breathy riff to a full-throated bellow, from a rhythmic vamp to a complex, spiralling solo, from harsh punctuation to a rich, mellow tone that had never been achieved before, he did what Sonny Boy might have done had he lived – he put the harmonica firmly at the front of the bandstand, and opened the door to a generation of harp stylists who would decorate the great years of Chicago blues – James Cotton, Snooky Pryor, Walter Horton – himself an early influence on Little Walter – Junior Wells, George Smith, Carey Bell and the others who helped to shape the distinctive Chicago sound.

The following Muddy Waters session was held

on 23 October 1950, and featured Walter, Crawford and Rogers in the band, with the addition of drummer Elgin Evans as percussionist. 'Louisiana Blues' added to the rapidly growing catalogue of classic Waters blues, and was yet another example of how the singer, now comfortably established as top dog in Chicago, was looking due south for his inspiration. The singer is yearning for Louisiana as an escape route from his troubles, and to equip himself with a 'mojo hand' to ensure greater sexual success. The voodoo theme was to prove a recurrent one in his work, notably of course in the rollicking 1956 classic 'Got My Mojo Working'.

'Louisiana Blues' is taken at a loping pace,

when the company became just a back catalogue rather than a creative unit. His mellowed attitude is confirmed in the remark: 'I thought Leonard was the best man in the business.' This reflection, delivered when Chess had moved into the past tense, contrasts with Waters's assertions as a young man that Chess had a tin ear for the blues.

'Louisiana Blues' proved to be a strong coupling with the contrasting 'Evans Shuffle', based on Joe Liggins's hit 'The Honeydripper', and shrewdly dedicated to radio disc jockey Sam Evans, who responded with plenty of helpful airplay. The b-side skips along delightfully, as light as a soufflé compared to the downhome blues of the top deck. It is a Little Walter solo feature, vamped over a simple two-beat rhythm,

with the instruments intuitively integrated and Waters giving his lyric a lazy, confident vocal. But the integration was not only intuitive – Waters worked hard to achieve this Delta sound in exile that he had largely invented, and Leonard Chess, if not always seeing eye to eye with his star, was also a diligent stickler for detail. Any abrasion between the Mississippi bluesman and the Polish entrepreneur was clearly working as a stimulus, not as a dampener. After all, Waters often referred in later years to Chess Records as a family, pointing out that he never had a formal contract, and indeed he remained on the label throughout the time it was a going concern. He looked elsewhere only when forced to, late in life,

tricked out with a false ending before the actual climax.

It was now becoming clear, in retrospect at least, that Muddy Waters was helping to give new life to a blues form that many had thought died out in the war as a commercial force – this was country blues, revived by an alliance of electricity and an ironic urban perspective, capable of combining sophistication and world-weariness with nostalgia and superstition, and it owed its survival to the genius of Muddy Waters and the pool of remarkable musicians that were beginning to gather in his shade.

A further session on 23 January 1951 continued to build that stunning Muddy Waters catalogue. The title 'Long Distance Call' – a slow, meditative and soulful strut – suggests accurately that he continued to exploit migration as a commercial theme, together with 'Too Young To Know', 'Honey Bee' and 'Howlin' Wolf'. The highlight of the last three titles is 'Honey Bee', with Little Walter switching to second guitar behind Muddy's distinctive slide.

At the same time as booking Little Walter for Muddy's sessions, Chess also gave Jimmy Rogers an opportunity to be the front-liner. 'That's All Right' may have been cut in time left over from a Waters session, on 15 August 1950, but the latter does not appear on the track – Rogers is backed by Walter and Crawford alone. The number was a revelation, lighter and more resigned in tone than the brooding Waters style, and it is one of the most tuneful and instantly memorable of all variations on the basic blues format. Rogers plays in picking style rather than copying the Waters slide, and the record was a hit, with 'Ludella' on the flip. As with all Rogers's compositions, they were published under his real name, James A Lane.

Up to this point Gene Ammons was Leonard Chess's other big star. An August 1950 session credited to Ammons and his Septet produced two single releases, 'Jug Head Ramble'/'Can Anyone Explain' and 'Don't Do Me Wrong'/'Prelude to a Kiss', and is notable for a new recruit in the band. Baritone saxophonist Sonny Stitt came to Ammons after a couple of years with Dizzy Gillespie, became effectively co-leader of the Ammons outfit, and went on to play with Miles

Big mouth:
Little Walter was the temperamental virtuoso of the harmonica.

Davis as well as fronting his own groups.

Other early Chess releases teamed Andrew Tibbs and Sax Mallard for 'You Can't Win'/'Achin' Heart' and the Claude McLin Sextet with a version of 'Mona Lisa', which was comprehensively gazumped by the Nat 'King' Cole hit version on Capitol. A potentially historic session, numbered ready for issue but in fact remaining unreleased until 1970, was credited to Shoe Shine Johnny, singing 'Joliet Blues' and 'So Glad I Found You'. Backed by Walter, Rogers and Crawford, the singer was Johnny Shines, the Tennessee-born bluesman who had worked with Robert Johnson in the 1930s and kept alive Johnson's rural bottleneck style. Unfortunately Shines was not destined to become one of the pantheon of 1950s blues greats on the Chess label, but later in life (he was born in 1915 and died in 1992) his career was revived by the 1960s blues boom, and his position as one of the pioneer southern bluesmen became better recognized.

That this did not happen on Chess was due to the brothers' reservations about him. Phil Chess has referred to Shines as 'just a run-of-the-mill blues singer', but what probably informed this harsh opinion was that they already had Muddy Waters, and Shines was a similar performer. Shines himself was disappointed. 'Anybody that Chess fool around with, to me it seems like he was going to get the best out of. He had a knack for getting the best out of musicians. See, I might have hooked up with 25 other companies, but wanted to go with Chess. 'Cause he had the patience to work with a guy, to find out what made him react, what he react to.' Well, this faith was not totally reciprocated, but Shines was to enjoy his deserved reinstatement later.

Jimmy Rogers followed up his hit with 'Going Away Baby', backed by 'Today, Today Blues'. This time Muddy Waters was on hand to help out, and the a-side is as instantly attractive in its own way as was 'That's All Right'. The mood is now jaunty and up-tempo, with an intricate little riff running through the song. Rogers makes the unlikely claim, for a bluesman at least, that he has loved only four women, and then caps this with the revelation that they are his mother, his sister, his sweetheart and his wife.

Pianist Calvin Bostick was another Chess artist at the time, with 'All Of My Life' (his version of 'Danny Boy' was not, however, offered to the Chicago public); and at around the same time as Muddy Waters was in the studio cutting 'Long Distance Call' (two weeks earlier, in fact, on 8 January 1951) there was another landmark session. Sax Mallard's instrumental 'Slow Caboose', backed by 'Darling, Let's Give Love a Chance', was to be the first release on the subsidiary label, Checker, with the catalogue number Checker 750. From Chess to Checker, the imprint on which Bo Diddley had all his hits – the Chess brothers were branching out.

Jimmy Rogers was enjoying his own taste of stardom in 1951. Billed on his headline releases as 'Jimmy Rogers and his Rocking Four', he seems to have toyed with the idea of leaving Muddy and setting up on his own. The 'four' were bassist Big Crawford, saxophonist Ernest Cotton, drummer Elgin Evans and pianist Eddie Ware. Maybe the fact that Rogers's tentative plans as a band leader came to nothing at this time were in part due to the erratic behaviour of Ware, who had a habit of disappearing when life got a little quiet. Ware had a wildly decorative style of playing, heard to good effect on such tracks as 'Back Door Friend', where, whenever Rogers pauses for breath, Ware hammers in with an exploration of the keyboard.

He in turn was rewarded with opportunities as the featured artist, using spare time on Rogers's sessions just as Rogers had previously done when Muddy Waters had cut his quota. 'Wandering Lover' and the novelty number 'Lima Beans', with Eddie Chamblee on vocals, was the first result, followed a year later by 'Jealous' (actually recorded at the 'Wandering Lover' session) and 'Give Love Another Chance'.

From his family tree of some of Chicago's finest blues artists, Leonard Chess was fashioning a new era for the city's music. Quite how conscious this was must be in doubt. 'The only reason Chess went along with the blues was because he lost out on his other recording company [Aristocrat] by not having the blues. They actually didn't know as much about the blues as people might think.' This is the opinion of Willie Dixon, expressed in his autobiography, and he should know. It substantiates Muddy Waters's opinion, expressed above, which credited Leonard Chess's business acumen rather than his feeling for the music. And yet there will be other testimonies to suggest that Chess had the feeling as well.

It would be remarkable if a man with little sympathy for the music accidentally assembled the greatest roster of talent ever to appear on one label. Moreover, Leonard Chess's pedantic attention to detail in the studio suggests an untutored love of the music, rather than indifference.

ROCKET 88

It was inevitable that Leonard Chess would soon come into contact with Sam Phillips in Memphis. Indeed it was a record presser in that city who had suggested that Chess was a good name for the relaunched label. With the new venture underway, and brother Phil now working full time on the record company in Chicago, Leonard was constantly commuting to the southern states with a car boot full of records, visiting a growing network of dealers and other outlets, as well as seeking out new talent and new contacts.

He reckoned to cover five thousand miles every three months, and his son Marshall has recalled: 'We'd stop off at a farmer's and record

some guy out in a cotton field. He'd be set up on a couple of bales and my father would record him on the wire recorder–not even a tape in those days.' Leonard's boast was that 'I always paid for the electricity.'

In 1950 the Alabama disc jockey Sam Phillips had been in Memphis for four years, working for local radio station WREC and later promoting gigs at the Hotel Peabody. In 1950 he went a step

---

PRAISE!! PRAISE!! AND STILL MORE PRAISE FOR
"ROCKET 88"
by Jackie Brenston And His Delta Cats
ON
"The Hottest Little Label in the Nation"
★ CHESS RECORD No. 1458 ★

"Rocket 88" is speedily zooming to the top everywhere in the country! DIS-
TRIBUTORS—A few territories still available. Hop on the bandwagon for bigger
profits with CHESS. Contact us immediately! Write NOW!!
CHESS RECORDS, 5249 Cottage Grove Ave., Chicago, Ill.

---

further, and opened a recording studio. The Memphis Recording Service was based at 706 Union Avenue at a rent of $150 a month. As quoted in *Sun Records*, by Colin Escott and Martin Hawkins, Phillips had a clear reason for wanting to move into the record business. 'The Negroes had no place to record in the South. They had to go up to Chicago or New York to get on record and even the most successful of the local entertainers had a hard time doing that. Rhythm & blues men like Jules and Saul Bihari [owners of Modern Records in Los Angeles]

would come south into Tennessee from the West Coast and set up studio in a garage to record the Negro blues singers of the South. So I set up a studio in 1950 just to make records of those great Negro artists.'

Saul Bihari has remembered giving Chess valuable advice. 'We were talking to Leonard Chess, and he told us around 1950 he started realizing that here he was, five years in the record business and not getting anywhere. So he looked around to see who he thought was doing best in the area he was working in, and he chose us. So then he started asking around to find out what we were doing that enabled us to be so successful, and the answer was that we went around the South, meeting the jocks, finding new singers, keeping in close contact with the distributors... And he got to be more and more successful, while we weren't so consistent.'

Initially Phillips simply sold his master tapes to Modern Records, beginning with recordings by jazz pianist Phineas Newborn. Modern were proving more successful than their rivals – for example, the Nashville label Bullet, who had more feel for 40s-style r&b and jazz – in capturing and marketing the southern blues sound, partly because of their willingness to capture the musicians in their natural habitat. They also had a superior distribution set-up, with an important hold on the Californian market.

At this time an almost stillborn venture by Phillips to launch a record label with another disc jockey, Dewey Phillips (they were not related), called The Phillips', saw only one unsuccessful release, 'Gotta Let You Go'/'Boogie in the Park', by one-man band Joe Hill Louis. The artist had just inherited a sponsored radio spot on local station WDIA from BB King, advertising an indigestion remedy called Peptikon. Among the other artists who performed on this slot were Rufus Thomas, Johnny Ace and Roscoe Gordon. The radio station was just down the road from Sam Phillips's newly founded studio.

WDIA played an important part in the story of the development of American local radio, since in 1948 it had launched the first programme (a tentative 30 minutes) aimed directly at a black audience. A music teacher from a Memphis high school, Nat Williams, was the disc jockey, and the huge and favourable audience reaction – which flew in the face of wary advertisers and openly racist critics of the move – made Williams a star. Within a year WDIA was programming specifically for blacks, and was dubbed 'Mother Station of the Negroes'.

After the failure of his first record release Phillips went back to dealing with Modern, and subsequently recorded Louis for both Modern and Chess. In 1951 he also leased sides to Modern by BB King, Walter Horton and Roscoe Gordon, and first met Leonard Chess later that year. It was the other Phillips, Dewey, who made the introduction.

For a while Phillips must have hoped that he could cover the lucrative southern beat for both Modern on the West Coast and Chess in the North, but almost inevitably when he provided Chess with a monster r&b hit in 1951, his longer-standing client took umbrage. And when Phillips later compounded the slight by sending Howlin' Wolf to Chess, his tie-up with Modern was over. By this time there was another independent label, Trumpet in Jackson, fighting for a share of the same market, and competition was fierce.

That big hit was 'Rocket 88', backed by 'Come Back Where You Belong' (Chess 1458), recorded on 3 March 1951 and credited to Jackie Brenston and his Delta Cats. In fact this was a band based in Clarksdale, Mississippi, formed by young local

disc jockey Ike Turner and called the Kings of Rhythm. Brenston was usually one of the saxophone players, but was headlined on 'Rocket 88' as its writer and singer, with Turner on piano, Willie Kizart on guitar, Raymond Hill on tenor saxophone, bassist Jessie Knight and drummer Willie Sims. Turner took the band to Phillips, who turned the song into a jump boogie classic and sent it on to Chess.

Phillips has referred to 'Rocket 88' as 'the first rock 'n' roll record' in that it began the process of pulling together 'blues, country and pop' into a form of music that, according to him, hadn't quite existed before. Suffice to say that if such a concept as the first rock 'n' roll record could actually exist – in a situation where it is easier to

see evolution than revolution – then Jackie Brenston's moment of glory is a prime candidate.

Certainly a hillbilly band leader called Bill Haley thought so. His group, the Saddlemen, recorded it, the first of their many cover versions of black records that culminated, after they had been renamed the Comets, in Sonny Dae's 'Rock Around the Clock'. This made Haley the first rock 'n' roll star – if there is such a thing, of course.

One outcome was that Brenston signed with Phillips as a solo artist, with his records appearing on Chess. He had fallen out with Turner, who remained faithful to Modern as a talent scout. Sadly, Turner will be best remembered by younger rock enthusiasts as a wife-beating drug addict, whose star waned as Tina's rose. But in the 1950s (he was born in 1931) he was a prodigious musical renaissance man – an accomplished guitarist and pianist, a disc jockey, talent spotter and band leader, and the creative force behind the Ike and Tina Turner Revue, one of the greatest live acts in rhythm and blues. The 'Rocket 88' session also produced a later Chess single credited to Ike Turner and his Kings of Rhythm, 'Heartbroken and Worried'/'I'm Lonesome Baby', with Brenston returning to baritone sax duties. Brenston's later Chess titles included 'Tuckered Out', which featured both the pianist Phineas Newborn and, on drums, his father, Phineas Newborn Sr.

Although Leonard Chess picked up singles from other sources – including, in Detroit, sides by John Lee Hooker, of whom more later – his most significant deal in the early days was this hot line to Memphis. A historic release, which was credited to Roscoe Gordon but effectively featuring the Beale Street Blues Boys, included BB King, Bobby Bland and drummer Earl Forrest on 'I'll Search Heaven' and 'Good Religion', while the same line-up, now fronted by and credited to Bland, cut 'Crying'/'A Letter from a Trench in Korea'. Gordon's 'Booted' was a hit on both the Chess and Modern labels.

Sam Phillips must now have been aware that as an independent supplier of master tapes he could serve only one master. It was soon, of course, to be himself. For in 1952 he founded Sun Records, and when Elvis Presley wandered in on his lunch break to cut an acetate of 'My Happiness' as a present to his mother, the label was on course to become one of the legendary independents, alongside Chess. After Elvis came Carl Perkins, Johnny Cash, Jerry Lee Lewis, Roy Orbison, Charlie Rich and a lengthy roster of rockabillies – indeed, as an identifiable form of white rock 'n' roll stiffened by southern blues influences, rockabilly was created in Phillips's tiny Memphis studio.

But in the meantime, there was Howlin' Wolf, the final blow to Phillips's relationship with Modern in that initially the singer appeared both on Modern and Chess, with the tapes sent in one direction by Phillips, in the other by Turner.

HOW MANY MORE YEARS

Nineteen fifty-two marked a turning point for Chicago blues. On 17 May Chess launched the subsidiary label Checker, and the early fruits of the tie-up with Sam Phillips were being enjoyed. Inevitably this gave new impetus to the revived taste for unalloyed, rural-based southern blues. The 'old guard' of city blues players, exemplified by Broonzy, Washboard Sam and Memphis Minnie, recorded but failed to revive their careers – Sam and Minnie soon retired, while Broonzy shrewdly reinvented himself as a folk-blues entertainer appealing to both coffee-house and concert-hall audiences.

Back door man: when Howlin' Wolf moved north he soon rivalled Muddy Waters as an extrovert club performer.

Some of the old Aristocrat artists were moving on as well. On 9 January 1952, for example, Andrew Tibbs and Sax Mallard, with Big Crawford on bass and Jump Jackson on drums, cut a session for the rival Mercury label. 'Leap Year Blues' also featured the great barrelhouse pianist Roosevelt Sykes, who was nicknamed 'The Honeydripper'. Meanwhile Chess was going from strength to strength. It would be a year until the only effective rival, Vee-Jay Records, appeared, and so Chess was gaining an ever-stronger foothold in the market.

Chess gave Claude Smith – 'Blue Smitty' – a brief opportunity to revive his career with a single session on 11 July, which resulted in 'Sad Story'/'Crying'. It was an impassioned piece of work, and the sad story was that of his mother's death – though this was in fact a revival of 'The Other Woman', a wartime release by Walter Davis. The other cuts, the mournful 'Elgin Movements' and a boogie called 'Date Bait', did not surface until later, on album collections, and Smith faded from the scene.

There were also releases for two musicians from Louisiana, guitarist Morris Pejoe and keyboard player Henry Gray, Mississippi guitarist Arthur 'Big Boy' Spires, the Kentucky bluesman John Brim and Mississippi pianist Eddie Boyd. Boyd was hot at this time with his huge JOB hit 'Five Long Years', but he was to spend the next five years on Chess, making the r&b top ten with two 1953 cuts, '24 Hours' and 'Third Degree'.

But, after Muddy Waters, the next important artist to break through on Chess – 'important' in that he became one of the biggest of all blues stars and had a huge influence on the blues revival of the 1960s – was Howlin' Wolf. 'Biggest' and 'huge' are appropriate words for him.

Chester Arthur Burnett was born in West Point, Mississippi, on 10 June 1910, sang in the Baptist church in Aberdeen and moved to the Young & Myers plantation near Ruleville in his early teens. Nearby was the Dockery plantation, where the man who has more claim that anyone to be the first of the Delta blues singers, Charley Patton, was working. From Patton the Wolf learned not only the blues, but showmanship, the ways of selling a song.

In a studio conversation added as a coda to the Charly boxed set of his work, which like all Chess material on the Charly label was deleted in 1996 when MCA Records won the rights to the catalogue, after a long and bitter dispute, the Wolf recalled his start in music. 'I was ploughing, ploughing four mules on the plantation. And a man come there picking a guitar called Charley Patton. And I liked his sound, so I always did wanna play guitar. So I got him to show me a few chords, y'know, and so every night that I'd get off work I'd go his house and he'd learn me how to pick the guitar. So I got good with it and I went out for myself. I got out there and everything was great, with the people seeing what I was putting down. Then I decided I would play so I asked my father to get me a guitar. 1928 – fifteenth day of January...

'Then along comes Sonny Boy with the harp, Rice Miller, he married my sister then he learned me how to blow the harp. Then I went to play from there. I been playing ever since. I been playing through Arkansas, Mississippi, Louisiana, Alabama and around in Kentucky. I never was in Texas but I played all over the cotton-belt country, y'know, so that's what started me playing the blues.

'Then I had a woman, she was kinda nice to me, then she pulled off and left me. And that give me the blues sure 'nuff. I went to howlin' like a dog then, you know what I mean. So I's been playing ever since.'

'Pop' Staples, head of the family gospel group the Staples Singers, has recalled seeing Patton and the Wolf working at this time. 'My daddy thought the blues was the devil's music. Wouldn't even let me play the guitar, said that was the instrument of the devil too. So I'd sneak out of the house, and that's how I saw Charley Patton and Wolf, when I was 12 or 13. It would be where someone had a big house, and on Saturday night they'd organize a dance. Ladies would be cooking chicken and chitlin' in the kitchen, and they'd have a room for gambling, playing cards, drinking bootleg liquor, and a big room out in front where they'd play and dance.

'Charley and me was on the same plantation, he'd always be playing there, and Wolf came along later. Wolf was my main man. Charley Patton was a good man, far as I know – I was young, and didn't know about his life or anything. But Wolf, I thought he was the greatest thing. A big guy, a real tall handsome man, he was really something else. He was just a few years older than me, but he was so powerful I wouldn't even dare speak to him. They were already calling him Wolf then. He was playing with Charley, I think he was maybe playing Charley's songs, but he was something different altogether. As far as I was concerned, he was the blues.'

There could be no more eloquent first-hand testimony of the almost supernatural power that the Wolf's physical presence, charisma and forceful musicianship exerted, even at a young and unseasoned age. One thing he would certainly have learned from Patton was that passion lay at the heart of the music's power.

Very frequently Patton's own singing was incoherent, a wordless, emotional moan. A howl, indeed. And the Wolf's first single was to be 'Moanin' at Midnight'.

There is some dispute as to when Chester Burnett became Howlin' Wolf. There is no doubt that on the plantation, and in his early days as a performer, he had two other nicknames inspired by his physical bulk – Big Foot and Bull Cow – and he certainly sometimes performed as 'Big Foot Chester'. As far as Pop Staples was concerned, though, he seems to have known him as the Wolf since the start of their acquaintanceship – and the Wolf himself will take it back further, to the age of three.

'My grandfather give me that name, 'fore he died, John Jones. He used to sit down and tell me tall stories about what the wolf would do, y'know, 'cos I was a bad boy. I was always in devilment. So he told me the story about what the wolf done to Little Red Riding Hood. Every time the girl'd ask him, "Mr Wolf, what makes your teeth so big?" he said, "So I can eat you, my dear." And she said, "What makes your eyes so red?" "The better I can see you, my dear."

'And then they finally killed a wolf, and drove it up to the house, and I told 'em it was a dog. He said, "No, that's a wolf." I said, "What's a wolf do?" He said, "Howl, y'know. Whoo-oo-oo." So I got afraid of the wolf and every time I'd kill some of my mother's chickens she'd go "Whoo-oo-oo", and that scared me and made me mad. And that's how they called me Wolf, and I gets mad about this. So they just kept on calling me Wolf and so I got so I didn't care *what* they called me. But first I was afraid of the wolf, y'know?

'I was three years old when they started calling me the Wolf. You know how it is, when people find out you get mad about something they always slip that in. The Wolf, it upset me. I didn't know it was going to be a great name for me!'

In spite of the early charisma and skill admired by such as Pop Staples, it took the Wolf until he was nearly 40 years old to convince himself that music should be his career. Until the late 1940s he would mix largely weekend work as a blues entertainer with farm chores on the plantations. But during the 1930s he also wandered with some of the biggest names of the day, including Robert Johnson, the second Sonny Boy Williamson – as he confirmed above – and Robert Jr Lockwood. When Sonny Boy married the Wolf's half-sister, Mary, he persuaded the younger man out on the road with him, but after each trip the Wolf would return to his tractor. He married twice, first to Delta singer Willie Brown's sister, who died soon afterwards, and then to Lillie Handley, with whom he stayed for the rest of his life. He spent three years in the army during the war.

By 1948 he was based in West Memphis, Arkansas, and at last took up music full time, touring with his own band and working for the local radio station, KWEM, as performer, disc jockey, producer and advertising salesman. The station had only just opened, and the reputation of the part-time bluesman working just to the south was strong enough for the radio executives to come looking for him. He was given a daily 3.00p.m. slot. 'This is the Wolf comin' at ya from KWEM in West Memphis, your only real home for the real downhome blues. Now Howlin' Wolf and the House Rockers is gonna play you an old-time Charley Patton number, but we kinda jazzed it up a little, and I think you cats are gonna like it.'

Not surprisingly, his raw, powerful style soon came to the attention of Sam Phillips. A 1951 session with the Wolf playing harmonica as well as singing, guitarist Willie Johnson, drummer Willie Steel and, on the b-side, Albert Williams or Ike Turner on piano, produced the single 'Moanin' at Midnight'/'How Many More Years'. This at least is how discographies usually chart this session, but harmonica player James Cotton, who was also to journey up to Chicago in the 1950s but who was at this time playing with the Wolf in Memphis, and was certainly present on later sessions, recalled in conversation with Paul Trynka being in on the Wolf's recording career from the start. The aural evidence of this decidedly low-fi session is in Cotton's favour, with the voice often distorting but not the harmonica.

'It was Ike Turner got us recording,' said Cotton. 'He played piano and was acting as some kind of talent scout for the Sun label. They was paying him to find people to record, so we went in there and recorded "Moanin' at Midnight" and "How Many More Years". It was a little old room, we just played how we felt and Sam Phillips kept himself busy getting the microphones right. We didn't think we were making a new sound or anything, we were just playing the way we played. Sam Phillips got real excited, he was real friendly and far as I was concerned he was a real nice person... Then Wolf decided he was gonna go up to Chicago, so he left Willie [Johnson] behind and took Hubert [Sumlin] along with him.'

Not for some time, though. At this stage Phillips was trying to juggle deals for the Wolf's material with both the Biharis in Los Angeles and Leonard Chess in Chicago. The tape of this first session went to Chess, but the next, produced by Ike Turner over in West Memphis, also included a version of 'Moanin' at Midnight' and was sent to the Biharis, appearing on RPM. This situation could clearly not last, and by the following year all Howlin' Wolf sides were going to Chess, and Phillips had burned his boats as far as the Biharis were concerned.

The début single is a stunning piece of work. Although the Wolf will always be remembered in tandem with his later Chicago guitarist Sumlin, it is clear that the younger man learned much from Johnson's belligerent, driving guitar style. There is little to suggest that, if Johnson had been willing to travel north a couple of years later, the Wolf catalogue would be any the weaker. Musically, that is – though one of them might well have killed the other before too long. 'Willie and Wolf would just argue all the time like cat and dog,' said Cotton. 'Willie could be pretty mean, too. It just got to be too much trouble for the old man.' Maybe as truculent and bone-headed a man as Howlin' Wolf needed the gentler, more equable Sumlin as a long-term partner – and even then there were to be many disagreements and fallings-out over the years.

On 'How Many More Years', in contrast to Johnson's striding, intricate guitar riff on 'Moanin', the mood is set by Williams's stomping, double-fisted piano style, as irresistible as anything by Jerry Lee Lewis. On top of them all, the icing on the cake, is the deepest, most reverberating howl ever yet heard on record, a voice that audibly sent all the needles in the control room jerking over into the red danger zone. It was an extraordinary début, 40 years in the making.

Although he had a hit coming out of the radio from Chicago, the Wolf was in no greater hurry to relocate than he had been to commit himself full time to music. He recorded in Memphis through 1952, and added to his schedule a Saturday-morning radio show for another station, KXJK, in Forrest City, Arkansas. But inevitably the Chess brothers were anxious for him to migrate to Chicago, to capitalize on his success, and in late 1952 he eventually agreed. 'I left the other guys back in West Memphis and came up to Chicago by myself,' he told writer Pete Welding. 'They were afraid to take the chance. I went back down there a year later and picked up some of them [notably, of course, Hubert Sumlin] – brought them back with me. But at first I was using guys that Chess furnished – the studio band that I recorded with – bassist Willie Dixon, guitarist Robert Jr Lockwood and so on. After moving to Chicago I found it easy to get into those clubs, playing my music, 'cos the people had heard about me before I came. Right off I started playing at a place at 13th and Ashland. Muddy Waters had been playing there. Then I went to stretching out all across town.'

In fact, there is no firm evidence that Leonard Chess put Howlin' Wolf into the Chicago studio until early 1954, since he had such a stockpile of Memphis-cut material to use up , like 'Howlin' for My Baby', 'Saddle My Pony', 'Oh, Red!' and 'All Night Boogie'. In the meantime, though, in 1952, the Muddy Waters band had spawned the next great Chess star – Little Walter. 'I never had anything to do with Little Walter,' said the Wolf, dismissively. "Cos he was always smoking dope and all that jive and I don't go for that... My reputation is too high to let someone drag it down with a weed. I'll take a drink of whisky but I ain't fooling with no cigarettes...'

JUKE

Jimmy Rogers once related in *Blues Unlimited* magazine how Leonard Chess would get actively involved in the studio. Referring specifically to his own sessions, though it clearly held true for all the Chess artists – particularly in the days before Willie Dixon effectively took over control of production – he said: 'Most times Leonard would have quite a bit to do with it… [He] mostly confused me by changing the beat, but he would never change my lyrics. You'd built a number with a certain tempo or beat and he would sometimes change the beat and that would throw you off in getting your words to blend in.'

A notable, and somewhat lumpen, example is the next Muddy Waters session, on 11 July 1951. The songs are as effective as ever, adorned in the first three instances by a heavily amplified Little Walter harmonica – 'Country Boy', the hit 'She Moves Me', 'My Fault' and the heavy 'Still a Fool' – but Chess took over the drum stool to indicate exactly the sound he wanted. And what he wanted, it seems, was a four-square thump on the bass drum, two beats to the bar without any frills, and it doggedly prevents the songs from taking flight.

Waters later recalled Chess's brief career as a drummer. 'Leonard Chess played the bass drum because my drummer couldn't get the beat on "She Moves Me". The verse was too long. You know, it says, "She moves a crazy man", he says, "Now I'm not so dumb. I took her to a funeral, the dead jump up and run." She spoke to a deaf and dumb boy, he said "Now I can speak," and that's where he couldn't hold it, 'cos it goes on, She took her finger in a blind man's face, he say, "I once was blind but now I see." "She moves me, man…"

'My drummer wanted to play a turnaround there. I had to go another six or eight bars more to get it turned around. My drummer wasn't doin' nothing, just dum-chick dum, but he couldn't hold it there to save his damn life, and Leonard Chess knew where it was. So Leonard told him, "Get the fuck out of the way. I'll do that."' A later Chess house drummer, Odie Payne, described this

as 'trying to be as a Negro'. But Elgin Evans's 'dum-chick dum' might, in retrospect, have served the songs better. Chess solved the problem of timing the turnaround by ignoring it.

Muddy returned to the studio on 29 December, now mercifully with Evans on drums, to proclaim 'They Call Me Muddy Waters' and to cut one of the many variations on Arthur Crudup's 'Rock Me Mama' theme called 'All Night Long'. It was the next studio date, on 12 May 1952, which produced the Waters single 'Please Have Mercy', which changed the role of blues harmonica and made it as defining a sound of 1950s Chicago blues as the guitar.

With Waters, Rogers and Evans as his backing group, Little Walter vamped his way through an instrumental that the band had been using for a while as a closing 'signature tune' on live dates, now given the title 'Your Cat Will Play'. At least, that's what they came up with on the spur of the moment to write in the session log, but when he selected it as a single to release on his new Checker label, Leonard Chess shrewdly gave the number the punchy, evocative name 'Juke'. Writer Neil Slaven has identified two earlier instrumentals that, when combined, could well have been the source of the tune – 'Snooky and Moody's Boogie', with Snooky Pryor on harmonica, and one that Sunnyland Slim similarly used as a theme, and which he called 'Get Up Those Stairs Mademoiselle'.

Fortunately, Chess was also shrewd enough to keep away from the drum stool on this occasion, and Evans gives the piece a simple, padding brush rhythm over which Walter can lay his virtuoso fantasies, with Waters and Rogers boogying away in the middle distance. Effective though the drumming is in this instance, however, there were signs developing that the

Muddy Waters band and its various recording spin-offs were beginning to outgrow the limitations of Evans's technique.

After this record had become a success, as Jimmy Rogers put it: 'If a harmonica player couldn't play "Juke", he couldn't play harmonica.' This makes the problem faced by a generation of British would-be guitarists ten years later, of mastering the mysteries of the Shadows' 'Apache', seem like the child's play that it actually was. 'Juke' remains a glorious statement of genius.

Inevitably, it was not a genius that appeared from nowhere. As well as undergoing his long apprenticeship, and in addition to the audible influence of the first Sonny Boy (and the second, for that matter), Little Walter had undoubtedly listened carefully to the aforementioned Pryor, who was on the Chicago scene at the time, and Jimmy Rogers has attested to the effect that another of the contemporary players, the Memphis-based Walter Horton, had on the younger man. Horton would show Walter something new and would have his advice arrogantly rejected – only for Walter to practise it and add it to his harmonica language.

Marshall Chess recalled in *Living Blues* magazine that a version of the 'old grey whistle test' (can the elderly janitor whistle the tune?) came into play once the record was cut. 'Well, blues, you know, has always been a woman's market. And "Juke" ... what prompted my father to put it out, it was a rainy day, we had a canopy over the place and the door was open, 'cos it gets very hot here in the summer, and he was playing "Juke", it had just been recorded a few days before at the tail end of a session. Well, he was listening to the record, and there was this old lady, an old colored lady, standing under the canopy to keep out of the rain, and he saw her

digging it. So he played it again, and then they rushed it into release, and it was one of our biggest hits ever. You know, they didn't really want to admit they dug the blues, but that's the effect it had.'

With the record pressed and distributed, the Muddy Waters band left town for a lengthy tour of the southern states, sharing the bill with John Lee Hooker. When they reached Shreveport, Louisiana, Little Walter's record was on all the juke boxes, and was constantly being selected by club customers. Walter's reaction to this sudden celebrity was the first serious sign of a temperamental weakness that was effectively to curtail his career, in this case irresponsible unreliability prompted by overeagerness.

As Jimmy Rogers recalls it in *Chicago Blues*: 'We all went to get some uniforms in Shreveport, Louisiana. We went downtown to have some pants, shirts combinations... This fella said pick them up about two o'clock... He [Walter] told me to bring his back. And when we left, *he* left ... and when we got back the girl at the desk said, "You talking about the little guy? He got a cab and left as soon as y'all left – he went to the train station." Yeah, we left one way and he left in the other and came back to Chicago.'

When the band, minus their harmonica player, arrived back home after the tour, Walter even had the nerve to ask for his full wage. Muddy forgave the errant virtuoso enough to continue booking him on record dates for some time to come, though it was surely at Leonard Chess's insistence – he was, after all, the best in town – and Walter even played a few more gigs with the band, but inevitably his ambitions lay in fronting his own outfit. The last straw for the tempestuous young man was at the Club Zanzibar, when a customer requested 'Juke' and tipped Muddy and Jimmy Rogers a quarter each, but had only a dime left for Walter.

He soon found a band, ready made – The Four Aces. The only problem was that another member of the Chicago harmonica Mafia, Junior Wells, was one of the quartet. It seems, however, that Muddy contacted Wells from the South after Walter's defection and persuaded him to join the band – it is more likely that the two men simply swapped places than that Wells, no fading violet himself, was meekly usurped against his will by Walter. The result was that Walter joined guitarist brothers Louis and David Myers, and drummer Fred Below, renaming the band Little Walter and his Night Cats. The swap arrangement was confirmed by Below in conversation with Bill Greensmith: 'Junior Wells went with Muddy because Muddy was a big name at that particular time. And you couldn't blame Junior for going with Muddy. Little Walter didn't have no group so Dave and Louis accepted him into our group.'

Below, who was to contribute to many of the finest Chicago blues records of the 1950s, was a more sophisticated technician that Evans. 'I was able to play the beat and put something to it that was a lot different... My musical experience helped me a lot to really play these blues.' He was born in Chicago in

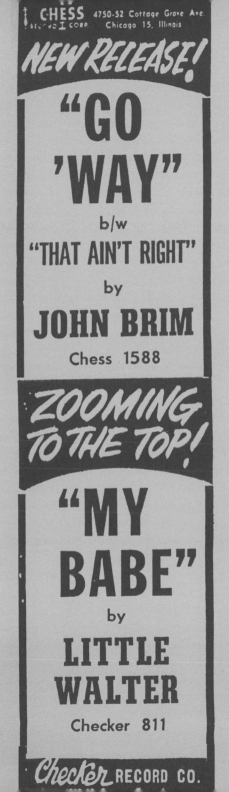

1926, learned music in school and broadened his experience during two stints in the army – in Alabama on war service he played with fellow soldier Lester Young, soon to be recognized as one of the greatest of all jazz tenor saxophonists, and while in Germany in the late 1940s he played the clubs during his time off, booked by the promoter Horst Lippman.

When Below returned to Chicago in 1951 it was his friend Elgin Evans who found him a job, playing at the Brookmount Hotel with Louis and David Myers, who needed a drummer. The only problem was that Below was by now a jazz man, whereas in his absence the blues had become the city's dominant music. Nevertheless, the Myers brothers were sufficiently impressed by his drumming to teach him to play the blues.

The brothers came from Byhalia, Mississippi, where David was born in 1926 and Louis in 1929. On moving to Chicago in 1941 the family lived in the same apartment house as Lonnie Johnson, then one of the city's big blues stars. They had to content themselves with playing at house parties until 1950, when they were both 21, since minors was not allowed into the licensed clubs, and by this time they were part of a trio with Arthur 'Big Boy' Spires. He was soon to be replaced by Junior Wells, and they were billed as the Three Aces – Below made it Four for the Brookmount Hotel gig.

The first Night Cats studio session took place in October 1952, by which time 'Juke' had been to the top of the r&b chart. Although two of the cuts remained unreleased for many years – the haunting 'Blue Midnight' and an exuberant and self-explanatory 'Boogie' – the rest of a brief night's work did the trick, producing a double-sided follow-up hit. 'Mean Old World' features Walter's singing – distinctive, but coming from

the greatest harmonica player of the day only adequate – while the expressive 'Sad Hours' is a slow instrumental tour de force. The latter peaked at number two.

After the session they left immediately for New York, and played a season at the Apollo. 'One of the largest crowds they ever had,' recalls Below. 'It was something they had never seen ... this is what you call southern music, downhome music.' Below also claims that they could have continued travelling eastwards for what would have been a pioneering trip to Europe, including a London Palladium date, but Walter got cold feet. Unlike Below, he had never left the States and was in no hurry to do so.

Back in the Chicago studio in January 1953, the sound fattened by 'Big' Crawford's bass, they could not produce a usable number – effectively, they were composing on tape. After another tour they returned to the studio three months later, now with Willie Dixon on bass for some tracks and a pianist, probably Henry Gray, on others. 'Tonight With a Fool' was rush-released but equally hurriedly withdrawn in favour of a remake of one of January's instrumental attempts, 'Off the Wall'. Backed by 'Tell Me Mama', it is an assured and practised boogie, the closest yet to the 'Juke' style, and it reveals Below now thoroughly at home with the demands of Chicago blues. Indeed, so confident was he that he introduced the drum solo to the genre. The record hit in April.

Commercially, Walter's next visit to the studio in September also did the trick. The flip side of the chosen single, 'Quarter to Twelve', is a slow and seductive instrumental. And 'Blues with a Feeling', probably with Jimmy Rogers on one of the backing guitars, is a familiar-sounding meditation that reached number six in October.

The session was fruitful indeed, because it also produced his next hit. The crisp, rocking 'You're So Fine' made it a good Christmas for Walter, peaking at number four in January 1954, while the b-side introduced a technical innovation that all other blues harmonica players had so far steered clear of. On 'Lights Out' Walter turns to the comparatively unwieldy, double-decker chromatic instrument, discovering a tonal richness and depth previously thought to be beyond the 'bent note' demands of the blues.

By this time Louis Myers had had enough and decided to leave the band, which was no longer the Four Aces as he recognized them, but simply a vehicle for Walter. This might have been an acceptable and profitable evolution given a front man of more generous, less arrogant personality. 'Walter was a greedy man, he want it all for himself,' Myers recalled. 'He didn't want to pay right... I got on to him time after time. I said, "I'm not trying to get into your business or nothing like that but why should one cat be professional out here... One cat ain't nothing without the other one." "Yeah, but I got a name. I'm Little Walter."' At one gig Myers was sharp enough to spot that Walter was being ripped off over his agreed share of the door money, but Walter showed no gratitude, and so came the first defection from the Night Cats.

Walter's luck held, however – first he had found a ready-made band after running out on Muddy Waters's group, then he found that he was still hired to play with the man he had let down, and now he found the ideal replacement for Louis Myers in Robert Johnson's old sidekick, Robert Jr Lockwood, born in Arkansas in 1915. Lockwood played on Louis Myers's last session in February, deputizing for the absent Dave Myers on a night that produced a hit single, 'Oh Baby'/'Rocker', and

three months later joined Waters's pianist Otis Spann for another Walter session. Spann crashes into 'I Got to Find My Baby' and Lockwood plays some dazzling rhythm/lead guitar, but the track mysteriously stayed on the shelf until 1961.

In his turn Dave Myers was also becoming disenchanted with Walter's arrogance, and two sessions in July marked his last work with the band. Of historical, if not aesthetic, importance is an early version of the Willie Dixon song 'My Babe', which borrows heavily from the happy-clappy gospel number 'This Train', a skiffle favourite. 'I felt Little Walter had the feeling for this "My Babe" song,' said Dixon. 'He was the type of fellow who wanted to brag about some chick, somebody he loved, something he was doing or getting away with. He fought it for two long years and I wasn't going to give the song to nobody but him. He said many times he just didn't like it but, by 1955, the Chess people had gained confidence enough in me that they felt if I wanted him to do it, it must be his type of thing. The minute he did it, BOOM! she went right up the charts.'

Not quite BOOM!, because Dixon is overlooking this first, reluctant attempt at the song, where Walter is clearly still to be convinced of the merits of what would prove his biggest hit.

At this time Muddy Waters, to whom we shall return in the next chapter, was scoring repeatedly in the charts – with Walter on harmonica – but the Night Cats were in flux. The first 'My Babe' session included another first attempt, at the slow blues 'Last Night'. These were followed by the tracks that produced the next Walter single, before Dave Myers in turn called it a day. The single combined a lively vocal boogie, 'You'd Better Watch Yourself', with another technical *tour de force* – on the strolling, moody instrumental 'Blue Light' Walter used four harmonicas, including the chromatic, to build his virtuoso effects. This was a September hit, which reached number nine. Yet again Walter was lucky in his new recruit – Luther Tucker, who was born in Memphis in 1936 but grew up in Chicago, was one of the most in-demand backing guitarists playing on the club scene at the time, and took over from Dave.

In October 1954 Tucker played on the next Walter single, the 'achieved' version of 'Last Night', and a Dixon dance song, 'Mellow Down Easy', whose swirling riff makes it the clear forerunner of one of the biggest hits in the Dixon catalogue, 'Wang Dang Doodle'. Then, in January 1955, came the sly, confident, bubbling shuffle of 'My Babe', with Dixon, Below and Lockwood supplemented by bass player Leonard Caston. Born in Mississippi in 1917, Caston was actually a pianist, and a member of Dixon's 1940s band the Big Three. This suggests that this was indeed a good example of Chess's spontaneous approach to recording – not only was Dixon's old chum grabbed in off the street, but to play an unfamiliar instrument.

Chess and Dixon were confident enough of the quality of 'My Babe' to put what is clearly just a warm-up instrumental, 'Thunderbird', on the flip side. By the beginning of March the record had reached number one in the r&b chart, and, with a stay of 17 weeks, it lingered in the list for a week longer than 'Juke'. It was credited with reaching the top of the lists that logged juke-box plays and radio spins by disc jockeys, and even – most unusual in the days before Fats Domino, Little Richard, Chuck Berry and Bo Diddley knocked down the racial barriers – it also lurked just outside the Hot 100 on the national, and therefore white, pop charts.

However, as Les Fancourt notes drily in his booklet to the Charly box set devoted to Little Walter's Chess career: 'Actual sales figures were not a feature Chess bragged about.' Of course not – the artists might begin to detect a discrepancy between the figures and the occasional hand-outs that Chess gave them. These were still the days when it suited record-company owners to encourage the idea that discs were simply a way of promoting an artist's live-performance career, increasing their box-office power – not an earner in their own right.

So Dixon's persistence with his song paid off, and cemented him in Chess's mind as a huge company asset, able to deal with musicians in all aspects of the business. It also established Little Walter as the label's biggest star, outselling even his old boss Muddy Waters. It is neat, therefore, that a newcomer to the label who was to rise even further, Bo Diddley, contributed to the next Walter single in April 1955. The instrumental 'Roller Coaster' is built as much around Bo's soon-to-be-distinctive, plangent guitar tone as it is around Walter's brilliant harp work. During the next month, incidentally, Walter turned up at a Diddley session, taking over from Billy Boy Arnold on 'Diddley Daddy'.

'My Babe' was, of course, a peak of Walter's career, but that did not have to mean that it was downhill all the way from there. Indeed there were three more hits to carry him through the rest of the decade – 'Who', 'Key to the Highway' and 'Everything Gonna Be Alright', the middle one reaching number six. But even this comparative success is confirmation of decline after the constant hit-making of the period 1952-5. It is not as if Walter, like so many more traditional bluesmen, was being swept away by the tide of rock 'n' roll. We have already noted that he could appeal to the white market, and 'My Babe' was his passport to the package shows that, under the banner of pioneering rock 'n' roll disc jockey Alan Freed, were to become characteristic of the new era.

The next blow to his career was the departure late in 1955 of Fred Below, the last survivor of the Four Aces, though he remained the first choice for sessions until 1957. Although Walter was capable of spontaneous gestures of generosity – the southern bluesman Houston Stackhouse, who encouraged the young Walter, is witness to an impulsive gift of a $50 bill – they were the exceptions. What was constant was his meanness as a band leader. And so, increasingly, were unreliability, heavy drinking and bouts of violence. The quickest way for a performing artist to arrest his career is to gain a reputation for not showing up to gigs. And so, at the peak of his popularity, Little Walter was not building his career, but at best was treading water, and before long was beginning to sink. He took to carrying a gun, and his face began to collect evidence of his drunken willingness to argue with a knife.

'I could see from the handwriting on the wall, instead of getting better jobs we were staying in the same trend,' says Below. 'We wasn't getting any better and we were getting less jobs.' But the drummer had no need to

Kingpin: songwriter, musician, producer and manager Willie Dixon was the heart of Chicago blues.

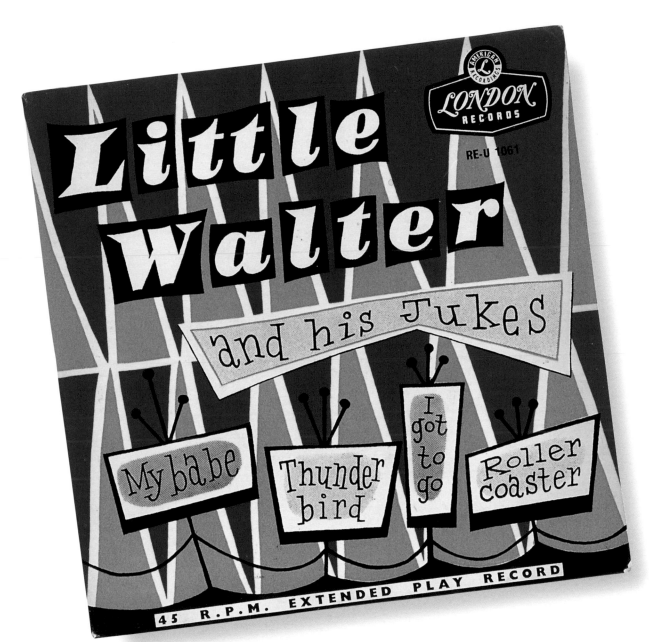

worry about his own future – such was his reputation that his telephone was bound to ring. He was soon hired by Memphis Slim, then he freelanced in the studio for a while with John Lee Hooker among others, went with one of the city's new stars Otis Rush and finished the decade playing with Buddy Guy.

For Walter, the remaining studio sessions of 1955 produced some quality sides, and continued his input to the Checker label. 'Hate to See You Go' has an instantly attractive riff in the Diddley style, though it was not a hit, while 'One More Chance with You' is relaxed and jazz-tinged, reminiscent of Hooker's 'One Scotch, One Bourbon, One Beer'. 'Who' was a hit, while 'Boom Boom, Out Go the Lights', a novelty number, has gone on to be a standard – British revivalists the Blues Band, for example, use it as an audience-participation rabble-rouser. 'It Ain't Right' has an infectious country-style riff.

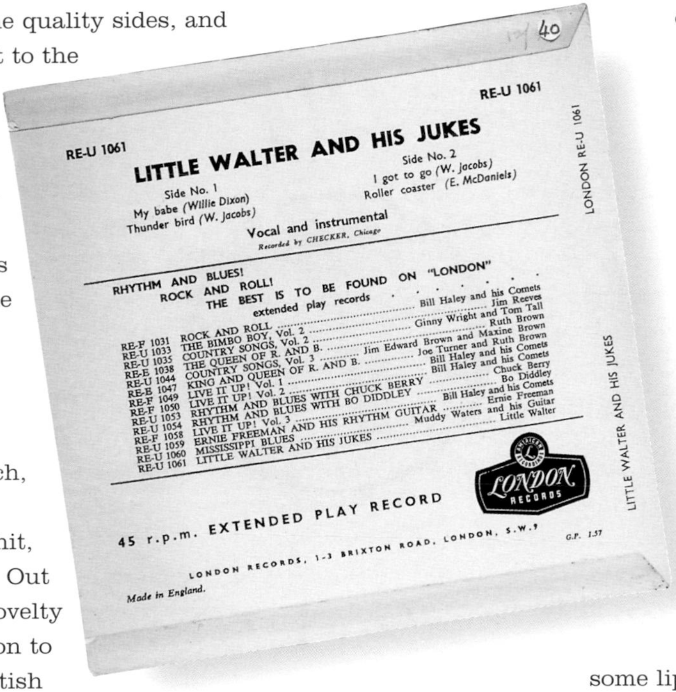

It would seem that Chess took Walter into the studio just twice in 1956, by which time Bo Diddley and Chuck Berry were fashioning a new image for the label. Walter's temperament and drunken tantrums meant that he was swimming against the tide, the tide of rock 'n' roll. There were some creative compensations, though.

'Flying Saucers' is another virtuoso performance mixing chromatic and the bluesman's more usual 'marine band' instruments. 'It's Too Late, Brother' is clearly a search for a clone of 'My Babe'. The instrumental 'Teenage Beat' has some Berry-ish guitar work by Lockwood (and its title stresses the attempt to come to terms with the new era), while 'Take Me Back' is an effective blues in classic style. By this time, however, Little Walter could have been privately grateful that he was still being booked for Muddy Waters studio dates.

As far as his own career was concerned, he seemed hell-bent on destroying it. One fight resulted in a gun wound, and Luther Tucker recalls Walter's inability to walk away from a fight, and that 'he beat women too. If a woman give him some lip, he'd fatten it up for her.'

A session in March 1957 produced a single in the 'Fever'-styled rocker 'Nobody But You' and a laid-back, appealing blues reminiscent of Jimmy Reed, 'Everybody Needs Somebody'. Walter also made the first attempt at a song called 'Temperature', and when he returned to the studio in July the band persisted through nearly 40 takes of this catchy number before producing the version selected for single release, with the piece given structure by some acidic guitar work on Tucker's part. Another strong side, 'Ah'w

---

40

RE-U 1061

RE-U 1061

LITTLE WALTER AND HIS JUKES

Side No. 1
My babe (Willie Dixon)
Thunder bird (W. Jacobs)

Side No. 2
I got to go (W. Jacobs)
Roller coaster (E. McDaniels)

Vocal and instrumental
Recorded by CHECKER, Chicago

LONDON RE-U 1061

LITTLE WALTER AND HIS JUKES

RHYTHM AND BLUES!
ROCK AND ROLL!
THE BEST IS TO BE FOUND ON "LONDON"
extended play records

RE-F 1031	ROCK AND ROLL	Bill Haley and his Comets
RE-U 1033	THE BIMBO BOY, Vol. 2	Jim Reeves
RE-U 1035	COUNTRY SONGS, Vol. 2	Ginny Wright and Tom Tall
RE-E 1038	THE QUEEN OF R. AND B.	Ruth Brown
RE-U 1044	COUNTRY SONGS, Vol. 3	Jim Edward Brown and Maxine Brown
RE-E 1047	KING AND QUEEN OF R. AND B.	Joe Turner and Ruth Brown
RE-F 1049	LIVE IT UP! Vol. 1	Bill Haley and his Comets
RE-F 1050	LIVE IT UP! Vol. 2	Bo Diddley
RE-U 1053	RHYTHM AND BLUES WITH CHUCK BERRY	Chuck Berry
RE-U 1054	RHYTHM AND BLUES WITH BO DIDDLEY	Bo Diddley
RE-F 1058	LIVE IT UP! Vol. 3	Bill Haley and his Comets
RE-U 1059	ERNIE FREEMAN AND HIS RHYTHM GUITAR	Ernie Freeman
RE-U 1060	MISSISSIPPI BLUES	Muddy Waters
RE-U 1061	LITTLE WALTER AND HIS JUKES	Little Walter

45 r.p.m. EXTENDED PLAY RECORD

LONDON RECORDS

LONDON RECORDS, 1-3 BRIXTON ROAD, LONDON, S.W.9
Made in England.

G.P. 137

Baby', completed the session, together with a first crack at the James Oden standard 'Goin' Down Slow', here called 'I Had My Fun'.

This guilt-ridden classic, presumably seen as being sung by someone stricken with syphilis but gaining even more mournful power in the AIDS era, was also cut by Howlin' Wolf, with extraordinary guitar work by Hubert Sumlin and a portentous opening monologue by Willie Dixon. Since this is one of the most spine-chilling of all Chess records, no one else, including Walter, need apply. He turns it into a light, wistful shuffle adorned by a spot-on solo.

Towards the end of the year there was another personnel change in the Walter band, with Lockwood leaving, Tucker remaining as lead guitarist and Jimmy Lee Robinson joining on bass. George Hunter was Below's most usual replacement on drums by this time. In January 1958 they cut another standard from the 1940s – the Jay McShann hit written and first performed by McShann's vocalist Walter Brown, 'Confessin' the Blues'. Again, to my ears, Walter was eventually gazumped by another Chess artist – Chuck Berry cut a beautiful version of the song two years later, and then the Rolling Stones pitched a respectful cover somewhere between the two.

An August session came up with a hit in the old Big Bill Broonzy war-horse 'Key to the Highway', with Walter in plaintive voice and Otis Spann and Muddy Waters strengthening the band. It climbed to number six and remained in the charts for 14 weeks. But two months later came an abortive session, with Walter singing drably on 'Someday Baby' and Phil Chess testily saying at one point: 'Put some feeling into it – take six.' The next studio visit, in February 1959, was a mixed affair, and by now there are signs that Walter's tempestuous life was taking its toll on his skills. Luther Tucker kicks into an up-tempo rocker, 'Baby', but Walter's voice seems to be fading and his harmonica losing its subtlety. However, he improves on the routine Willie Dixon number 'My Baby's Sweeter' and raises his game even further on Dixon's lively 'Crazy Mixed-Up World', but loses out once more to Berry in reviving Big Maceo's 'Worried Life Blues', which Chuck was to revive a year later.

July brought Walter his last hit, 'Everything's Gonna Be Alright', with Spann on cracking form, plus a lively revival of Arthur Crudup's 'Mean Old Frisco', while an August date suggested – misleadingly – that all was not yet lost. Walter's impassioned singing, Tucker's frenetic guitar fingering and some crashing back-up chords make 'Blue and Lonesome' one of Walter's finest sides. The year ended with another strong number, 'Me and Piney Brown', urged on by Otis Spann, who plays in similar manner to his work on the Muddy Waters hit 'Got My Mojo Working', and an improved attempt at 'Goin' Down Slow'.

Chess did not invite Walter back into the studio until December 1960, a sure sign that his drink problems and violent nature were now far outweighing his ability to produce hits. Surprisingly, the session was quite successful. The single 'I Don't Play' is a strong Dixon riff number, and there's still a little life in Walter's drink-coarsened voice. But studio backchat from Walter before cutting the pleasantly melodic 'You Don't Know' – the observation that 'this is a nauseating situation' and an unhealthy sprinkling of 'motherfuckers' – confirm that time was running out.

By this time Buddy Guy was the new king of Chess, and therefore it is fitting that he was around three years later, in February 1963, for

Walter's penultimate Chess session. Although 'Up the Line' is quite a strong rocker, beefed up by Jarrett Gibson's saxophone as well as Guy's guitar, 'I'm a Business Man' marks a sad farewell – repetitive, tired, slurred and clearly drunken. In between times Walter continued to make some sort of living playing the clubs, and he could even garner the occasional compliment, like Hound Dog Taylor's endorsement: 'He was the best – the harder you drove, the more he would play.' But for the man who just a few years previously had been on the top of the blues world with 'My Babe', there were few interruptions to the downward spiral.

By this time, though, the British blues revival was in full swing. Muddy Waters's red-blooded, heavily amplified music may have been something of a shock to the beard-and-sandals British jazz fans on his first visit in 1958, but by 1963 he was a hero. Walter's own visit took place in September 1964, a six-week club tour together with spots on BBC radio and on the best television pop show of the day, *Ready Steady Go*. But this belated opportunity to revive his career did not improve his behaviour. He would make it clear when he found his backing musicians wanting, and would occasionally insult them by deciding on an ill-tempered impulse to perform solo. He wasn't invited back to the UK, not as a headline attraction anyway. Others, like Muddy, Buddy Guy, John Lee Hooker and even Sonny Boy Williamson – no more sober nor even-tempered a man than Walter – knew how to play the British game better, and were grateful to discover an adoring overseas audience they never knew existed. Chuck Berry, of course, recorded his biggest British hit here, though unfortunately it consisted of the schoolboy rudeness of 'My Ding-a-Ling'.

Walter continued Chicago club work when he could get it, and played a session as a backing musician to Robert Nighthawk and Johnny Young for the Testament label. Chess did make one last attempt to coax another hit out of him, in February 1966, but could not bring themselves to release any of the three tracks, and a year later they invited him to play on an album project called *Super Blues Join Forces*, with Bo Diddley, Muddy Waters, Otis Spann and Buddy Guy. He does not give a good account of himself, and it would even seem that it is one of the backing group, Cookie Vee, and not Walter himself singing on 'My Babe'. His other main contribution, 'Juke', wasn't included on the Checker album culled from the session and had to wait for later bootleg release.

In autumn 1967 Walter was included on a Chicago blues package tour of Europe, including some British dates, with Hound Dog Taylor and Koko Taylor, but again he bickered with his musicians, his fellow artists, the promoters and anyone else who stood in his way, and turned in a generally listless performance.

Back in Chicago, on 14 February 1968 Walter, as was all too common, picked a drunken fight in the street. During the fracas he was kicked in the head, and staggered off to a friend's house, saying that he needed a gun. But his headache was so bad that he lay down instead, lost consciousness and died in his sleep. Said his bass player Jerome Arnold, as a melancholy epitaph: 'He sought out the worst kind of riff-raff ... he seemed to be comfortable with them.' Walter was just 38 when he died. He is buried at St Mary's Cemetery in Evergreen, Illinois, and a belated headstone erected by fans in 1992 describes him as the 'Blues Harp Master'. No one would want to argue with that.

CHAPTER 3

IN COMMAND OF THE GAME

I'M READY

Although Little Walter's Chicago career lasted some 20 years its peak was sadly shorter, perhaps between 'Juke' and the late 1950s. Therefore it seems appropriate to have pursued his life to its melancholy end before returning to our chronological discipline, and to the heart of Chicago blues in the Muddy Waters band of the early 50s.

Junior Wells replaced Walter on stage and also, briefly, in the studio for a four-song session in September 1952, at which time Walter was on the road with his new band. It was a half-success, producing a single, though not a hit, in 'Standing Around Crying', with Wells's harmonica handling the crying, and a pleasantly riffing jump blues in 'Gone to Main Street'. Walter was virtually impossible to replace, so much had he advanced the potential of his instrument, but Wells was already proving more than adequate as a member of the band.

He was even younger than Walter, born in Memphis in 1934, and as a kid would undoubtedly have heard such local celebrities as Howlin' Wolf and Junior Parker. He moved to Chicago when he was 11, and, like Walter, soon became known to the resident musicians. His trio with the Myers brothers was originally but

briefly called the Little Chicago Devils, changed its name to the Three Deuces, then the Three Aces, and when Fred Below expanded the sound they were, naturally, rechristened the Four Aces. After his job swap with Walter, Wells recorded as Junior Wells and his Eagle Rockers for the States label in 1953.

As if to confirm that the swap was amicable, his backing group on the session were what was by then Walter's band – the Myers brothers and Below – together with pianist Henry Gray and Muddy Waters himself on a couple of tracks. The first single was 'Cut That Out' and 'Eagle Rock', followed by 'Hoodoo Man' and 'Junior's Wail'. Neither made the r&b chart but, along with his position in the most prestigious band in town, they consolidated his local reputation.

Wells's career was soon interrupted by his being drafted into the US Army, and his job in the Waters band went to Walter Horton. Back in Chicago in 1957 Wells returned to recording, and had a small hit on Profile in 1960 with 'Little By Little', which featured Earl Hooker on guitar. Soon after this he cut 'Messin' with the Kid' for the Chief label, and though this wasn't a hit at the time it has long been his best-known theme. In the mid-60s Wells teamed up with Buddy Guy for a double act that was to last some 25 years,

'Then I had a woman,
she was kinda nice to me,
then she pulled off and left me.
And that give me the blues sure 'nuff.
I went to Howlin' like a dog then,
you know what I mean.
So I's been playing
ever since.'

Supergroup:
Muddy Waters, maracas shaker Jerome Green, pianist Otis Spann, harmonica man Henry Strong, drummer Elgin Evans and guitarist Jimmy Rogers, circa 1954.

and he is still working, the senior statesman of the blues harp.

Muddy Waters returned to the studio in January 1953, with Horton in place of Wells, and two of the numbers make a fascinating contrast. Whereas 'She's All Right' deliberately looks back in style to his late-40s 'Delta in Chicago' sound, the richer, stronger groove of 'My Life is Ruined' looks forward, to that fully achieved mid-50s style of such numbers as 'Got My Mojo Working', in which Muddy once again redefined the character of Chicago blues. Clearly he was making this transition, consciously or not, in his stage act early in 1953.

In May Little Walter was once again available, and Leonard Chess was anxious to use him. Indeed he dominates a version of 'Baby Please Don't Go', the Big Joe Williams classic, which is here called 'Turn the Lamp Down Low'. Waters agreed with Chess anyway. 'I had the best harmonica player in the business,' he later recalled. 'He put a lot of trick things in there, getting all different sounds ... he always had ideas.' And it now seems as a result of stylistic analysis by Tony Glover in America that it was Little Walter rather than Horton, who has been credited up until now, present on the next Waters session in, making the most of a roistering blues in Elmore James style, 'Blow Wind Blow' and contributing a stunning solo to 'Mad Love (I Want You To Love Me)', a stop-rhythm rocker in Muddy's new mid-50s mode.

Willie Dixon has suggested, however, that in his view Walter Horton was even better than Little Walter, rating the latter as 'very good' and Big Walter as a 'helluva harmonica player'. The problem was that he was 'loaded most of the time but once you'd get him in good condition, he could run rings around all of them.' He could, for example, use a drinking glass or a tin can with the top cut out to make the instrument sound like a trombone.

Horton was more of Muddy's generation than that of Little Walter and Junior Wells, being born in Mississippi in 1918. Although he was certainly employed as a session player from the late 1930s onwards, he didn't cut a record in his own right until a Memphis date in 1951, and by this time he was a fully formed artist – even if he was billed under his nickname Mumbles. Regular

subsequent sessions as a solo artist, along with his 1950s work with Muddy and also with Johnny Shines, confirm him as Little Walter's main rival when it comes to technical command and richness of tone. Horton remained in work throughout his life, recording and touring – including European blues packages – and died in Chicago in 1981.

The next Muddy Waters session, in January 1954, featured the other Walter, however, and it was a historic one. By this time, anyway, Horton had left the Waters live band in favour of Henry Strong, who was reckoned to be more reliable. With Otis Spann, Jimmy Rogers and Elgin Evans completing the line-up, they cut a number that was to be a compulsory component of every subsequent Waters gig until the end of his life – 'Hoochie Coochie Man'. Willie Dixon was now approaching his peak as a songwriter and producer, constantly refreshing the Chicago blues sound in his work with, in particular, Muddy and later on with Howlin' Wolf, and this boastful classic – 'Gonna make pretty womens jump and shout' – is a prime example. It harks back to the early Muddy Waters numbers that dabbled in southern voodoo for their appeal.

Until this time Dixon had struggled to get Leonard Chess to take him seriously as a songwriter. He had a contract to 'assist' the company in any way required, which by and large meant menial duties, and as he wryly observed: '...They weren't giving me much of a pay thing ... every week, I'd have to damn near fight or beg for the money.'

And so the man who is now seen as being at the very heart of 1950s Chicago blues was actually regarded by the head of the company as a dogsbody, more exploited than encouraged. Chess raised no objections, however, to Dixon's desire to pitch 'Hoochie Coochie Man' to Muddy Waters, who was approached by Dixon during the interval at a Club Zanzibar gig and, after initial reluctance, performed the song that very night. As soon as the recorded version of the song started selling, Chess revised his opinion of Dixon's usefulness as a songwriter, and came to rely on him to have a suitable song ready whenever an artist needed one.

For those who feel that Fred Below added just a little more to the Muddy Waters sound than Evans could manage, the line-up for the next session in April 1954 marks the greatest of all Waters line-ups – Dixon on stand-up bass interplaying with Below, Little Walter and Otis Spann decorating the songs, Jimmy Rogers in perfect support of the leader. 'Just Make Love to Me' is the defining song of this period (more easily recalled, perhaps, under an alternative title that is also a line of the lyric, 'I Just Want to Make Love To You').

With the obvious exception of 'Juke', Walter often produced his finest work when corralled by the contributions of others, forcing him to make the most of his solo opportunity, and his playing here is peerless. And as with so many of the classic numbers that Waters was now compiling, it is Spann's tough, confrontational piano pounding that helps define the song's character. The flip side, a confident rocker called 'Oh Yeh', has sometimes been credited to Bo Diddley, who, at the time, was still playing for dimes on Maxwell Street – a confusion with Diddley's 1958 'Oh Yea'.

Two months after this session, in June, tragedy caused another shift in the live-band personnel – Henry Strong was murdered, and the latest in the lengthening line of Muddy's harp players was George Smith, an Arkansas-born

Big bass man:
Willie Dixon was part of the classic 1954 Muddy Waters line-up.

virtuoso who, like Little Walter, had adapted the chromatic instrument to the blues.

In September the stellar April line-up cut the next classic, 'I'm Ready', kicked off by Spann's sly piano riff and Below's slap-happy drums. This three-minute catalogue of sexual boasting contains one of Dixon's finest tongue-in-cheek lines – 'I hope some schoolboy starts a fight, 'cos I'm ready, ready as a man can be...!' The session also produced a curiosity in a version of 'Smokestack Lightnin'', credited to Howlin' Wolf. Although the Wolf had moved to Chicago by this time and was recording with Dixon, he didn't cut his own version of the song until 1956, so definitive that after this there was not much point in anyone else bothering with it. Though that didn't stop Manfred Mann!

The Muddy Waters song is not, however, a mysteriously early reading of the Wolf classic, although there are similarities – rather it borrows from the same source, an old Tommy Johnson number. Johnson (1896–1956), a Mississippi bluesman whose best-known song gave its name to the revivalists Canned Heat, was known to sing a falsetto number about 'smoke like lightning', though where *he* got this atmospheric tribute to the power of steam trains from is not known.

For the next two sessions local drummer Francis Clay replaced Below. An October date produced a distorted and badly balanced sound, but February 1953 was more fruitful. After the melodramatic 'This Pain' and a sprightly, defiant boogie called 'Young Fashioned Ways', built as so often on Spann's spirited piano, came the next classic. 'I Want to Be Loved' has a distinctive and sophisticated riff, and is decorated by an elegant Little Walter solo.

By May 1955, now with Wells back in the line-up while on leave from the army, Waters was aware that there was a new talent in town, Bo Diddley. So he took Bo's bragging 'I'm a Man' and created his own distinctive version, called 'Manish Boy' – that's how it appeared on the label, but it's hard to resist adding an extra 'n'. 'Oh yeh, oh

yeh,' shouts town-crier Waters. 'Everything's gonna be all right this morning.' The riff is Bo's but the boasting is pure Muddy. Although Bo was to prove an expert at tempering sexual braggadocio with self-mocking humour, Muddy Waters can also tread this tightrope. Just as he was looking for a schoolboy to fight in 'I'm Ready', note the deliberate change in the title of this song. The reigning king of Chicago blues is pretending to be adolescent, fully equipped below the waist but still with the appealing naivety of youth. Towards the end of his life Muddy re-recorded the song, and in 1988 it edged into the UK charts after being used in a TV commercial for denim jeans – at the time this was becoming a familiar way to revive the careers of old blues and soul singers, though in Muddy's case the honour was posthumous.

The next three Muddy Waters sessions, the first late in 1955, the others in January and June 1956, each produced an addition to what had become an unbroken sequence of hit records, respectively the light, up-tempo groove of 'Sugar Sweet', the forceful 'Forty Days and Forty Nights'

Phone OA. 4-3641

MUDDY WATERS - G
Chess Recorder
KING OF THE BLUES

4339 Lake Park Ave.   Chicago 15, Illinois

Europe and was still being recorded in the 1990s.

The Chess brothers assembled another solid-gold line-up for sessions either side of Christmas 1956, and three out of the four sides, at least, are now among the most celebrated of Waters's songs. Yet none of them made the r&b chart. The sophisticated wordplay of Dixon's 'I Live the Life I Love (and I Love the Life I Live)' soon became associated more with the white jazz stylist Mose Allison, and Waters adds the familiarly robust theme of 'Rock Me' and the rollicking energy of 'Got My Mojo Working', the song that summed up the power of the artist at his peak.

The musicians creating these classics were Waters, Little Walter and Cotton on two tracks each, Spann, Sumlin, Dixon and (probably) Clay, joined by Jimmy Rogers's replacement, Cotton's friend Pat Hare. Hare, born in Arkansas in 1930, had contributed the driving guitar sound to the early-50s hits by Junior Parker and had also worked with Howlin' Wolf during his Memphis days. He was to stay with Muddy into the 1960s, but his belligerent musical style unfortunately matched his personality. After recording in 1954 a song called 'I'm Gonna Murder My Baby', he did just that, and died in jail in 1980.

So how on earth could it have been these sessions that brought the Muddy Waters hit machine to a halt (with the sole exception of 'Close To You', a 1958 number nine on the r&b list)? It was certainly not because his faithful constituency had rejected the evolution from backwards-glancing Delta music to the tough, ensemble, club r&b that Waters and Dixon had

and the equally powerful 'Don't Go No Further', which also flirted with the national pop charts. 'They may not understand the lyric, but they respond to the beat,' was Phil Chess's comment on the white fans who were beginning to discover the blues. On the last two of these tracks, Howlin' Wolf's guitarist, Hubert Sumlin, was included in the mix.

By this time Junior Wells had left the army, rejoined the live band – and quit. His replacement, unlike any of those who had filled the harmonica vacancy since the late 1940s, stayed for a decade. James Cotton was born in Mississippi in 1925, worked with the second Sonny Boy in Arkansas and formed his first group in Memphis, with another émigré to Chicago, guitarist Pat Hare. They had a couple of singles released on Sun, 'My Baby' and 'Cotton Crop Blues', before Cotton made the Chicago trip. After his long stint with Waters, Cotton went solo in the 1960s, and his late-60s James Cotton Blues Band included guitarist Luther Tucker. He cut albums for many labels, worked extensively in created over the past few years. After all, earlier examples of the new sound had entered the charts with ease, and the Chess brothers' distribution system was working ever more smoothly. Muddy Waters remained the king of clubs – his kingdom may have consisted largely of down-at-heel juke joints and sweaty bars, but he was never short of work.

If Muddy was indeed selling records in lesser quantities (though this is not necessarily the case, with the market for pop music and everything else expanding as wartime privations receded), I suspect that the reason was 'the enemy within'. By this time Chuck Berry and Bo Diddley had rewritten the rules, and they had invented Chicago rock 'n' roll. Muddy Waters needn't have worried – he already had enough hits to fill every set for the rest of his life.

I DON'T KNOW

And so by 1952 the leading members of the Chess blues stable were Muddy Waters and Jimmy Rogers, Howlin' Wolf and Little Walter. The label's success had spawned many would-be competitors, mostly short-lived, and with Mercury too closely associated with a form of the blues that now sounded old-fashioned, Chess was undoubtedly the market leader.

Willie Mabon was the next major Chess star, and his smooth style added an extra dimension to the label's identity. In his early-50s sides one can hear the first hint of a form of r&b that was to become hugely popular later in the decade – the sharp, comic vignettes of the Coasters, the Clovers and the Olympics. If he is less remembered now than the mighty quartet referred to above, it may be in part because he left the label in 1956. When the ripples of the British blues revival reached back to America, the Chess stars were identified as being at its centre, and Mabon was no longer among them.

He was born in Tennessee in 1925 and moved to Chicago in 1942, where he studied piano at Sable High School. After service in the US Marine Corps he returned to Chicago, developing a style more akin to the sophisticated styling of Nat 'King' Cole or, in particular, Charles Brown than to the amplified rural blues of Muddy Waters. In 1947 he formed his own group, the Blues Rockers, to work in the Chicago clubs, and he first recorded for the Apollo label in 1949, cutting 'Bogey Man' under the somewhat ill-advised name of Big Willie.

He came to Aristocrat/Chess on the strength of his healthy club following, signed from Al Benson of Parrot Records, and soon hit it big with 'I Don't Know', a novelty blues which sounded ultra-contemporary but was in fact a reworking of a song recorded in the late 30s by one of the pre-war Chicago performers, Cripple Clarence Lofton. In November 1952 it reached the top of the r&b list, a feat which Mabon repeated with his next release, recorded in February 1953, 'I'm Mad'.

Although Mabon had only one more substantial r&b hit in 1954's 'Poison Ivy' (no relation to the Coasters' number), which reached number eight, he was by now an established star and was often billed on the r&b package tours that travelled the continent from a New York base.

After leaving Chess Mabon remained in Chicago, recording for a succession of local labels into the 1970s - Federal, Mad, Formal, USA and Antilles, without recapturing the Chess success. So why did he choose to leave the market leader? Eddie Boyd gave the answer to *Living Blues* magazine. After 'I Don't Know' had been one of the biggest r&b hits of 1952, according to Boyd,

Mabon eventually received a cheque for $3,700 from Leonard Chess in full settlement for the song. 'Willie put that cheque on the counter,' recalled Boyd, 'and said, "You just wait till I come back, motherfucker."'

He came back with a gun, by which time Chess had hidden in the locked storeroom. 'Willie hung around there a long time and he finally left,' continued Boyd. 'He really was gonna kill. Willie figured on his money from that and from his royalty and had went and purchased a six-flat building. He was trying to do something, you know. Then this cat gonna give him that, for after over a year, selling the record. So I talked to him and got him to promise that he wouldn't shoot nobody... Get you a good lawyer, man, and he'll be glad to take that case, because he'd probably get four times more than Chess would ever pay you.'

Willie Dixon confirmed the story: 'When it come reward time, Willie Mabon wasn't getting anything to amount to anything... I know every time he'd meet with Leonard, they would especially wind up in an argument.' And when Mabon took Boyd's advice on the matter, he lost out, according to Jimmy Rogers. 'He tried to sue Chess and Chess bought the lawyer and froze him out everywhere he turned to. So he mess hisself around.'

Once again, this gun-and-lawyer tale shows the darker side of the Chess organization. Leonard Chess was recording the artists and boosting their careers, sure; he was only doing what every other record company did, sure; he managed to maintain the loyalty of such artists as Muddy Waters – and even the mean-spirited, shrewd and suspicious Chuck Berry, sure. It is also true that it would be far too simplistic to make this the familiar tale of white businessmen ripping off black artists. The black-owned companies that were slowly entering the market didn't believe in full accounting either. It's just a pity that Chess, who, by a mixture of luck and judgement, played a major part in creating one of the most exciting genres in rock-music history, 1950s Chicago r&b, didn't break the mould rather than fit it all too exactly.

And so, inevitably, Mabon moved on to other labels. And, apart from a period in the late 60s when he took jobs outside music, his career continued to be healthy. In the 1970s and 80s he recorded in England, Germany and France, and indeed he found a new lease of musical life on the European festival circuit, before dying in Paris in 1986.

His friend Eddie Boyd came to Chess on the back of his self-financed 1952 number one on the JOB label, 'Five Long Years'. Boyd was born in 1914 on Stovall's Plantation in the Delta, and is a cousin of Muddy Waters. He left in a hurry, having defended himself with a pitchfork against the racial insults of one of the plantation overseers, and roamed the South before moving to Memphis. Having learned first kazoo, then guitar and finally piano, he busked locally and as an itinerant musician before settling in Chicago in 1941, where he worked in a steel mill and then in a meat-packing factory – essential industries that meant that he didn't have to do military service in the war.

He played piano in the clubs at night, notably with the first Sonny Boy Williamson and Muddy Waters before forming his own band in 1946. He first recorded, as a vocalist only with JT Brown's Boogie Band, in 1947 for the Victor label, and then as pianist/singer made a series of singles for Victor as Little Eddie Boyd and his Boogie Band. He claims to have also cut some sides for

Aristocrat, but nothing came of them. The reason was, he said, that he made it clear to Leonard Chess that he owned the copyright on his material. Chess was reputedly taken aback, since he was allegedly interested in purloining material for his one established blues star, Muddy Waters, and wasn't used to bluesmen who knew their legal rights. After a 1950 single on Regal he took his classic blues, 'Five Long Years', to JOB. Ironically, he then signed a management contract with Al Benson, who promptly sold it on to Leonard Chess, and so in 1952 Boyd ended up with the man he suspected of trying to rip him off a few years earlier. He was billed on record as Eddie Boyd and his Chess Men.

Two 1953 hits, '24 Hours' and 'Third Degree', confirmed him as a star alongside Willie Mabon, and he went into the studio for Chess each year until 1957, a relationship that resulted in 14 singles. Then life on the road had a tragic consequence – he and his road manager St Louis Jimmy crashed their station wagon south of Milwaukee, and Boyd was hospitalized for some time. Unlike Mabon, he had managed to get some money out of Chess over the years, because the label boss had had an early indication that he was no greenhorn financially, but it all disappeared in medical bills. When he was fit again he turned to farming, playing music part time and touring only occasionally, as on a series of dates with Jimmy McCracklin in 1962, until in 1965 he was invited to join the American Folk Blues Festival for a European tour. More and more European work, including a British tour with John Mayall's Bluesbreakers, led to him settling in Paris in the late 60s, a base from which he continued to work throughout Europe and Scandinavia.

In the 1950s Leonard Chess was lucky with his pianists. For example, Lafayette Leake was a marvellous session performer, Otis Spann was central to the Muddy Waters sound and Johnny Johnson to Chuck Berry's. But these were sidemen, recording under their own names, if at all, almost as an afterthought. Willie Mabon and Eddie Boyd brought greater depth to the label in the guitar and harmonica-dominated early 50s as headline performers, Mabon sophisticated and humorous, Boyd preserving the old virtues of the barrelhouse blues entertainer.

J B Lenoir (sometimes billed as the more phonetic Lenore) was another talented and highly individual artist who gave depth to the Chess roster, and it is a mystery that he is not now remembered for more hits – his engaging, almost feminine, high-pitched voice and relentless boogie style certainly deserved the accolade. Maybe his style was a little old-fashioned. On the other hand it is noticeable that he sold sufficiently well, and was regarded highly enough, to be retained on Chess until 1958, long after Bo Diddley and Chuck Berry had rewritten the rules, and to record for other labels until the mid-60s.

JB, it seems, was just JB – baptized with initials, not names. He was born on 5 March 1929 in Monticello, Mississippi, due south of Jackson and the Delta, to parents who combined farm work and music. When still very young he worked in the south with the second Sonny Boy Williamson and Elmore James, and settled in Chicago in 1949. Once there he worked with the top names in the 'old guard', like Bill Broonzy and Memphis Minnie, and formed his band, JB and His Bayou Boys. In 1951 he cut some sides for the JOB label with Sunnyland Slim in support that were leased to Chess, before a series of further singles were released on JOB itself.

After moving to Parrot in 1954 Lenoir cut his strongest song and only hit, the infectious boogie

"Hitting With The Hits!"

PARROT RECORDS

THE GROUP WITH THE NEW BEAT
THE FLAMINGOS
SING
THE BEST VERSION OF
"KO KO MO"
B/W
"I'M YOURS"
PARROT — 812
"A Killer Diller"

TOPS IN BLUES!
J. B. LENORE's
"MAMA TALK TO YOUR DAUGHTER"
B/W
"MAN WATCH YOUR WOMAN"
PARROT — 809
Big in Chicago, Memphis, Detroit

PARROT RECORD CO.
BLUE LAKE RECORD CO.
4858 COTTAGE GROVE
CHICAGO 15, ILLINOIS
(Phones: OAkland 4-5254-55)

recording, in 1965, his masterpiece, an acoustic album called *Alabama Blues*, which entwined re-recordings of songs like 'Talk to Your Daughter' with new writing reflecting the civil rights struggle. He also toured Europe that year as part of the American Folk Blues Festival, and surely would have found a new audience with his 'serious' material – a side of his work that had been apparent since 1951's 'Korea Blues' but which was now gaining strength in the era of black power – had he not been killed in a car crash in 1967.

'Mama Talk to Your Daughter', later acquired by Chess, and in 'Eisenhower Blues' revealed the talent for social satire that had already produced a song called 'Korea Blues'. Blaming the President for the fact that taxes made a poor man poorer got the record banned, so he rejigged it as 'Tax Paying Blues'. The Parrot sides also eventually found their way to Chess, and in the meantime in 1955 Lenoir signed with Checker. Some of his singles reworked his most familiar theme, as in '(Mama) What About Your Daughter' and 'Daddy Talk to Your Son', and he was never short of live work. Released by Chess in 1958, he cut further singles for Shad and Vee-Jay before

SMOKESTACK LIGHTNIN'

When guitarist Hubert Sumlin joined Howlin' Wolf in Chicago one of the most fruitful of all the partnerships that created Chicago blues was cemented. Sumlin recalled the summons in *Mojo* magazine: 'Wolf was already established... Scared me to death he did. Then one day I'm staying with [James] Cotton at this old hotel and I get this call from Wolf. He said, "Hubert, I'm putting this band down and I'm going to Chicago and forming me a new group, 'cos these guys, they think they're too good, they don't wanna play..." I said OK... Sure enough, two weeks later he calls the hotel, tells me that the train leaves at so and so time and you are going to be met by Otis Spann... And that's what happened... I got to see all these big lights, and I got scared, so we went straight back to Leonard Chess's daddy's apartment building. Wolf had his own apartment there. He got me an apartment there and done got my union card and everything.'

Although the image that one gets of the Wolf in later years, from the testimony of such as recording engineer Malcolm Chisholm and his 'minder' Willie Dixon, is of a bone-headed genius, he was also by contrast an efficient and well-organized bandleader, making sure that his musicians had somewhere to live and were up to date with their union dues. He even enrolled Sumlin at the Chicago Conservatory of Music, where he himself had been taking lessons. Jimmy Rogers confirms the Wolf's efficiency. 'Wolf was better at managing a bunch of people than Muddy or anybody else. Muddy would go along with the Chess company, Wolf would speak up for himself.' And obviously his band would also benefit from this, and so the stubborn, cussed streak in Howlin' Wolf's personality had its positive side.

Indeed the feeling was that Muddy was getting a little lazy, taking his status for granted and only making an appearance late into a club date, leaving the bulk of the set to James Cotton and the band. It was the Wolf who put him on his mettle – the newcomer ran an efficient and punctual outfit, and was the most powerful and charismatic performer in town.

When challenged about his rivalry with Muddy Waters, the diplomatic Wolf made it clear that, as far as he was concerned, he concentrated on business while Muddy could be too easily distracted. 'Muddy's a nice person, y'know, but he's a little jealous of me sometimes. See, Muddy loves women better than he love guitar... I've got a wife, she's a flower since the first day I saw her. No, I didn't always have a wife but I was never made up of the stuff Muddy Waters was made up of... I never fought Muddy, he was just jealous of me. He drew a gun on me once...'

There are records of some 60 completed tracks recorded by the Wolf at Sam Phillips's studio in Memphis and down the road in West Memphis. Most of this material found its way to Chess, although the open double-dealing whereby tapes

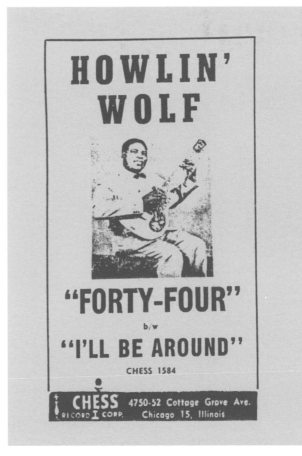

also went to RPM/Modern lingered for a while, as with the 1952 RPM single 'My Baby Stole Off'/'I Want Your Picture'. But it meant that Leonard Chess need not hurry the Wolf into a Chicago session, even though that initial hit was not repeated in such Memphis Chess releases as 'The Wolf Is At Your Door', 'Saddle My Pony', 'Oh! Red' and 'All Night Boogie', all of them powerful witnesses to the singer's outstanding talent. Sales ticked over while the Wolf established his club

Another Smash Hit on Chess . . .

"OH RED"

by

THE HOWLING WOLF

Chess No. 1528

CHESS RECORD CORP.

750 E. 49th Street
Chicago 15, Illinois

Oh! Red:
when **Howlin' Wolf** came to Chicago he had an enormous backlog of Memphis recordings available to Chess.

reputation, and Chess was kept busy with hits by other members of his growing blues stable.

However, 1954 saw a flurry of activity in the studio – it was time to try more positively to get the Wolf back into the r&b hit list. In March Chess assembled Spann, Dixon and Below, along with guitarist Lee Cooper, while for further sessions in May and October Cooper was replaced by Sumlin on bass and teenager Jody Williams. The latter line-up also played on the Wolf's one 1955 session in March. The search for a hit was unsuccessful – wearing his songwriter's hat, Dixon was heavily involved with Muddy Waters in particular, and was yet to find precisely the right sort of vehicle for the Wolf – but artistically the results are impressive.

There are a dozen tracks dating from this period, almost all written by Wolf himself. The first Willie Dixon song in his repertoire is the suitably titled 'Evil', a stop-rhythm number with threatening vocals. 'No Place to Go' is sung almost as a conventional blues sequence, but the pounding, repetitive and effective guitar-led riff doesn't bother to move out of its root chord. Cooper's jazzy, fluid style is best shown on the jaunty rocker 'Neighbors', 'I'm the Wolf' is one of the singer's many chest-thumping autobiographical lyrics, 'Rockin' Daddy' is a lively, good-humoured shuffle, while 'I'll Be Around' has an unusual, swampy guitar sound that lifts it way above the rest of the pack. Altogether, it's a satisfying mix, yielding a generous handful of singles.

The rivalry between the Wolf and Muddy had by now developed into band warfare, and at one point in 1956 Muddy openly poached Sumlin halfway through a gig at the Club Zanzibar, sending over his chauffeur with a huge billfold and an offer to triple Sumlin's pay. The Wolf found out and sacked his guitarist on the spot. In a telling image that sums up Howlin' Wolf's towering anger, Sumlin said that his face actually seemed to get blacker! The Wolf must have known, surely, that his Memphis guitarist Willie Johnson had moved to Chicago in the previous year, and was busking on Maxwell Street. And so Johnson rejoined the Wolf band while Sumlin went off on tour with Muddy.

But Sumlin found the comparatively lax organization of the Waters band, including a ridiculously taxing touring schedule that should never have been agreed to, too much to take, and meanwhile the Wolf and Johnson were getting on no better than before. And so it wasn't long before Sumlin was back in his rightful place, though Johnson stayed around and would frequently tour with the Wolf as well as playing on some of the Chess sessions, including the Wolf's greatest song, 'Smokestack Lightnin''.

This was the track that first unveiled the consummate Chicago sound of Howlin' Wolf, and made the most of Sumlin's eerie guitar work. The song is a perfect marriage of the Wolf's unparalleled vocal power, his lupine howls echoing into the distance, one of Johnson's most narcotic riffs, a mysterious lyrical landscape and a melody – if such a delicate word can possibly be associated with this artist – that immediately hoicks the number out of the run-of-the-mill blues bag. Deservedly, it put the singer back in the chart, peaking at number 11. There are few echoes of the raw Tommy Johnson song left in it now, and none of the Muddy Waters number – this is the pure and unadulterated howl of the wolfman, climbing one of the highest peaks of Chicago blues.

Buddy Guy arrived in town in the following year, when 'Smokestack Lightnin'' had made the

Wolf the hottest act in town, and he recalled in *Mojo* the impact that seeing the man in the flesh, after knowing his music for so many years, had on him. 'I came here to work in the day and watch people like Wolf at night – sit there and watch while I sat over one Coke for six hours. I could never explain really what seeing Wolf was like. I had his records, 78s, then I walked into a club and find this big man crawling around on his knees, dragging his tail and howling like a wolf!'

In the latter half of 1956, when Sumlin defected to the Muddy Waters band, Wolf cut two sessions, with Willie Johnson joined on guitar by Smokey Smothers, and the line-up was the same for a session in June of the following year. Although Sumlin's distinctive style is not there to urge on and give shape to the singer's ferocity, it remained business as before. Indeed on the first track is a deliberate attempt to follow up 'Smokestack Lightnin'' in similar style, with Johnson playing a reversed mirror image of Sumlin's riff. And once again the inspiration is Tommy Johnson, who earlier had reworked the traditional moan 'I Asked for Water (She Gave Me Gasoline)'. Other notable tracks of this period are 'The Natchez Burning', a powerful piece of

journalism based on a fatal fire in Natchez, Mississippi; a slow blues with intricate guitar work, 'Bluebird'; the up-tempo boogie 'You Ought To Know', with Hosea Lee Kennard hammering out some Otis Spann-styled piano; the threatening 'Who's Been Talking', revived decades later by Robert Cray; and the solid rocker 'Nature'. None was a big hit, but the Wolf's singles continued to sell strongly and his stage act remained unparalleled.

In fact the central significance of the Wolf in the development of Chicago blues is not reflected in the r&b chart – indeed the only other entry is a modest showing for a re-recording of 'Evil' in 1969. And as far as the wider audience was concerned he remained a total unknown until the Rolling Stones opened white American ears, and he never entered the Hot Hundred. The role of Britain in spreading the blues gospel in the 1960s is highlighted by the fact that Howlin' Wolf *did* feature once in the British charts – in 1964, when Pye released 'Smokestack Lightnin''.

In the second half of the 1950s the Chess brothers were distracted from their hard-core Delta artists by the success of the new generation, notably Chuck Berry and Bo Diddley. Nevertheless, they continued to put the older bluesmen into the studio regularly, for there was still a demand for singles even if the chart hits had stopped, and the Wolf was never short of club work. By December 1957 Sumlin was back in the fold for a session that included the standard 'Sittin' on Top of the World', and there were a surprising three sessions in 1958.

A productive studio date in July 1959 completed the decade, and in retrospect these years – from the time when artists like Howlin' Wolf and Waters were represented in the r&b chart to their 1960s rediscovery by British fans – saw a number of strong additions to the Wolf catalogue. As well as such incidental pleasures as the jaunty rocker 'I Didn't Know' and another 'Smokestack' retread called 'Mr Airplane Man', with its stomping guitar riff and echoing falsetto cries, there were two classics – 'Moaning for My Baby' is a relentless howl matched only by the similarly titled 'Howlin' for My Baby' (in some versions titled 'Howlin' for My Darling'), and the titles indicate the combination of barrel-chested robustness and lovelorn desperation that characterizes this type of Wolf song.

It was the new decade, however, that brought a stunning revival in the Wolf's work. Willie Dixon, who had spent the 1950s freelancing all over town while always being on hand to guide the fortunes of the Chess label, now turned his songwriting attention to the Wolf. The first fruits came in a midsummer session with Dixon himself on bass, surrounded by as strong a line-up as Chicago could offer – the wonderful Otis Spann on piano, Sumlin and Below, and (maybe) Freddy King on another guitar. (It seems to have been common practice for Sumlin to have been augmented by a shifting cast of further guitarists on Howlin' Wolf sessions, though since the departure of Willie Johnson he remained the common factor, and so deserves the credit for creating the distinctive guitar sound of the Wolf's best records.) A three-song session this, without a dud moment. Howlin' Wolf hated 'Wang-Dang-Doodle', rehearsing and recording it under constant grumbling protest. Dixon's faith in the song, however, was such that when the Wolf's version failed to make the charts he cut it, in 1966, with Koko Taylor, and was rewarded with the last blues hit on the label. It is an innovative piece of writing, and the Wolf was too set in his ways to appreciate innovation. Against a hypnotic, strutting riff Dixon conjures up a teeming cast

---

RE-U 1072   RE-U 1072

RHYTHM AND BLUES WITH HOWLIN' WOLF

Side No. 1
Come to me, baby (Burnett)
Don't mess with my baby (Graham)

Side No. 2
Smokestack lightning (Burnett)
You can't be beat (Burnett)

HOWLIN' WOLF BURNETT (vocal and harmonica) with instrumental accompaniment

At the conclusion of the Second World War the term "Race Music", which had hitherto described Negro folk musical forms, fell into disfavour with coloured musicians who objected to the hint of racial distinctions implicit in the phrase. "Rhythm and Blues"—or "R. and B."—admirably describes the contemporary Negro folk music with its structure founded on the traditional twelve-bar blues and its pronounced emphasis on rhythm which, if sometimes devoid of subtlety and complexity, is always compelling.

Howlin' Wolf Burnett is one of the most impressive of the tough, aggressive singers and musicians who have emerged during the last couple of years. In his rough-textured voice can be heard echoes of Mississippi singers like McLennan, whilst his declamatory phrasing recalls Joe Turner's Kansas City style. Gramophone records, intricate radio networks and the spread of Negro labour has compressed the characteristics of country and city blues into one music which shares the qualities of them all and is to be heard from New York to 'Frisco, from Chicago to Houston. The greatest influence on R. & B. has been exerted by the urban blues of the Chicago singers of the 'Forties and their accompaniments. Many of these men were Southern musicians whose music hardened under the pressure of Chicago life and the process has continued. Boogie pianists like Sunnyland Slim have replaced Big Maceo and Black Bob and singers like Muddy Waters, recently from the South, have adapted themselves to the new styles. Howlin' Wolf's own harmonica playing derives from that of Jazz Gillum and Sonny Boy Williamson: fierce, harsh, impassioned. Against a background of boogie piano, staccato drumming and the electric guitar, which has replaced the knife and bottleneck styles, he sings and blows his mouth harp with growling vibrato and relentless intensity, and on the railroad blues "Smokestack lightning" he demonstrates the aptness of his soubriquet.

PAUL OLIVER

Recorded by CHESS, Chicago

45 rpm EXTENDED PLAY RECORD
LONDON RECORDS, 1-3 BRIXTON ROAD, LONDON, S.W.9, ENGLAND

Made in England   R.S. 1/57/594

LONDON RECORDS

LONDON RE-U 1072 — RHYTHM AND BLUES WITH HOWLIN' WOLF

of low-life chancers, all of them ready and able to wang-dang-doodle all night long, whatever that might involve.

Next came the macho boastfulness of 'Back Door Man', perfectly geared to the Wolf persona, while exploring a cuckolding theme that has been the subject of blues songs since the beginning – from all three points of view, in fact. Not surprisingly, Jim Morrison later picked up on the song as being well suited to his swaggering style as singer with the Doors. And completing the hat trick came 'Spoonful', issued on a single with 'Howlin' for My Darling' and unaccountably failing to get the Wolf back into the r&b chart. Again there's an irresistible Sumlin riff, a beautifully crafted Dixon lyric and a hammering vocal performance. Any compiler of a Howlin' Wolf 'best of' would pencil this track in immediately after 'Smokestack Lightnin''. In the 1960s the song was covered by numerous bands, notably in an epic version by Cream.

A year later two mid-1961 sessions maintained the standard with another quartet of Dixon songs. 'Little Baby' attempts a rewrite of 'My Babe' but adds a stop-rhythm bridge to avoid too obvious a case of self-plagiarism. 'Down in the Bottom' is a forceful recreation of the old slide-guitar Delta style, with Jimmy Rogers on hand to give it authenticity, as the obvious model is Rogers's early-50s work with Muddy Waters. Little Johnny Jones played piano on these sessions – this Chicago stalwart, who was to die of pneumonia in 1964, was at the time part of the 'West Side' sound as a member of Magic Sam's band. The session also featured the drummer from the Wolf's stage band, Sam Lay.

Next comes 'Shake For Me', with its distinctive spiky, bustling riff, followed by another Dixon masterpiece, 'Little Red Rooster'. Sumlin's languorous, slippery guitar part conjures up a sleepy farmyard under a blistering sun, with a rooster who is 'too lazy to crow today' but who wakes up at night to go on the prowl. In November 1964 the Wolf's biggest fans, the Rolling Stones, created a respectful cover version – including a neat innovation by Keith Richards when his guitar echoes the phrase 'dogs begin to bark' – and took it to number one in the UK.

In *Mojo* Hubert Sumlin confirmed that this new and fertile period, with magnificent songwriting by Willie Dixon, was a deliberate attempt at moving on a step musically. 'We wanted to take this thing somewhere new, but we didn't wanna stray too far from our roots. Mostly, we was trying to get as lowdown and dirty as we could. We'd sit there and talk about the song – is this going to be somebody telling a story, who did this, who did that, did somebody kill somebody? You gotta think about what you saying and it better fit...'

A December 1961 session spawned two strong numbers in 'Just Like I Treat You' and 'I Ain't Superstitious', and two new masterpieces. On 'You'll Be Mine' Dixon seems to throw in every trick he can think of. There's an urgent rhythm reminiscent of 'Got My Mojo Working', whipped along by Henry Gray's piano, that climbs gloriously to its second chord when the Wolf declaims the title phrase. The bridge breaks into boogie but culminates in a stop-rhythm last line, and the single-note guitar solo is unusually fluid and frenetic for a Wolf record.

And his version of 'Goin' Down Slow' is simply as chilling as anything he ever did, decorated by Sumlin's baleful guitar lines, with Dixon adding a portentous monologue to the story of a man dying from too much pleasure. 'I did not say I was a millionaire,' he says. 'I said I have spent more money than a millionaire. 'Cos if I had kept the money I have already spent, I would have been a millionaire long time ago. And women? We-e-e-ll, googly-moogly.' Whatever googly-moogly might be, we know that it is rather enjoyable, very sinful and, in the context of the song, fatal.

The Wolf's stage bass player, Jerome Arnold, was present on the next session for the first time, but it was not until September 1962 that Chess brought him back to the studio. It was a mixed day, with 'Do the Do' probably as popular with the singer as was 'Wang-Dang-Doodle'. But he gives it everything, and it is a lively novelty. One more classic was added to the catalogue in 'Tail Dragger', another boastful manifesto rich in imagery. 'I'm a tail dragger, I wipe out my tracks,' he claims, and refers to 'the mighty Wolf making his midnight creep.' The granddaddy of heavy-rock guitar, Link Wray, who in his 60s still greases back his hair, peels on the black leather stage gear and turns his amplifier up full, turned this song into one of his most lascivious, macho performances.

The Chess label remained a going concern for a further decade, and continued to record the Wolf throughout this time. But the great era of Chicago blues had passed, and there were now signs that they were not quite sure what to do with the ageing and highly individual artist. Dixon tried to inject a mainstream pop feel

with such lighter numbers as 'Hidden Charms' and 'Three Hundred Pounds of Joy', and the theme of the latter is better explored in a song from the same 1963 session, 'Built for Comfort'. Significantly, however, this was the last Dixon number dished out to the Wolf. Buddy Guy was on the session, and returned in August 1964 to duel once more with Sumlin on the last new Howlin' Wolf classic, the powerful 'Killing Floor', which the singer imbues with all his old desperate passion. The song is decorated by an insistent, complex, swooping riff on the guitars.

Later, revivals of such numbers as the old folk-blues 'Louise' and the Robert Johnson/Elmore James 'Dust My Broom' add nothing to

Three Hundred Pounds of Joy:
the mighty Howlin' Wolf had the biggest voice in the blues.

Blues boom:
in the 1960s the Wolf was
a regular visitor to such
London clubs as the
Marquee and the 100.

Blues for sale:
the Wolf remained a draw
throughout the soul era.

the songs, and the Wolf is given arrangements
that vary from barrelhouse to traditional jazz.
Ironically it was that familiar indication of a
record company running out of ideas for an artist
– the re-recorded 'best of' package – that gave him
his final hit with 'Evil'. The song selection for
this November 1968 venture could not be faulted,
but not surprisingly no song was improved upon.

The project was Marshall Chess's idea, and he
misguidedly tried to sit the Wolf into a currently
modish psychedelic setting, wah-wah pedals and
all. An extraordinary misjudgement – the Wolf
was so disgusted that he insisted on overdubbing
his vocals without being able to hear the
squelching, squealing, fuzz-boxed backing tracks.
The experience inspired the singer to make a rare
foray into the world of record reviewing; 'dogshit'
was his verdict. And of 13 songs cut at a session
in July 1969, 11 remained in the can.

Not only is it not surprising that an old Delta
bluesman had said all that he had to say by the
time he was 55, it also didn't matter. Because by
now the white audience had discovered him, like
Muddy Waters, John Lee Hooker, Jimmy Reed
and all the surviving giants of the blues, and so
he was more popular than ever. And what his
new audience wanted, of course, was his old
classics. The fact that 'Killing Floor' was his last
little masterpiece was of no concern – indeed it
was still a recent recording. Least of all did it
matter to the Wolf himself – as Sumlin put it,
referring to a European trip: 'He thought he'd
died and gone to heaven. Those people over there,
they treated us like kings.'

Of course we did. We'd survived for so long on
a diet of imitation rock 'n' rollers. Some, like Billy
Fury, had their moments. Even Cliff occasionally
cut a rug before going off on a summer holiday
and finding God – not the God that put the
frighteners on Robert Johnson or Jerry Lee
Lewis, not the God who inspired the Baptist
fervour of the great gospel singers in the South,
but a God who smiled indulgently when the kids
played a little skiffle in the vestry. We'd had a
taste of the real thing in Buddy Holly, Eddie
Cochran and Gene Vincent, but now these exotic
black men with their diamond rings, their cool
attitudes and their voodoo lyrics were coming to
Britain out of the airwaves and into the clubs and
concert halls. They were kings.

The biggest breakthrough as far as Chess was concerned came in 1962, when the Pye label struck a licensing deal with the Chicago company whereby it released British pressings of Chuck Berry, Bo Diddley and the Delta bluesmen. Pye issued these albums at 14s 6d, making easily available the sounds that we were hearing on Radio Luxembourg and American Forces Network. As we have noted, the Wolf was one of those who even hit the pop charts as a result.

In May 1965 the Rolling Stones were booked to appear on the networked American rock show *Shindig*, devised by the English TV producer responsible for all the best pop shows on UK television up until that time, Jack Good. The Stones managed to get Howlin' Wolf included in the bill. It is hard now to imagine the impact that this caused – those white fans in both countries who were already familiar with the work of such performers, and whose ranks, of course, included the Stones, were still a minority. Now white high-school America saw its pop idols the Rolling Stones sitting at the feet of a huge, sweating black man, howling from coast to coast, and many viewers would have realized for the first time that the Stones hadn't invented the blues. 'We were all ignored until those

Teamwork: guitarist Hubert Sumlin was central to the Howlin' Wolf sound.

English kids came in,' is how Buddy Guy puts it.

After the ill-fated wah-wah re-recordings came the inevitable London album with a group of superstar fans, in 1970 – this was a familiar Chess device in the label's declining years. The Wolf's supporting cast included Eric Clapton, Steve Winwood, Bill Wyman, Charlie Watts and Ringo Starr, banging their way through a list of Wolf classics.

Engineer Glyn Johns recalls that the 'so-called' producer of the project was quite capable of playing a record on the turntable at the wrong speed, when reminding the band of the song they were about to revive. And clearly some of the musicians, attracted by admiration for the Wolf, were booked on the strength of their pop-music fame rather than their feel for the downhome blues. 'What am I doing here?' asked Ringo forlornly, during his brief tenure of the drum stool. He was swiftly replaced by Watts.

Clapton was equally uncertain. Why, he wondered, was he in the studio while the great Hubert Sumlin stood in the control room or emerged simply to play rhythm guitar? And so arose the bizarre situation of the Wolf teaching Clapton to play Sumlin's riff for 'Little Red Rooster', to which Sumlin himself added a modest second-guitar part. It is one thing to round up a few stellar white pop names and put them on an album cover in an attempt to spread the appeal of the real star of the project, quite another to force them reluctantly into the spotlight when they know they shouldn't be there. Clapton could have

played support guitar to Sumlin and been thrilled, rather than embarrassed. In the circumstances, it is surprising that the resulting album is as listenable as it is, and is a vast improvement on the 'dogshit' sessions. But it would undoubtedly have been better had it taken place *instead* of those sessions, when the Wolf was fitter and Clapton was still a blues player

There were a couple more albums in the Wolf's dotage, with Sumlin ever-present. And he sang every week at a club run by Eddie Shaw, who by now was also acting as the Wolf's bandleader and manager. The final album was called *Back Door Wolf*, a fitting image. He continued working though in increasingly frail health, looking older than his years, bespectacled and with his skin seemingly now too big for his body. Circulation problems confined him to a chair on the stage where once he had writhed and dragged his tail, and he was also suffering from cancer. The Wolf died of kidney failure in January 1976, having never fully recovered from a serious car accident three years earlier.

DON'T START ME TO TALKIN'

Of the unparalleled roster of great blues artists who signed to Chess from 1947 onwards, the last to arrive was also the oldest, a loner who had enjoyed a long itinerant career in the South without ever doing himself justice on record. Exactly how old Sonny Boy Williamson was when he first recorded for Chess in 1955, we will probably never know, but some estimates make him a child of the previous century.

He was certainly born in Glendora, Tallahatchie County, Mississippi, a settlement in the geographical heart of the Delta. His passport confirmed that he hailed from Tallahatchie, and claimed that he was born on 7 April 1909. This could be too late – those British fans who remember him from club dates in the 1960s seemed to be watching a comparatively elderly man, not one who was only in his mid-50s. There may be something in his rather murky past that made this passport useful, and he is on record, literally, as singing that he was born in Glendora in 1897. But he's also said 1894. Meanwhile, *Blues Who's Who* plumps for 5 December 1899. Recent research makes him younger that ever, suggesting 5 December 1912. From the very start, then, there was an air of mystery about the man.

And of course the mystery continued with his name. His aliases included Willie Williamson, Willie Williams and Willie Miller (the last of these is actually the name of his brother). And the name we now remember him by already belonged to the younger, but 'first', John Lee 'Sonny Boy' Williamson, and was appropriated by the 'second' for work in the South – he didn't make his way to Chicago until 1955, when the 'real' Sonny Boy had been safely dead for seven years.

In spite of all this self-mystification, it would seem that he was the son of a Glendora couple, James and Mildred Miller, and that his given name was Aleck (or Alec). Confusion continued because he was better known by the childhood nickname 'Rice'. By the age of five he had taught himself to play the harmonica.

As a teenager he began the life of the itinerant musician throughout the southern states, now often under the name Little Boy Blue, and there are inevitably few accurate records of his movements between the two wars. He was in New Orleans towards the end of the 1920s, and a few years later was working in Missouri with Sunnyland Slim, but mainly he seems to have been down south, moving around on his own, sometimes augmenting his harmonica-playing with a crude one-man-band set-up, and seeking out a paying audience wherever he could – fish fries and parties, carnivals and logging camps, or simply busking on street corners.

From the mid-30s he was in regular working contact with other big names in southern blues – as mentioned earlier, he was briefly married to Howlin' Wolf's half-sister Mary, he teamed up with Robert Johnson and Elmore James, and in the late 1930s he formed a more lasting partnership with Robert Jr Lockwood.

In 1941 the pair were in Helena, Arkansas, where a local radio station was being established by a businessman named Sam Anderson. They offered to perform for free, in return for being allowed to plug their upcoming appearances. Instead, Anderson brought them together with Max Moore, boss of the Interstate Grocery Company, which had a product called King Biscuit Flour. The result was that they were contracted as the King Biscuit Entertainers, and when Station KFFA began transmitting in November 1941 *King Biscuit Time*, featuring Miller and Lockwood, quickly became successful. It was broadcast five days a week, Monday to Friday, for a quarter of an hour at 12.15p.m. And Miller was billed as Sonny Boy Williamson.

Whether or not this change of name came from Miller or his sponsor, there can be little doubt – in spite of Sonny Boy's protestations for the remainder of his career that he was not only the older but the first artist to use the name – that it was deliberate theft. John Lee Williamson, well established in Chicago, had no particular wish to leave the clubs and streets that gave him a living, and so his name was stolen. He probably may even have benefited – anyone who enjoyed the show and went out to buy a Sonny Boy

Williamson record as a result would have been sold the latest by John Lee. Miller wasn't recording at this time, which could have had something to do with the deception. Ironically, they had totally different musical styles, and to many ears the 'second' Sonny Boy is superior.

Miller and Lockwood augmented their band in Helena with such local artists as drummer James 'Peck' Curtis, two pianists in Robert 'Dudlow' Taylor and Joe 'Pinetop' Perkins, and Robert Nighthawk's cousin, the Mississippi guitarist Houston Stackhouse. When Lockwood left to join the rival show, *Mother's Best Flour Hour*, he was replaced by Joe Willie Wilkins. The radio show and spin-off live gigs suited Sonny Boy for a while, but he was soon on the move again, cropping up in such places as New Orleans, Little Rock and Detroit. Quite often a lifestyle that, when he was not performing, revolved around gambling and drinking meant a stay in a prison cell. In 1947 he and Elmore James were in Yazoo City, Mississippi, appearing on the Talaho Syrup show on WAZF-radio, and two years later he joined Howlin' Wolf in West Memphis on KWEM's Hadacol show.

In 1951 a shop owner in Jackson, Mississippi, Lillian McMurry, started the Trumpet record label, and searched out Sonny Boy as one of her first

City gent:
Sonny Boy Williamson in his City of London-inspired stage suit.

signings. Thus, late in life, he began his recording career, and he stayed with Trumpet until the company failed in 1955. He cut the first versions of a number of tracks that were later to be recut for Chess, like his début 'Eyesight to the Blind' and the classic 'Nine Below Zero'. Among the label's biggest hits were Elmore James's 'Dust My Broom' and Sonny Boy's 'Mighty Long Time', and McMurry was a rarity among record-label owners in that she provided proper accounting and royalties. She also gave her artists the security of a contract, and it was this that took Sonny Boy to Chess – when Trumpet collapsed his contract passed to a local entrepreneur who sold it on to Leonard Chess. Nineteen fifty-five proved to be a crucial year in the history of the company, for not only did it sign the last of its great old-time bluesmen to join the label (Buddy Guy, still in Baton Rouge, was barely out of his teens by then), but it secured its future by contracting Bo Diddley and Chuck Berry.

On 12 August of that year Sonny Boy was furnished with the great Muddy Waters band for his first Chess session, and emerged with his first hit for the Checker label, 'Don't Start Me to Talkin'', which by mid-October had reached number seven in the r&b chart. This sly, anecdotal song, with its stop-beat verse and rocking chorus lines, established the Sonny Boy style, breathy and confidential, but with a hint of evil. All in all, the session was an impressive

ENRICHED

SONNY BOY

DEGERMINATED
WHITE
CORN MEAL
WATER WASHED FOR PURITY
PACKED FOR AND GUARANTEED BY
INTERSTATE GROCER CO.
HELENA, ARK. 72342
NET WT. 5 LBS.

Cornflour king:
a sponsored radio show made Sonny Boy's name, even if that name belonged to someone else.

début – the single's b-side was the meditative, jaunty 'All My Love in Vain', there is a frantic boogie led by Otis Spann, 'Good Evening Everybody', the sprightly 'Work with Me' and an impassioned slow blues, 'You Killing Me (On My Feet)', with an outstanding harmonica solo.

Chess was riding high at the time – 'My Babe' had charted early in the year, to be succeeded by 'Manish Boy' and now by 'Talkin''. The competition from Vee-Jay Records, in its second year, was obviously not troubling the Chess brothers too much. They dispatched their artists out across the country on promotional packages, established impressive offices at 4750/52 Cottage Grove Avenue, and took on more and more staff to handle the demand. Sonny Boy cut two sessions in 1956, which reunited him with Robert Jr Lockwood (who had made his own journey to Chicago in 1950) and introduced him to the 20-year-old Luther Tucker, from Little Walter's band. The impassioned, up-tempo 'Let Me Explain' was the chosen single from the first of these dates, in January, but the next hit came from the August session, without Otis Spann – the boogie 'Keep It to Yourself' crept into the hit list at number 14 for a week.

Williamson now worked more in the North than in his old stamping grounds, where many creditors may well have been lying in wait for him, and was often shuttling between Chicago and St Louis while also going into the Chess studios regularly. February 1957 added a new classic to the Sonny Boy catalogue, with the same band as had produced the August hit, in 'Fattening Frogs for Snakes': 'It took me a long time to find out my mistake, but I bet you my bottom dollar I ain't fattening no more frogs for snakes.' A September session showed that magic could not always be created in the studio no matter how long they tried – a song called 'Little Village' was cut 12 times without much success – but when the talents of Lockwood and Tucker, Dixon and Below were all interplaying smoothly and imaginatively with Sonny Boy's harp, a track like 'Fattening Frogs' was the result, a satisfying and integrated whole.

Otis Spann returned for that September date, and, despite 'Little Village', it proved to be a fruitful one. 'Cross My Heart' is a slow, deeply felt blues, 'Born Blind' a neat reworking of his first-ever Trumpet single and 'Ninety Nine' gains a thicker sound than usual from its rubbery, insistent guitar riff. Sonny Boy played amplified harmonica for the first time on this session. In March 1958, with Lafayette Leake now on piano, he cut another classic in 'Your Funeral and My Trial', both laid-back and menacing, while 'Wake Up Baby' is a curiosity, a jaunty pop blues with a traditional cuckolding theme that dates back to medieval times.

It was a year before Sonny Boy produced another Chess single, now with Odie Payne on drums, but it was a cracker, linking the Jimmy Reed-style boogie 'Let Your Conscience Be Your Guide' with the mysterious, mid-tempo 'Unseeing Eye', which 'remind me of a midnight dream – it remind me of somebody I have never seen'. In 1960 Sonny Boy cut five Chess sessions – remarkable considering this was the awkward period between rock 'n' roll and the blues revival

for such ageing artists. 'The Goat' is an amusing rocker, 'Open Road' is a variation on the Otis Spann/Muddy Waters song 'My Home is in the Delta', 'Santa Claus' is a clever variation on the Christmas theme, with Sonny Boy's hoarse voice miked up loud and allied to a strong lyric, 'Checkin' Up On My Baby' is an up-tempo jealousy riff, 'Somebody Help Me' has a desperately pleading vocal, affecting though breathless, while 'Trust My Baby' is a strong, slow confessional blues and 'Too Young to Die' is a cautionary tale of an old man with a dangerous younger girl. Nineteen sixty-one added another classic to the list with a return to 'Nine Below Zero'.

There were no invitations to record in 1962 but in the following year, with 'Bye Bye Bird' and his last hit, 'Help Me', the now elderly Sonny Boy became a star in Europe. 'Help Me', with its insistent riff reminiscent of Booker T and the MGs' 'Green Onions', reached the 20s in the charts and was picked up on by many a British r&b band, while the virtuoso 'Bye Bye Bird' was covered in the UK by John Mayall.

In September 1963 Sonny Boy cut a session with Buddy Guy's band, producing one strong track, 'Decoration Day', before joining a blues package tour to Europe. On reaching the UK and receiving more adulation than the shifty old rogue had ever enjoyed before, he decided to delay his return to Chicago. He invested in a curious cartoon version of a City gent's attire, with a neat suit, immaculately knotted tie, bowler hat and umbrella, and toured the country with the hottest possible backing groups – the Animals and the Yardbirds were blues-based chart bands and bill-toppers in their own right, but were quite happy to be upstaged by one of the great originals.

Back in America, and now living in Milwaukee, Sonny Boy cut two sessions in 1964 which evidenced a deterioration in quality due simply to old age and ill health, mainly due to heavy drinking. But of course he could not resist the opportunity of returning to Europe with that year's Blues Festival, and even cut a tune called 'I'm Trying to Make London My Home'. In 1965 things came full circle – he went back to Helena, where he had first made his name on *King Biscuit Time*, and bumped into Canadian rocker Ronnie Hawkins's backing band, the Hawks, later to be rechristened the Band. They jammed together, but by this time Sonny Boy was constantly spitting blood, and on 25 May he was found dead in bed.

I GOT MY BRAND ON YOU

By 1957 Muddy Waters had given up playing the guitar regularly, leaving this to the blend of Jimmy Rogers's subtlety and Pat Hare's attack, and with James Cotton acting as emcee the bandleader would now make his entrance a way into the set. The 'revue' feel to the show was stressed by the use of brass, and when he recorded in June 1957 with this augmented line-up Muddy now seemed part of a band, his vocals more integrated into the overall sound. Robert Jr Lockwood was also on the session, which produced one strong track in 'Evil', built on the same riff as 'Hoochie Coochie Man'.

Nineteen fifty-eight saw Muddy's last hit, when the Willie Dixon song 'Close to You', with the singer adopting a somewhat mannered laughing delivery, reached number nine in the charts. There were other pleasures in the year's three sessions, including the slinky 'I Won't Go On', another of his sexual boasts in 'Born Lover', and a sultry meditation on the young girl/old man theme, 'She's 19 Years Old'. Since Muddy was now in his 40s but showed no sign of easing

off on his spare-time pursuits, it may well have been sung from the heart.

In the UK, meanwhile, the most dynamic live music was being produced by the jazz bands, those who had fallen in love soon after the war with New Orleans music and hence with the blues. In 1956 the Humphrey Lyttelton band reached number 19 with the rollicking boogie 'Bad Penny Blues', the most exciting British record of the decade, while the bands of Ken Colyer and Chris Barber had within them a smaller outfit who would perform folk-blues during the band break at gigs. Barber's guitarist and banjo player, Lonnie Donegan, became the leading figure in what became known as skiffle, a home-made music based on traditional Negro blues and the songs of such performers as Huddie Ledbetter.

These enthusiasts were also aware, via the record import shops, of the music of Chicago, and it was Barber who brought over Muddy Waters for a British tour late in 1958. His audiences had until then only had the opportunity to hear the toned-down music of Big Bill Broonzy, and Waters's heavily amplified sound and biting slide guitar upset some 'purists', just as the electric Bob Dylan was to do in 1966. One critic referred to his 'vacuum cleaner' guitar, and objected to the fact that Otis Spann needed to amplify his piano. Although dissatisfied customers were in the minority, Waters noted that 'people in England like soft guitar and old blues'.

Of course, he was totally unaware, at this time at least, that his visit was to give birth to the British blues scene, a movement that later rebounded back over the Atlantic and brought overdue recognition for Chicago blues as the mainspring of rock 'n' roll. Among his audience were musicians like harmonica player Cyril

Davies and guitarist Alexis Korner, members of the Barber/Colyer circle who a year before, with guitarist Jeff Bradford, had cut the first tentative examples of British blues. When they saw Muddy perform it confirmed for them that this was the right direction, and they went on to form the Soho-based band Blues Incorporated, the seed-bed of the Rolling Stones and the entire British blues revival. Chris Barber, in the meantime, brought over Muddy's harmonica player James Cotton, gospel singer Alex Bradford, folk-blues duo Sonny Terry and Brownie McGhee and jump-jive band leader Louis Jordan to provide further inspiration.

Rebranding the product: the Newport Jazz Festival brought the Muddy Waters sound to a new audience.

But to Muddy the lesson was that folk-blues was the way forward, and in the summer of 1959 he cut an album's worth of songs consisting mainly of Broonzy material, plus a couple by his then lodger James Oden, composer of 'Goin' Down Slow'. Although he gives a sprightly rereading to 'Moppers Blues', among others, these sessions seem, with hindsight, to be at best a temporary diversion. Broonzy stood for the 1930s and 40s, and his attempts to adapt to what he perceived to be the requirements of the white coffee-house crowd were no longer relevant – Broonzy had died in 1958. Waters, at very least of Broonzy's stature in the unfolding story of the blues, was his own man, and indeed his time would come again.

The start of his 'crossover' appeal, after the mixed success in the UK, began with a 1959 performance at New York's Carnegie Hall. A session in June 1960 added two more classics to his catalogue, both of them snapped up by Blues Incorporated in the Soho clubs – the strutting 'Tiger in Your Tank', with Muddy playing some urgent slide guitar, and 'I Got My Brand on You'. And then, building on his Carnegie Hall experience, Muddy accepted a booking for the 1960 Newport Jazz Festival.

The Chess brothers were shrewd enough to see a live album as the next stage in broadening Muddy's base. His band at the time was exceptionally strong, and since this was to be their last recording together it was doubly timely. Cotton, Spann and Hare were still with him, and the rhythm section was now Andrew Stephens on electric Fender bass and Francis Clay on drums. Listening to the album now, it reminds one of the plot of so many cheap rock 'n' roll movies, where the mayor and the school governors begin in a mood of cold outrage at the jungle music being perpetrated on stage, but by the end are twisting

Mojo working:
Muddy Waters followed
Big Bill Broonzy on to
the concert stage.

and finger-popping over by the soft-drinks bar.

Muddy starts a little nervously, and the audience are polite but cold. But the atmosphere gradually builds, and by the time he gets to 'Got My Mojo Working' he and the band have clearly won. Indeed a long and dynamic version of the song is immediately reprised as 'Got My Mojo Working Part 2', before Otis Spann leads into the coda, singing 'Goodbye Newport Blues' with great feeling.

There were not many recording opportunities for Muddy over the next couple of years, though he remained as busy as ever in his own Chicago club kingdom, and those tracks that were cut often included brass in the line-up. This was Chess's reaction to the increasing popularity of a more sophisticated big-band blues style epitomized by BB King, who signed with ABC Records in 1962 and whose success at around this time was to culminate in his marvellous 1964 album *Live at the Regal.* But this was not the Muddy Waters way, and he never sounds quite at home with saxophones, any more than he does with the electric organ that in 1962 replaced the briefly absent Otis Spann, who was off making his own album for the Candid label. However much his music had evolved and pulled the sound of Chicago blues along with it, Muddy was still in essence a Delta singer, and the dusty roads and plantations were no place for a Hammond organ.

The period had its recorded pleasures, though, notably a jokily arrogant answer to Junior Wells's anthem 'Messin' with the Kid' called 'Messin' with the Man' and a lovely slow blues, 'Tough Times'. It also had a horrid aberration – one can only imagine Waters's private feelings when Leonard Chess pressed on him the 1962 masterwork 'Muddy Waters Twist'. Lacking Bo Diddley's creative, self-mocking sense of humour, Waters was unable to subvert such modish rubbish by sending it up. Another experiment which could have failed as badly, in fact emerged as something of a triumph – Chess had bought some instrumental tracks by John Lee's cousin Earl Hooker, a masterly guitarist in the Delta slide mould, which Willie Dixon refashioned while dubbing on Muddy's voice. They emerged as 'You Shook Me', a variation on the 'Rock Me Baby' theme, and 'You Need Love', later to be purloined by Led Zeppelin.

Two early-summer sessions in 1963 saw Muddy reviving songs associated with other artists, which suggests that his engine had temporarily run out of steam, though some of the results are strong enough – his versions of Eddie Boyd's two big hits, 'Five Long Years' and '24 Hours', for example. But he also allowed himself to sing 'She'll Be Coming Round the Mountain'! This, however, was followed by a triumph – a set cut live at the Copacabana club in Chicago, meaning that, in intriguing contrast to the Newport album, Muddy was now firmly on home base, with an audience who neither need warming up nor winning over. Buddy Guy, with two hits of his own under his belt by this time, joins Spann, Below and guest vocalist Dixon among the band, and it is this version of 'Mojo' that we best remember these days, with Spann storming into a supercharged boogie piano riff and Donald Hankins's bass part urging the whole thing irresistibly forward. The hits were long gone by now, but rather than sleepwalk

through them Waters was still capable of improving on them.

From black to white – the next project, cut in September 1963, was a 'don't frighten our new audience away' exercise. Muddy went into the studio with an acoustic guitar, Buddy Guy was similarly equipped, and on some tracks Willie Dixon contributes his plummy stand-up bass and Clifton James slaps a little drum kit. This is the album *Muddy Waters – Folk Singer*, and it is another masterpiece. Although one feels that Muddy may be mistaken in thinking that his growing number of white fans are still scared off by amplifiers, this mature re-examination of his roots is a wonderful piece of work – it makes it seem that it was the trumpets, saxophones and electric organs that were the defensive measures, whereas this back-porch project is at the very core of his genius. He's got a bottleneck back on his finger, Buddy Guy is in prime form, and everything from his robust revival of 'My Home Is in the Delta' to a spare, thoughtful revisit to one side of his first Aristocrat hit, 'I Feel Like Going Home', is a pleasure.

And so it was a confident Muddy Waters who immediately left for Europe once more as part of the American Folk Blues Festival. By this time the Rolling Stones had scored their first hit with a slightly bowdlerized version of Chuck Berry's 'Come On', and when their début album appeared early in 1964 it consisted almost entirely of Chicago blues. My generation of blues fans, the Stones generation, found that their record collection was clearly matched by that of this new British band, and Muddy Waters was a hero to all of us. The 'coals to Newcastle' operation by the Stones was to guarantee him work for the rest of his life. He still had his local base, of course, but it was being increasingly augmented by college dates, concert halls and European visits – he was back in 1964 for the next of many visits that continued into old age. Any dissenters had vanished in the previous five years.

By now the Chess mainstream was moving towards soul, together with the licensing-in of product from elsewhere (of which the finest example was Tommy Tucker's wonderful 1964 hit 'Hi-Heel Sneakers', recorded in New York). They seemed uncertain of what to do with Muddy as with the rest of their surviving old guard. The early-1964 pairing of 'You Can't Lose' and 'The Same Thing' was strong enough, but by October he was being given a 'Sneakers'-style song in 'Short Dress Woman', somewhat compromised by getting saxophonist JT Brown to switch to clarinet – not an instrument one immediately associates with downhome blues. But at least he was back driving his slide guitar on most of the tracks dating from this period, a particularly frantic example being the otherwise gimmicky 'My Dog Can't Bark'.

Muddy's diversifying gig schedule reduced recording opportunities at this time in any case, though a 1966 album project put him together with yet more brass and, on some tracks, a soul-styled organ. His stage band now included two other guitarists, Sam Lawhorn and Pee Wee Madison, who were also present on the sporadic mid-60s sessions. But James Cotton left around this time, to be briefly replaced by George Smith.

In the last years of Chess as a creative label Waters's output continued to be a mixture of the acceptable and the disappointing. Best among the former is a project with his celebrated white American fans, the harmonica bluesman Paul Butterfield and the guitarist Mike Bloomfield, called *Fathers and Sons*. By this time Norman Dayron, a young white producer, was working for Chess, and he was also a member of the white

A band leader with bottle:
Willie Dixon toured throughout Europe on the blues package shows.

Muddy Waters at the
Fairfield Halls, Croydon,
in 1964.

blues fraternity in Chicago. He had first joined
the company as a janitor and had risen to be
assistant engineer, working with Willie Dixon
and learning from him. He was involved,
uncredited, on the Butterfield band's *East-West*
album, which was cut at Chess studios.

He told *Blues Access* magazine in 1996 about
his visits to blues clubs with Bloomfield and
Butterfield. 'On the South Side and West Side,
Paul and Mike would regularly sit in with
everyone, from Muddy to Wolf, Chuck Berry,
Little Milton, BB King and Sonny Boy
Williamson. White people didn't go into these
clubs then, and there was no precedent for them
being there. When Paul and Mike went in it
would be expressly out of their intention to sit in,
and blow whoever it was – Muddy or whoever –
right off the stage. Those two guys were focused
on demonstrating that they could play as well as
and with anybody up there. And what they did
when they sat in was extraordinary.' Dayron
also described how, in the late 50s and
early 60s, it was rare 'to find a truly
impeccable performance on harmonica
… and you rarely saw a good lead
guitar player'. In this environment
Butterfield and Bloomfield gained a

Big hair day
Muddy Waters backstage
at Hammersmith Odeon,
in 1968.

Main man:
in the 1970s Muddy Waters was revered as the catalyst of postwar Chicago blues.

foothold, and soon came to impress even the superstars like Muddy.

Bloomfield came up with the *Father and Sons* idea, and knew that they had to pitch it to Marshall Chess rather than the brothers, since Leonard's son was of the generation to whom

white blues bands were now commonplace. It took a couple of years to come to fruition, with the addition of other big names like drummer Buddy Miles and Booker T's bass player, Duck Dunn, and when Bloomfield turned up at the session and saw not only those involved, like Muddy and Otis Spann, but all the other Chess stars who had turned up to watch, he fled to the airport and had to be dragged back.

'I think this was one of the greatest sessions we did since Little Walter's time and Jimmy Rogers's. We was close to that ole sound,' said

Muddy Waters. 'People say the white kids can't play the blues, but that's wrong,' was Otis Spann's view.

Among the disappointing projects, by contrast, is the squelchy psychedelia of *Electric Mud*, trying to find a new market and failing. And somewhere in between is 1971's *The London Sessions*, featuring Irish blues guitarist Rory Gallagher. The last Chess album of note is the 1973 set *Can't Get No Grindin'*, produced by Ralph Bass at the Chess studios and consisting largely of Waters originals. There is no longer any need to fashion Muddy into something he is not, and Bass settles instead for a contemporary version of the familiar style.

The last decade of Muddy's life was a rewarding one, in which he was able to take pride in his stature as the king of postwar Chicago blues. Though a serious car accident in 1969 had restricted his mobility, and he was still liable to leave most of the guitar playing to others, his majestic voice and dignified charisma were intact. He signed a deal with the Blue Sky label, distributed through the major CBS (now part of the Sony conglomerate) and made four albums with albino bluesman Johnny Winter as producer. *Hard Again*, *Muddy 'Mississippi' Waters Live*, *I'm Ready* and *King Bee* mixed recuts of Waters classics, covers of other artists' material and new songs into a satisfying whole, respectfully overseen by Winter.

However, increasing health problems, aggravated by the long-term debilitating effects of the car crash, made Muddy seem older than his years, and on 30 April 1983 he died of heart

failure. He had helped to launch the Chess brothers' career as record-company entrepreneurs, with both Aristocrat and Chess itself, and had remained loyal throughout the latter label's life. In the process, he had played a major role in forging that link between the Mississippi Delta and Chicago which has proved to be one of the most dynamic and fruitful in all of the blues.

SINCERELY

If the best years of postwar Chicago blues began with Muddy Waters's first Aristocrat hit, maybe they ended at around the time of his penultimate r&b chart entry, 'Don't Go No Farther', in August 1956. Certainly within a few more years both Chess and its main rival, Vee-Jay, were finding it much harder to sell product by the old-style bluesmen, and towards the end of the decade only John Lee Hooker and Jimmy Reed really came into this category as far as Vee-Jay was concerned, while over at Chess just the 'big four' – Muddy Waters, Howlin' Wolf, Little Walter and Sonny Boy Williamson – remained, along with the locally popular JB Lenoir, who last recorded new material for the company in 1958. Although Chess took the blues into the next decade with Buddy Guy and Little Milton, by the mid-50s it was clear that something new was needed to inject life into the label.

But this was surely only clear in retrospect. The decision by Leonard and Phil Chess to sign Bo Diddley and Chuck Berry in 1955 was inspired – it gave the label its essential link between the blues and soul in rock 'n' roll. It must be said, though, that this inspiration was more luck than shrewd judgement. Although Berry came almost out of nowhere and found his potential instantly recognized, Bo had been banging out the blues on Maxwell Street and elsewhere since he was a teenager in the early 1940s, without ever being lured indoors by a Chess contract. In the meantime there was another link in the chain of black music which Chess was in a position to exploit – doo-wop.

Teenagers used to be invisible – they filled an awkward gap between childhood and adulthood, but had the status of neither, existing in a limbo between innocence and responsibility. Before the 1950s, when the world recovered from the Second World War and began to dish out pocket money, they hadn't been invented. Records, and specifically here the product of the Delta bluesmen, sold to adults. Their songs, after all, dealt with adult concerns – of lost love, of unemployment, of poverty, of racism, of a yearning for one's roots. The furtive excitements of teenage years were ignored. And it wouldn't have occurred to anyone before Chuck Berry to write about 'Lonely Schooldays'.

But now, as television spread into every American home, providing accessible cheap entertainment day and night, record sales to adults diminished. And in the early-to-middle 1950s there was no one else to sell them to. The blues felt the pinch as much as any kind of music, and indeed more than most. While teenage rock 'n' roll had to wait for Chuck Berry, in the interim the doo-wop groups were found to hold appeal for the younger audience that was beginning to emerge.

Growing out of the gospel choirs and the 1940s close-harmony ensembles like the Inkspots, doo-wop was the ultimate in poor-boys' music. Unlike skiffle, it didn't even require a Woolworth's guitar and a tea-chest bass – just a quartet of blending voices and, if possible, a subway tunnel to amplify the harmonies and impress a passing record-company executive.

The Moonglows were the most successful of mid-50s doo-wop groups, and they were on Chess. Their influence was to linger way beyond their chart life – the lead singer with the Drifters in the early 1960s, Ben E King, observed, 'If you could sing Moonglows, you could *kill* the neighborhood' – and the seduction routines of Philadelphia groups in the 1970s were in part a homage to the Moonglows.

The group, led by Harvey Fuqua, came from Louisville, Kentucky – four singers and an extra luxury in the form of guitarist Billy Johnson – and it was disc jockey Alan Freed who secured them a deal with the Chance label in Cleveland, Ohio. As with Berry's 'Maybelline', there was a price tag to Freed's assistance, and when the group moved to Chess in 1954 on the collapse of Chance his name appeared with Fuqua's as co-writer of 'Sincerely', the group's first and biggest hit, which made number two in the r&b chart in November.

Alan Freed, credited with coining the term 'rock 'n' roll' for his Cleveland radio show *Moondog's Rock 'n' Roll Party* in 1951, was the chief scapegoat in the payola investigation that ran through the record business in 1962. Like everyone else at the time, he took money and in his case sometimes a writer's credit for playing records, a system that Leonard Chess simply

Take it easy: physically restricted late in life, Muddy Waters nevertheless retained his powerful stage charisma.

accepted and stumped up for. But in Freed's defence it should be added that, unlike such apparently squeaky-clean disc jockeys as Dick Clark, he was a fervent champion of black music and would always support the cause of the meaty original over the pallid white cover version. Clark hedged his bets far more, and felt safer with the Frankies and the Bobbys – though it should be added that Bo Diddley won't hear a word said against him. In the case of 'Sincerely', the white cover came courtesy of the McGuire Sisters. Freed's career was destroyed by the payola scandal, and he died in 1965.

Chess sometimes tried to double their money by issuing Moonglows' cuts on Checker credited to Bobby Lester and the Moonlighters, which indeed they were. The hits, however, came under their proper name – 'Most of All' in 1955, a breakthrough into the pop Top 30 in 1956 with the upbeat 'See Saw', another r&b hit in 1957 with 'Please Send Me Someone to Love' and in 1958 their biggest moment and most enduring classic, the pop hit 'Ten Commandments of Love', which reached number 22 in the national charts and number nine in the r&b list, credited to Harvey and the Moonglows.

The group split up in 1959, by which time Fuqua was well in with the Chess brothers – he joined the company in a similar role to Willie Dixon, as director of a&r. In the meantime he

assembled another set of Moonglows, a group until then called the Marquees and who included Marvin Gaye. But there were no further chart successes. Fuqua worked with artists like Etta James for Chess in the early 60s before marrying the owner of the Anna label, Gwen Gordy. With her he set up further labels, Harvey and Tri-Star, which Berry Gordy bought out and absorbed into Tamla Motown. Fuqua then worked at Motown through the rest of the 60s as a writer and producer, later setting up his own production company and re-forming the Moonglows for the 1970s rock 'n' roll revival circuit.

After the Orioles first hit the r&b list in 1949 with 'Tell Me So' there developed a craze for ornithological doo-wop, and it was two of the many bird groups that established an early bridgehead for black music in the 'white' pop charts – the Orioles themselves with 1954's 'Crying in the Chapel' and the Crows with 'Gee' in the following year. The Ravens had two r&b hits in the early 50s, and would later record 'Kneel and Pray' for Chess. The Penguins created one of the most beautiful and successful doo-wop records of all with 'Earth Angel' in 1954. The Robins were rejigged as the greatest of all the black vocal groups, the Coasters, and the Falcons, who were only one secular stride from the chapel pew, spanned the 1950s and 60s with the assistance of their rasping, impassioned lead singer Wilson Pickett.

In Gerri Hirshey's *Nowhere to Run* Pickett gives a telling definition of the vocal group style. 'You got no cash for music lessons, arrangers, uniforms, back-up bands, guitars. No nothin'. So you look around for a good, solid used chassis. This be your 12-bar blues. R&b ain't nothin' if it ain't the 12-bar blues. Then you look around for what else you got. And if you come up like most of us, that would be gospel.' Pickett demonstrated his theory on such soaring classics as 'I Found a Love'.

And so Chess got their own bird group – one of the best and most versatile, although it was after a move to the End label in 1959 that they really piled up their hit list – as much in the Hot Hundred as in the r&b equivalent. The Flamingos were a Chicago ensemble formed in 1952, first recording, as did the Moonglows, for Chance. They hit on Checker in 1956 with 'I'll Be Home', a romantic ballad written by Fats Washington, but unfortunately for them and the Chess company the big hit version was the customary white cover – in this case by crooner Pat Boone. This musical magpie compounded the insult to black music by making it a double-sided top tenner, coupled with his somewhat baffled reading of Little Richard's revolutionary scream 'Tutti Frutti'.

The Flamingos, sporting a changing cast list as was the way with all vocal groups, continued to score hits until 1970's 'Buffalo Soldier', by which time one of the original members, Johnny Carter, had joined Chess's major success with 1960s vocal-group soul, the Dells.

Chess's other success with 1950s doo-wop was a song licensed in, rather than originating on, the label. Lee Andrews and the Hearts were a group from Philadelphia who first recorded in 1954, and in 1957 they cut 'Tear Drops' for the Main-Line label. When the number was picked up for release on Chess, it gave them their biggest hit and only Top 20 entry, reaching number 13 at Christmas.

Chess also recorded groups called the Sparrows and the Clouds, although no singles resulted. Doo-wop proved useful to the Chess company in that it provided welcome chart action at the very time when interest in the hard-core blues was beginning to fade, and papered over the gap between that and the new sound of Chuck Berry and Bo Diddley.

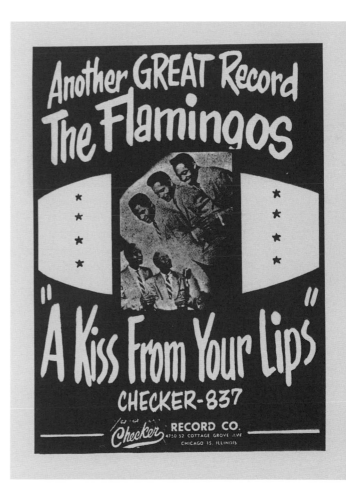

CHAPTER 4

THE TWO KINGS

I'M A MAN

If doo-wop was a bridge between Chess's mainstream dependence on Delta-derived blues and the company's future, then Bo Diddley and Chuck Berry, by and large, were that future. Bo was first into the studio, on 2 March 1955, and Chuck followed some ten weeks later.

Unlike the musical genius of Muddy Waters, which has direct and clearly audible links with pre-war Delta blues, that of Bo Diddley is impossible to trace back to its source. It must start somewhere in his complex lineage, which perhaps gives him a subconscious inner ear for many different regional and national styles of music. 'I'm classed as a negro,' he once said, 'but I'm not. I'm what you call a black Frenchman, a creole.' He also threw African and native American blood into the mix, and pointed out that some members of his extended family could pass for white. If there ever was a straight line to be drawn from the West African base of the slave trade to Mississippi, it surely wandered off in many different directions before coming up with Bo Diddley.

The next element in his unique style, and one that he points to himself, is that he learned to play the violin as a child and simply transferred the finger positions to the fretboard of a guitar.

'One day I saw a dude playin' a violin,' he told his biographer George R White. 'I didn't even know what it was, you know, so I told my mother that I wanted one of them things that that man had [with] a stick on it, you know.'

In fact it was his local Baptist church who presented the young Bo with a violin, having taken up a collection, and he soon got bored of '...playin' "Drink to Me Only with Thine Eyes" an' concertos... I wanted to play some jazz an' *get down*.' This caused him some disciplinary problems as a member of the church orchestra, but he persisted with violin lessons until he broke a finger at the age of 15, after which he found that his dexterity had been affected. By this time, however, his sister had bought him a guitar, and he would fool around until he could reproduce the single-note runs and chords on the guitar that he could play on the violin. 'My [guitar] technique comes from bowin' the violin, that fast wrist action.'

The next enforced difference in Bo's technique comes from what he calls his 'meathook' fingers,

All jacket and short trousers:
Bo Diddley gave new life to Chess in the mid-1950s.

too big to shape the chords on a guitar conventionally (and one reason he's never felt comfortable with the celebrated but narrow-necked Fender guitars). And so he soon learned to tune the instrument to an open chord, in his case E major, so that he could create chords simply by 'barring' across a fret. From there he developed his single-note runs as well.

Bo has always been a musical magpie, able to listen to classical music, Spanish flamenco or reggae for pleasure. He has something of Robert Johnson's celebrated ability to hear something once and assimilate it. Whatever he has heard is likely to sink into his subconscious and eventually colour his sound. Add to this his long apprenticeship on the streets of Chicago, only parting the bystanders from their dimes and quarters if he could come up with something they wanted to hear, and we begin to understand how Bo Diddley could arrive at a sound that no one had made before. It's African and it's the blues, it's the earliest rock 'n' roll, it's funk before its time. He can play a blues as if he's a moonlighting classical violinist ('The Clock Strikes Twelve') or out-Moonglow the Moonglows with a reverberating slice of doo-wop, as in 'I'm Sorry'. In all cases, the sound is Bo Diddley's and no one else's.

Bo was born on 30 December, 1928 in McComb, Mississippi, a dusty settlement down near the border with Louisiana, less than 100 miles due north of New Orleans. As the illegitimate son of Eugene Bates, whom he never knew, and the teenaged Ethel Wilson, his original name was Ellas Bates, but he was raised by his mother's first cousin, Gussie McDaniel. When his adoptive father Robert died in 1934 he was taken by Gussie to Chicago, at first staying with relatives, and his name became Ellas B McDaniel.

He grew up on Langley Avenue, in the tough, rundown South Side, an experience which stood him in good stead later when he took up boxing.

After his introduction to the violin and guitar he left school prematurely to live as a streetwise but law-abiding hustler, good with his hands, able to figure out how things worked and mend them when they went wrong, ingenious in devising ways to earn a dollar. After meeting fellow guitarist Joe 'Jody' Williams and washtub-bass player Roosevelt he formed a street band, originally known as the Hipsters, later the Langley Avenue Jive Cats, and they were sometimes joined by Earl Hooker, who himself became a distinguished Chicago bluesman before dying of tuberculosis in 1970.

At some point Ellas gained the nickname Bo Diddley, for reasons that have always been obscure. The 'diddley bow' is one name for the crude instrument, neither violin nor guitar, that so many bluesmen started with – usually a length of wire nailed to a wooden wall, fretted with metal. But Bo has never felt that this was the source of his name.

His first harmonica player, Billy Boy Arnold, has recalled the Hipsters' bass player Roosevelt pointing out a bow-legged man walking down the street and referring to him as Bo Diddley. Arnold says that he remembered this at Bo's first Chess session, and thus a legend was born. But Bo himself recalls his 'mother' Gussie referring to an old man she called Bo Diddley – a former slave, a dancing and singing busker.

Bo says that people have often said to him, 'Are you the Bo Diddley that used to live in...?', which he never is, while George R White refers to a nightclub advertisement in a 1935 edition of the *Chicago Defender* announcing 'Efus & Bo Diddley and band'. It could surely have been a extent that he took to carrying a knife to protect his earnings. He left home at 16 – at first only as far as next door – and his band's orbit soon included Maxwell Street in 'Jew Town', the celebrated centre of Chicago street music. He recalls listening to the Muddy Waters band when he was 16, too young to be allowed into clubs, and so he hid behind the juke box until the bouncers spotted him. If so, this would have been soon after Muddy's arrival in town, though Bo also remembers Little Walter in the band. However old Bo was, he was certainly below the minimum 21 years for attending licensed clubs.

The group graduated to talent shows at the Indiana Theater and elsewhere. The Indiana, on 43rd Street, was a movie house during the day but at night it had the Midnight Ramble, an informal blues gig. Bo also began working out in the gym, and took up amateur boxing as a light-heavyweight. But he abandoned the idea of turning professional at about the time, at the age of 18, that he married Louise Woolingham, though the marriage lasted for less than a year. He also began the first of a long series of short-lived labouring jobs.

When he was 19, claiming to be 21, Bo landed the band's first residency, at the 708 Club on E 47th Street, and in 1949 he married for the second time, to Ethel Smith. When not at his day job or working at the 708, he continued to play on the streets, and in 1950 Billy Boy Arnold

Showtime:
Bo in the mid-50s with guitarist Bobby Parker.

school nickname, and yet Bo says he was known as 'Mac'. Take your pick.

Playing on street corners did not, of course, please Bo's family – 'Baptist people think *breathin'* is bad, you dig?' But he thrived, to the joined the band. Arnold, born in 1935, was a kid at the time and happened to be walking past a restaurant when he heard the band, just the acoustic guitars of Bo and Jody plus the washtub. As he recalled in *Blues Unlimited* in 1978: 'I told them I played harmonica so Bo Diddley said, "We're going up to the Midway Theater to do an amateur show. Come up there with us."'

They played more and more in clubs, invariably unsavoury ones, although it was hard to improve on their street earnings – sometimes it was a case of 'five bucks split between four or five musicians'. At this time Bo continued to see music as a supplementary income, an addition to his regular work, and the more ambitious Arnold left in 1952, the year that Little Walter's 'Juke' launched their common instrument as a star attraction. Arnold would later return to play with Bo, including his first recording session, but in the meantime broadened his experience with such artists as Otis Rush and Johnny Shines.

At this time, according to Arnold, Bo 'didn't play a lot of that "Bo Diddley" type stuff. He played a lot of boogie-woogies like the song "Noxema" which was a version of "Dirty Mother Fucker" and he would play a boogie-woogie type of riff on the guitar.' Apart from the inevitable Muddy Waters, Bo himself cites Louis Jordan as an influence at this time, and the 'Noxema' riff had similarities to Jordan's 'Caldonia'. But when Bo finally got the chance to record in 1955, the rude lyrics of 'Noxema' and 'Dirty Mother Fucker', familiar 'public domain' rhymes involving girls sitting on the grass and hens clucking, became transmuted into the chant of 'Bo Diddley', with the dirty bits cut out.

In the meantime Bo's curiosity about how things worked – washing machines, radios, automobiles, anything – was leading him towards the next element in his distinctive musical style, its amplification. Arnold says that Bo could, for example, 'take a motor out of a car and lay it down on this floor and when he got through with it, each part of that motor be no bigger than a cigarette, he could take a motor like that and put it back together.' He electrified his guitar with a pick-up cannibalized from a record player and the entrails of an old radio, he married the valves and speakers of cheap amplifiers to create a bigger sound, and he worked out how to 'break up' the sound with circuits pirated from the mechanism of an electric clock.

Les Paul, the pioneer of the electric guitar, sometimes with his wife Mary Ford as co-vocalist, had been creating remarkable electronic multi-tracked sounds since the late 1940s, and now Bo Diddley was inventing a funky, bluesy, home-made version.

Then came the next element of the early Bo Diddley sound, the portable percussion of Jerome Green's maracas. Bo hit on the idea of maracas by recalling the sound made by Sandman, one of the Langley Street buskers, who would spread sand on a board and perform a shuffling, rhythmic dance. Naturally the impecunious, ingenious Bo Diddley did not walk into a music shop and buy a pair of factory-made maracas. Instead he scavenged the scrapyards for lavatory-cistern ballcocks, and filled them with black-eyed beans! He then worked out various rhythmic patterns and taught them to Jerome, an aspiring musician who lived downstairs. 'I picked the right dude,' Bo told George R White. 'That cat could shake the hell outta them things.' Thus the Bo Diddley sound was born, from lashed-together electrical goods and a pair of ballcocks.

For a couple of years the apprenticeship continued – day jobs, street and club music, technological curiosity, and attempts to get on record. 'I went for a while of gettin' doors slammed in my face.' But seemingly Bo didn't even realize that Chess Records was only about three blocks from his house until he saw someone coming out of the back door to dump a pile of broken records. He lived at 48th and Langley, while Chess was at 48th and Cottage. One of the rejections was by Vee-Jay, who didn't like his 'jungle music'.

In the meantime, late in 1954, Arnold returned to the band, which at that stage consisted of Jerome, James Bradford on stand-up bass and a second guitarist called Buttercup, who soon had to go because his wife completely wrecked a bar after they had had an argument. The next recruitment was a significant one – drummer Clifton James, one of the many great session musicians associated with Chess and one with the skill to help create the original 'Bo Diddley sound', with its complex cross-rhythms. James went on to a long career with the label – he came to Europe with the 1964 Folk Blues Festival, for example, and was later one of Willie Dixon's Chicago Blues All-Stars.

Bo told *Rolling Stone* of his arrival at Chess. 'I said, "Man, y'all make records in here?" And Phil [Chess] was there, he said, "Yeah, whaddya want?" I said, "Well, I gotta song." He said, "Let us hear it." And when I started playin' Phil called his brother Leonard in... They told me to rewrite it. The words was a little rough. It had lyrics like, "Bowlegged rooster told a cocklegged duck, 'Say you ain't good-lookin' but you sure can ... crow.'" It took me about seven days to rewrite it, and that song became "Bo Diddley".'

Bo, with Jerome, Arnold, James and Bradford, were rewarded with a session on 2 March, with the loan of Otis Spann on piano and Willie Dixon

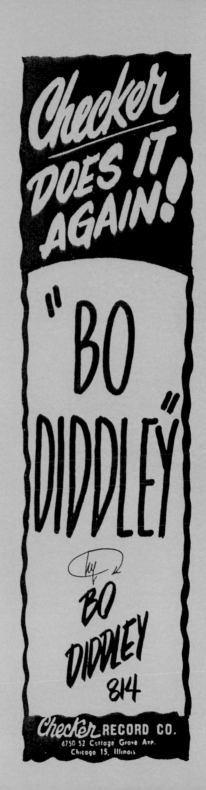

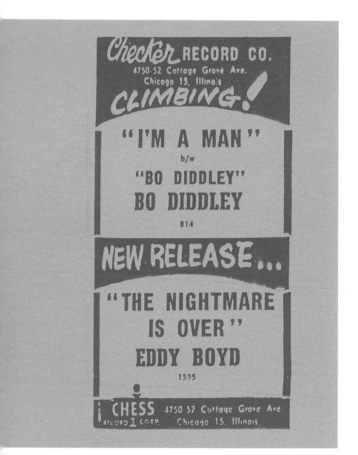

Diddley', supported strongly by two further songs that would eventually appear on his exceptional 1959 Checker album *Go Bo Diddley*, the stomping 'Little Girl' and 'You Don't Love Me (You Don't Care)'.

Dixon was impressed. 'I heard Bo Diddley playing in the streets lots of times. He had a little band that would go from corner to corner, set up and start playing... One day somebody brought him into the studio. He did this song "I'm a Man" and kept developing it... I knew Bo had a very good rhythmic style.' Referring to the percussive impact of the Diddley style, Dixon noted: 'The drums have always been giving messages. In slavery times they didn't allow black people to tap or drum on wooden things because they could talk the message of rhythms. That's why Bo Diddley always carries this particular pattern. The drums are speaking and he'll tell you what the drums are saying.'

'I'm a Man' required about 30 takes, partly because the Chess brothers came up with the idea of spelling out the word 'Man' as part of the lyric, but then found it hard to convey to Bo what was wanted, since they didn't think to spell it out in the correct, slow, deliberate tempo. 'They couldn't tell me what the hell they was talkin' about,' recalled Bo.

Released on Checker 814, the double-sider reached number two in the r&b list in May. It secured Bo a slot on the most powerful television vehicle of the day, the syndicated *Ed Sullivan Show*, which was a disaster. Sullivan wanted Bo to sing the Tennessee Ernie Ford hit 'Sixteen Tons', which Bo did as part of his stage act. Bo naturally assumed Sullivan meant in *addition* to his own hit, and so went out and sang 'Bo Diddley'. An argument ensued during which Sullivan accused Bo of being the first 'colored

in attendance as supervisor of the session and playing bass on some tracks. Arnold, already an artist with one single to his name ('I Ain't Got No Money' on Cool, 1953), cut three tracks, but Chess did nothing with them. This was because Arnold had meantime done a deal with Chess's rival Vee-Jay, resulting in what Willie Dixon has described as a 'heated discussion'. The settlement required that Chess should keep Bo and Arnold should stay with Vee-Jay.

Bo's contributions to the day were historic – a double-sided début hit single in the boastful, staccato 'I'm a Man' and the revolutionary 'Bo boy' to double-cross him, an insult that earned him an attempted right hook.

To complete the day, Bo was forced to sign for his fee, $750, and then give the cheque straight back. For a 'colored boy' it was apparently considered enough to simply appear on Sullivan's show, and this was Bo's first lesson in the racism and corruption that riddled the industry. Later it became clear to him that this rip-off wasn't confined to television – whether he appeared live as a solo attraction or as part of one of the treadmill of package shows that this new hit-maker soon embarked upon, there seemed to be two fees – the one that the promoter paid for the act, and the one that the act actually received. Artists like Bo Diddley were caught in a trap – record companies didn't pay well or at all, because they insisted that record sales were simply a way of promoting live gigs, and promoters didn't pay up either. Bo has claimed that this massive hit earned him a station wagon and a cheque for about $1200.

Willie Dixon certainly played on the follow-up session on 15 May (six days before Chuck Berry continued the revival of the company's fortunes with 'Maybelline' – what a week!) because he felt that Bradford lacked the 'firepower' to complement Bo's muscular style. For the next distinctive chant and second hit, 'Diddley Daddy', Harvey Fuqua's Moonglows were also on hand, with Fuqua scoring a co-credit with Bo, and when coupled with 'She's Fine, She's Mine' (sometimes called 'You Don't Love Me') the record made number 11 in July.

This was the summer when black artists, the real rock 'n' rollers, made their first inroads into the white market, into the national consciousness. There was Bo and Chuck, there was Little Richard and Fats Domino. Elvis Presley was making waves wherever he played, of course, but it was another year before he moved to the RCA label and 'Heartbreak Hotel'. After 1955 black artists no longer had to croon to cross racial barriers – they could brag and bluster like Bo and Little Richard.

But what happened to the money? Marshall Chess has always insisted that Chess was fair, but admittedly. 'I think they paid low royalties, but everyone did, y'know... I don't know of any overt ripping off ever,' he told Ray Topping. 'I used to see my father go through the royalty statements and all I ever saw him do was once take money from one artist and give it to another. Because one guy, y'know, he needed the money to live, from the big one... I'll say this, they were two to three per cent artist's royalties ... cheap royalties...'

He confirms that session fees were also paid, at union scale. His counter-argument to claims, most vociferously by Bo Diddley, that due royalties were not paid is that the artists were always coming to the office for advances and hand-outs, and that they were without exception actually in debt to the company. He expanded on the theme in *Living Blues*.

'None of those artists ... ever discussed their own habits... constantly coming in to borrow money... The one thing I wish I would have would be the book that we had with all the money owed back to us... I say it's bullshit... It was constant trouble and bailings out... Who in the hell knows what went down 30 years ago in some little room somewhere with two people, you know, one guy begging for money, the other guy, he's already given him a lot, says, "Look, if you want more you've got to do this," and the guy says, "I'll do it."' One of them was indeed Bo Diddley, who, at a low point in his career, sold off the rights to his songs.

He, of course, sees it differently, calling Leonard Chess a 'motherfuck thief'. To which the engineer on the Chess sessions, Malcolm Chisholm, claims that the artists are 'inclined to think that everyone is a thief. They are genuinely paranoid. So far as I know, Leonard would never actually steal from anybody.'

But Bo Diddley warmed to his theme in *Rolling Stone*. 'Well, Bo Diddley ain't got shit. My records are sold all over the world, and I ain't got a fuckin' dime. If Chess Records gave me, in all the time that I dealt with them, if they gave me $75,000 in royalty checks, I'll eat my hat. Boil it and eat it. Somebody got the money – everybody in this business has big mansions and stuff, you know? I got a *log* mansion. When I left Chess Records, they said I owed them $125,000... How? Where is the money? Bo Diddley did not get it.'

'When they started buyin' radio stations an' stuff,' he said to George R White, 'I began to wonder where they was gettin' the money from. Now ... I've figured it out: they used *my* money, an' Muddy Waters's, an' Willie Dixon's... Jimmy Rogers got shafted around by Chess Records. They got rid of him *right quick* because he started to askin' about money. They did Willie Mabon the same way...

'I started hearin' less Bo Diddley records bein' played on the station that *they owned*! They was tryin' to cut my throat *quick*, popularity wise. You know, let's shut this nigger down, because this nigger is *dangerous*!'

To illustrate the complexity of this situation – it is clearly not a case of outright rip-off by the Chess Brothers, nor on the other hand of sheer paranoia on the part of uneducated, suspicious black men in a white man's business world – a year after talking to *Rolling Stone* Bo was telling *Blues Unlimited*: 'I wanted to stay with Chess Records from the beginning to the end. I feel like we were like a family ... I felt I was for them and they was for me and we was for each other.'

The family feeling was certainly apparent in 1955, and Chess devoted a lot of time to their new star. With 'Diddley Daddy' in the charts Bo was brought back to the studio in July and created another classic single (though, surprisingly, he didn't chart again until 1959). Willie Dixon's 'Pretty Thing', which, like Muddy's 'Rollin' Stone', gave its name to an admiring British r&b band, is irresistible, clearly tailored specifically for Bo, and for the b-side Bo gave the spotlight to his maracas player for the catchy 'Bring It to Jerome'. In November the next single comprised Willie Dixon's revival of an old Blind Blake theme, 'Diddy Wah Diddy', and the pounding 'I'm Looking for a Woman'.

In the meantime, on the back of 'Diddley Daddy' Bo topped the bill on an Alan Freed coast-to-coast package tour that included Little Walter and the Moonglows, Dakota Staton and Dinah Washington. At a time when Elvis's gyrations were known only to his growing band of fans down south, and before James Brown ever took to the road, Bo was one of the wildest showmen around. As one reviewer put it: 'Bo usually starts stomping on one side of the stage and high-kicks, spins, dips, taps and waddles his way to the other. By the time he's across the stage, man, everybody's jumping.' Chuck Berry's duck walk

Bo's band, sometime in the early 60s:
(clockwise from left) Norma Jean 'The Duchess' Wofford, Frank Kirkland, Jesse James Johnson, Bo Diddley, Jerome Green.

was to become world-famous, and it was surely born as a response to the antics of his label-mate and friendly rival. Bo has claimed that Elvis was smuggled into the Apollo Theater in Harlem to get some tips on stagecraft. He has no hard feelings towards Elvis, but does not like to hear it claimed that Presley 'invented' rock 'n' roll.

As the new music took hold it was getting crowded in the charts, but Bo remained a top live attraction throughout the rest of the 1950s, criss-crossing the country constantly as a headline attraction on the package tours. His friend Bobby Parker was guitarist for a while, then Jody Williams was in the band again until he was called up for army service in 1957, when Bo had the good fortune to bump into a talented 19-year-old female guitarist, Peggy Jones. As second guitarist on a number of Bo's sessions in the late 1950s, Peggy would either play lead lines over his reverberating rhythm guitar, duplicate his sound to give it greater depth, or even, she says, play the guitar in his style while he concentrated on singing.

By this time Bo had two drummers on call, Clifton James and Frank Kirkland, who would alternate on the long tours and in the studio.

A year after his recorded début, in March (possibly May) 1956, Bo Diddley recorded one of his masterpieces, 'Who Do You Love'. The line 'I walk forty-seven miles of barbed wire' was already in his head, but he couldn't think what to do with it – although he knew that it clearly

implied a 'tough guy' stance. For some reason the words 'Use a cobra snake' occurred to him, and Clifton James immediately completed the line – 'for a necktie'.

Gradually the surreal lyric took shape – his house is of rattlesnake hide with a human skull for a chimney, the night was black and the sky was blue. But the twist in the song is evidence of Bo Diddley's genius – this is no simple 'I'm a Man' boast, since the singer is constantly asking his girlfriend Arlene for reassurance, prompted by jealousy, and the question in the song's title hovers between confidence and despair. The music itself is a muddy, choppy stew of sound, urgent and neurotic, out of which Jody Williams's spiky, harsh guitar lines stab their way clear and then fall back again. It is an eerie piece of work.

At around this time, in Washington, DC, Bo heard a young singer and pianist with an unusual vocal mannerism, swooping and stuttering and reshaping the lyric. Billy Stewart was an ex-gospel performer, now a confident 18-year-old, and Bo cut an instrumental with him called 'Billy's Blues'. What distinguished it, though, was not Stewart's piano or Bo's guitar, but the delicate guitar figure contributed by Jody Williams.

When, later in the year, the New York duo Mickey and Sylvia enjoyed a huge hit with their 'Love is Strange' – eventually a million-seller – the Chess brothers immediately recognized the guitar part running through it, and sued the duo's record company RCA. It would seem that

BO DIDDLEY

"WHOM DO YOU LOVE"

CHECKER # 842

Checker RECORD CO.
4750-52 COTTAGE GROVE AVE.
CHICAGO 15, ILLINOIS

Williams had played the tune to Sylvia, and that the lyrics were in fact by Bo, though the courts decided that the similarity to 'Billy's Blues' itself had not been established sufficiently. Later, in the difficult late 1960s, Bo sold his share of 'Love is Strange' to Sylvia and later still, as Sylvia Robinson, she became the president of All-Platinum Records – whose assets included the Chess catalogue. Stewart himself was to become one of Chess's mainstays in the 1960s, notably with his extraordinary assault on George Gershwin's 'Summertime'.

The next Bo Diddley single, 'Down Home Train', cut in October 1956, created a soundscape of a speeding express engine carrying a man home to his girlfriend, and Otis Spann enlivened the humorous, jive-talking b-side, 'Cops and Robbers', another of Bo's strongest songs, though not in his view, since 'they had me talkin' like a cissy'.

Peggy Jones, renamed Lady Bo, made her studio début on the next single, a double-sided winner. 'Hey Bo Diddley' proved that the singer could continue to ring the changes on ways of chanting his name while making each one distinctive, and 'Mona' – crisply covered by the Rolling Stones at the start of their career – is a mating call set to a shimmering rhythm that proves, if proof were still required, the extraordinary power and depth of Bo's voice. The real-life Mona was a Detroit stripper whom Bo 'had the pleasure of working with' once.

Through 1957 and into 1958 Bo continued to make stunning records, and yet his name had disappeared from the r&b chart. One reason is that the pioneer of rock 'n' roll was now one of many, fighting for a share of the 'youth' market. But the fact is that his records continued to sell well enough, if not in the quantities of his first two hits, and George R White identifies the main

explanation for this discrepancy – sales but no chart listing. Chess Records continued largely to be a 'car-boot' company, with their pluggers (originally, of course, it had been Leonard alone) driving to a particular area with a load of discs, distributing them to the radio stations and shops, and returning to base for another load. Disc jockeys would pick up on a particular single in a specific region, and it would sell there, before breaking out elsewhere as a result of the next plugging trip. And so, when sales were collated for the purposes of publishing a countrywide

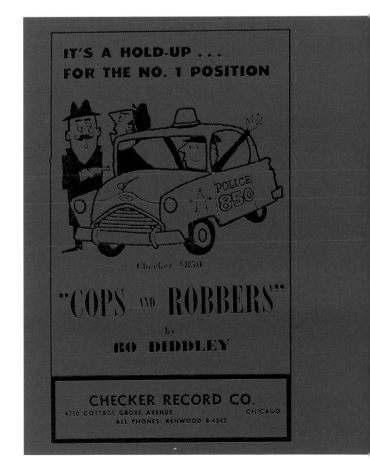

IT'S A HOLD-UP . . .
FOR THE NO. 1 POSITION

Checker #850

"COPS AND ROBBERS"
by
BO DIDDLEY

CHECKER RECORD CO.
4750 COTTAGE GROVE AVENUE   CHICAGO
ALL PHONES: KENWOOD 8-4342

chart, such a regional hit might well fail to make it, though over a period of time it could sell as well as, or even better than, any instant, nationally distributed chart success.

Bo Diddley also noticed that his appeal among black audiences was fading somewhat, and so he made a deliberate decision to 'quit the chitlin' circuit' and aim at bookings among the growing white, often college-based, market that, just a few years before, would have been closed to him. With the uncompromising blackness of his music, compared with the shrewd and revolutionary teenage-oriented rock 'n' roll of Chuck Berry, it was a hard road to take.

In summer 1957 Chess opened a new studio, having moved from 2120 South Michigan Avenue to 320 East 21st Street, and in August, now with Lafayette Leake on piano and the Moonglows once more on hand, Bo cut his next single – the joky, hard-time blues 'Say Boss Man' and a quite remarkable noise called 'Before You Accuse Me'. If one didn't respect Bo's professionalism one would suspect that drink had been taken. The song is in the standard blues format (and indeed, in spite of the fact that Bo never got round to re-recording it, the song has *become* a blues standard), and it is attacked with exhilarating energy. And yet Bo's guitar is out of tune, everyone seems to be at cross purposes, and they just boogie on regardless. In a more clinical age this tape would have been discarded immediately, and it is still hard to understand why Chess allowed it on to a single – and yet it has undeniable charm as one of rock 'n' roll's curiosities.

The jive humour of 'Say Man', with Bo and Jerome trading insults, marked a strong start to 1958 but remained in the can for more than a year, and in September Bo went to the other extreme and cut a novelty number, 'Bo Meets the Monster', the month after white actor and country singer Sheb Wooley had charted (even in the r&b list) with his 'Purple People Eater'. But the trick didn't work twice. Bo's career seemed to be at a low ebb, and he could not have guessed that 1959 was to mark his resurrection as a chart artist, and would prove to be the most successful period of his entire career. Not only did he score four times in the r&b chart, but the pop audience was at long last ready for him.

A session late in 1958 was to produce two hits, including his pop-chart breakthrough. With a dubbed Bo, and Jerome and Lady Bo crooning in the background, 'I'm Sorry' was a slow, vibrant doo-wop song that reached number 17 in the r&b list in March, while the infectious 'Crackin' Up', set to a languorous rhythm and built around the repeated question, 'What's bugging you?', climbed three rungs higher in August and also reached 62 in the Hot Hundred. 'Say Man', mysteriously overlooked until now, proved to be Bo's biggest r&b hit since his début, peaking at number three, while in the pop charts it was his most successful of all, just edging into the Top 20. And so in September, after a couple of unproductive sessions, Bo was rushed back to the studio for a follow-up, 'Say Man, Back Again', consisting of more humorous backchat with Jerome. Although it missed out in the national list, it was an r&b number 23.

The success of 1959 extended into the next spring when another September cut was released, as 'Say Man, Back Again' faded in the charts. 'Road Runner' is one of Bo's finest numbers, sprouting more than 20 cover versions (these don't, of course, include Junior Walker, who gave the same title to one of his own Tamla Motown hits). It combines all of the artist's distinctive strengths – a pounding, unforgettable riff, offbeat humour, strange noises (in this case produced by scraping the plectrum up the bass string of his guitar), and his ability to latch on to some novelty, craze or aspect of popular culture and turn it into prime rock 'n' roll. Here it is the cartoon hero Road Runner, a supercharged member of the cuckoo family characterized by its habit of running down the road in front of cars. Bo turned this into one of his comic boasts, 'I'm a road runner, honey, and you can't catch up with me.' The record reached number 20 on the r&b list, 75 on the Hot Hundred, and carried Bo triumphantly into the new decade.

However, in the meantime he had cut his next single, which proved to be his first chart failure for over a year. 'Walkin' and Talkin'' apes the cowboy theme of the Coasters' hit 'Along Came Jones', whereas Bo's strength is his individuality. By this time, though, he was an established album artist. Chess had first simply collected together a handful of singles for an eponymous 1958 LP, and this was followed a year later by the hit-packed *Go Bo Diddley* and then, in 1960, by two albums, *Have Guitar – Will Travel* and the delightfully varied collection *In the Spotlight*.

Bo had been spending increasing amounts of time working in Washington, and now decided to move there. He built a basement studio and began to work with a mixture of Chicago and Washington musicians, with some of his tapes being sent over to Chess for extra instruments to be added – Lafayette Leake's piano or Willie Dixon's bass, for example. It was at this time that he first met a young white girl, Kay Reynolds, who

Dude ranch:
a fancy-dress outfit and no specs make for one of the all-time great album covers.

was to become his next wife. Their marriage lasted for two decades.

Throughout his career Bo Diddley has reinvented himself as the hero of his songs in different guises, and in August 1960, having been to see *The Magnificent Seven*, he cut 'Bo Diddley is a Gunslinger'. It was first pressed up on his own label, BoKay, as a promotional give-

Tin Pan Alley:
Bo Diddley visits a
London music store, 1965.

away, but the Chess brothers also picked up on it as the next Chess single. They perpetuated the 'black cowboy' persona by making it the title track of his next 1960 album, which contains Bo's nods towards country and western in such tracks as 'Sixteen Tons', 'Cheyenne' and 'Whoa Mule (Shine)'. Since gunslingers didn't usually wear horn-rimmed glasses, the cover uses a shot of Bo for once without his trademark specs.

The remarkable and enduring influence of the Bo Diddley sound is stressed in a list, compiled by George R White, of singles released at around this period which make use of his distinctive beat – Chuck Berry's 'Broken Arrow', the Big Bopper's 'It's the Truth, Ruth', Freddy Cannon's 'Buzz-Buzz A-Diddle-It', Dee Clark's 'Hey Little Girl', Duane Eddy's 'Cannonball', Bill Haley's 'Skinny Minny' and 'Lean Jean', Ronnie Hawkins's 'Clara', Buddy Holly's 'Not Fade Away', Elvis Presley's 'His Latest Flame' and Johnny Otis's 'Willie and the Hand Jive'.

A somewhat stronger album – though Bo's decline in popularity at this time is reflected in its comparative commercial failure – revealed his next persona, in 1961's *Bo Diddley Is a Lover*. From the Jimmy Reed-styled 'Bo's Blues', with its weird violin solo like a crying cat, to the tight riff and off-the-wall lyric of 'Hong Kong, Mississippi', from a reworking of 'Road Runner' as an instrumental, 'Congo', to the rap humour of 'Bo's Vacation', another tussle with Jerome, it is further testament to Bo's versatility, surrealism and continuing creativity.

He was invited to play at President Kennedy's inauguration early in 1961, but suffered a setback that summer when

Peggy Jones formed her own band, the Jewels, and left him. Although he remained in constant demand as a live act, the Chess brothers did him no favours in releasing his next album, the sub-standard *Bo Diddley's a Twister*. It was remarkable, then, that the second album of 1962 was a masterpiece, and contained a single that restored him to the charts after more than two years. *Bo Diddley* is a delight throughout, and the chosen single was a pairing of 'You Can't Judge a Book By Looking at the Cover' and 'I Can Tell', both passionate, brooding riff numbers as strong as anything he ever did. It reached 21 in the r&b chart and 48 on the Hot Hundred. Also outstanding is the no less dramatic 'Who May Your Lover Be', the surreal 'You All Green', about 'the baddest hombre y'all seen', and a handful of virtuoso instrumentals.

Lady Bo was replaced by another outstandingly attractive guitarist, the Duchess. Norma-Jean Wofford was from Pittsburgh, and was a permanent member of Bo's band until she got married in 1966. Her first sessions made up the next album, *Bo Diddley & Company*, which not surprisingly could not quite maintain the standard of its predecessor, but was a work of genius compared to the first 1963 LP. *Surfin' with Bo Diddley* is an unfocused mess, and eight of the tracks aren't even by him – they feature Billy Lee Riley's backing group the Megatons.

This year saw Bo tour the UK on one of the greatest of all package tours – he joined his

Small screen hero: the Rolling Stones helped artists like Bo Diddley gain exposure on television.

fans the Rolling Stones, the Everly Brothers and, back after a brief return to the church, Little Richard. One of the magazine interviews at the time quoted Bo as saying, 'I can go down the highway to a little town and totally destroy the place.' As I recall, the management of the dignified and historic Castle Hotel in Taunton, my own little town, might well agree with him. He and Jerome relaxed somewhat boisterously after delighting us at the Gaumont cinema.

The tour brought him his first UK hit, the shimmering 'Pretty Thing', released under Chess's new licensing deal with the London-based label Pye. This 1956 classic reached 34. He was even more successful in the British album chart, making the Top Twenty with *Bo Diddley*, *Bo Diddley Is a Gunslinger*, *Bo Diddley Rides Again* and *Beach Party* over the course of five months. The last-named was cut live at the Beach Club, Myrtle Beach, South Carolina on 5 and 6 July 1963, and has a pleasant, if chaotic atmosphere beneath the murky sound quality.

In 1964 Bo jammed with Chuck Berry on the *Two Great Guitars* album and eventually earned a gold disc for *Bo Diddley's All-Time Greatest Hits*, one of those 'best of' compilations that defines rock 'n' roll as surely as those by Elvis, Buddy Holly, Eddie Cochran or the Everly Brothers. The results of sessions cut in this year, which ended with Jerome Green leaving the band, appeared in 1965 and saw Bo trying to adapt somewhat to the arrival of soul music, on the album *Hey! Good Lookin'* (the title track of which was his second and last UK hit) and in particular on its successor, *500% More Man*. It didn't work – his old fans wanted the Bo they knew, and he didn't really break into a new market. In addition, his return to the UK in autumn 1965 ended prematurely as a result of a dispute with the promoter over pay. However, the year ended on a better note with a Hollywood TV booking, *The Big TNT Show*, which was also briefly released to the cinemas.

After an abortive recording session in Canada early in 1966 Bo cut a final, and surprising, hit record in September, produced by Marshall Chess and featuring Eddie Drennon on electric violin. The uncharacteristic 'Ooh Baby' reached 88 in the Hot Hundred and 17 on the r&b list. In the meantime Chess had released an album called *The Originator*, a strong selection even though it was made up of bits and pieces from various 1960s sessions. The novelty 'Pills', with the surprising subtitle 'Love's Labours Lost', a bluesy rap on the unlikely subject of 'Two Flies' and another bizarre rap with Jerome, 'Background to a Music', are among the pleasures. Bo then revived his blues roots in two collaborations produced by Ralph Bass, a staff man in the final years of Chess, which enjoyed some commercial success: *Super Blues* teamed him with Muddy Waters and Little Walter, just before the latter's death, and *The Super Super Blues Band* replaced the late harmonica player with Howlin' Wolf.

The musical tide was ebbing away from Bo, however, and a move to Los Angeles in 1969 could not revive his chart career. It was at this point that his conviction that Chess Records had been ripping him off over the years developed into an ongoing and unresolved slanging match, and matters reached their nadir when Leonard Chess died on 16 October 1969. Marshall Chess was later to say: 'Bo Diddley's disappointed me a

Axe man:
Bo finds an instrument even more bizarre than his guitars, London 1965.

lot. I've seen a lot of interviews where he's said a
lot of bad shit. I know what went down with him.
He used to suck money and ... in his mind,
everyone was cheatin' him.'

But if Chess as a force was coming towards
the end of its life – though admittedly it was still
releasing a significant amount in the r&b/soul
field, and Little Milton retained his popularity –
rock 'n' roll was reviving. Music had become

pretentious, creating a new hunger for its roots.
Not only did tongue-in-cheek groups like Sha Na
Na spring up to exploit a nostalgia for the music
of a decade previously, but the great originals
were still around, fit, reasonably young and still
rocking. In autumn 1969 Bo was booked for the
Toronto Rock 'n' Roll Revival Festival, along with
Chuck Berry, Little Richard, Jerry Lee Lewis and
Gene Vincent – as well as rocker John Lennon

and non-rocker Yoko Ono. Although Vincent's sad, drunken and tearful performance was cut out of the film that DA Pennebaker made of this event, *Keep on Rockin'*, and though the film in its original form ended with Eric Clapton resignedly leaving his guitar to feed back on its own as a comment on Yoko's dreadful screaming, the rock 'n' roll segments that survive precluded another upturn in the careers of such as Bo and Chuck. The impresario Richard Nader began to stage regular revival concerts, hundreds in all. Wembley Stadium hosted its own equivalent of Toronto in 1972, an exhilarating experience which climaxed with a burning forest of matches and cigarette lighters encouraged by Chuck Berry, and the movie *Let the Good Times Roll* showed such artists as Bo in excellent light.

Bo, perhaps against his better judgement, remained faithful to Chess until 1974, but only 1972's *Where It All Began* album came close to recapturing his unique magic. That was also the year when he cut the now obligatory *London Sessions* superstar album, but on this he sounds like a guest at his own party. A couple of unsuccessful mid-70s albums on other labels followed, but his career revived yet again at the end of the decade thanks to three inspired tours. In 1978 he came to Europe as a double attraction with Carl Perkins, between them uncovering the very roots of rock 'n' roll, the punk group the Clash revealed themselves as lifelong fans and booked Bo as their support act for a US tour in February 1979, introducing him to an entirely new audience, and later that year he toured with the bass-slapping rockabilly Ray Campi and the young and modish slide-guitar band George Thorogood and the Destroyers.

In the 1980s he was in as much demand as ever as a live touring act, he appeared on TV, video and even feature films (a small role in *Trading Places*, for example), and when the Chess catalogue was revived as a result of its purchase by MCA in 1985 (as well as disputed releases on the UK independent Charly, which also claimed the rights to exploit the catalogue), he was back in the record racks as well. He returned to recording, with mixed success, most promisingly with British producer Mike Vernon in the 1990s. Given his health and a sympathetic promoter, Bo Diddley remains the vibrant, living bedrock of rhythm & blues, a unique talent, looking more like a corporate lawyer than a rock 'n' roll legend (if it wasn't for the trademark stetson hat, that is), creaking his guitar strings self-mockingly to imitate arthritic knee joints, and still blasting out that shimmering, reverberating Bo Diddley sound.

ROLL OVER BEETHOVEN

There are hints of Chuck Berry's music in that of other artists, unlike Bo Diddley, who seemed to spring almost from nowhere, but Berry's effect on rock 'n' roll was greater than any other individual. Whereas Elvis caused a revolutionary change in pop music with a voice and an image, Berry was the complete article, a writer and musician with the imagination to show that rock could venture into previously uncharted territory.

His guitar playing, admittedly, had the tone of jazzman Charlie Christian, the 'chicken-cluck' soloing technique across two strings taken from T-Bone Walker, the bounce of Louis Jordan's guitarist Carl Hogan – but none of Berry's predecessors could have dreamed of playing the introduction to 'Johnny B Goode', 12 bars of sheer magic that epitomize the excitement of rock 'n' roll. His voice, in particular on slow, reflective numbers early in his career like 'Wee Wee Hours',

Crazy legs:
Chuck Berry unfolds
himself for an early
publicity shot.

'How You've Changed' and 'Time Was', confirms his admiration for Nat 'King' Cole, but crooner Cole could never have rocked into the line, 'When I got on a city bus and found a vacant seat, I thought I saw my future bride walking down the street' – a story which is neatly set up in one couplet – nor could he have bawled 'Let it rock!' with much conviction.

As an affable human being Chuck Berry has no qualifications whatsoever – his lifelong fan Keith Richards, who tangled with him in making Chuck's sixtieth-birthday tribute movie *Hail, Hail, Rock 'n' Roll*, once made the memorable observation: 'I love his work but I couldn't warm to him even if I was cremated next to him.' Berry seems mean-spirited and suspicious, and he has several times come into conflict with the law – youthful robbery, 'transporting a minor across a state line for immoral purposes', tax evasion, installing video cameras in the women's lavatories at his country club.

He would say that his insistence on being paid in advance for a gig, and his habit of playing for the contracted time almost to the second before leaving, is a natural reaction to being ripped off early in his career (although by the late 50s, unlike any of his label-mates, he was a comparatively wealthy man, laying out plans for his country club with its guitar-shaped pool and

guest chalets). He would say that his habit of picking up unrehearsed and often intimidated musicians *en route* is an economic necessity, because he could not possibly afford to keep a salaried band together. He would say, with justification, that at least one of those convictions was racist in origin, and indeed when it first came to trial the clearly racist opinions of the

Full circle: a compilation album by the Originator capitalizes on the fame of his transatlantic fans the Beatles.

judge caused it to be thrown out. On the other hand, it was perhaps not prudent to pick up a 14-year-old immigrant prostitute in El Paso, take her to St Louis and install her as a waitress in his club, though there can be no doubt that the American legal system would pursue such a case against a black man with greater zeal than it would against a good ol' boy.

In his defence, his modestly titled *The Autobiography* (which, surprisingly, proves that his remarkably pared-down, witty skill with a lyric does not translate to prose) does nothing to hide his turbulent, adulterous past. It is a pity that he's not a nice chap, but we're talking about a rock 'n' roll idol, not a next-door neighbour.

As suggested earlier, it would be only a slight exaggeration to suggest that there was no teenage music before Berry. Before the 1950s there were children and adults, separated by a murky, furtive, spotty, gawky period of purdah. An early rock 'n' roll song like 'Shake, Rattle and Roll', whether shouted by Big Joe Turner or bowdlerized by Bill Haley, remains a bawdy, adult song. The blues itself was dealing exclusively with adult themes of poverty, sex and racism, while rhythm & blues was built for dancing in clubs that excluded minors. Suddenly along came Berry chanting, 'Ring, ring goes the bell, cook in the lunchroom's ready to sell.'

Charles Edward Anderson Berry was born in St Louis on 18 October 1926, the fourth child of Martha and Henry Berry. His father was a carpenter, who enlisted the young Chuck's help in making his rounds. As was the custom, Chuck joined the church choir as a youngster, but the first sign of his future musical direction came at 15, when he made the bold choice of Jay McShann's 'Confessin' the Blues' to sing at a high-school concert. He borrowed a guitar and swiftly taught himself the rudiments.

When he was 18, incited by a friend, he took part in a robbery on a bakery, and was sentenced to ten years. He continued his musical education by forming a quartet in prison, and after three years he was released on parole. After a number of manual jobs he became an apprentice hairdresser, married Themetta Suggs in 1948, and began to supplement his earnings by singing in bars. It is revealing that they tended to be bars patronized by a white clientele. The strains of country music were never far from his work – indeed he originally wrote his first hit, 'Maybelline', in hillbilly style and called it 'Ida Red'. It has famously been observed that Elvis's success was founded on the fact that he was a white boy who sounded black, and the opposite

was true of Chuck. Of course, after more than 40 years of his music it is impossible to hear him as a white singer, but that was not the case when 'Maybelline' was first shipped to the radio stations, and the single received useful airplay on some that would never knowingly have played 'nigger music'. Compared, say, with Bo Diddley, Berry's singing has always been distinguished by the clarity of enunciation that his ingenious lyrics demand.

In June 1952 the former school friend who had accompanied him on 'Confessin' the Blues', Tommy Stevens, invited him to play a Saturday-night booking. The group drew a crowd, so the proprietor added Friday nights and raised their pay from $6 to $8. In December local pianist and band leader Johnny Johnson asked Chuck to join a trio, completed by drummer Ebby Hardy, for a New Year's Eve gig at the Cosmopolitan Club. By Easter they were playing to packed houses – part 'black hillbilly', part Nat Cole, part Muddy Waters – and the club's name was reflected in a racially mixed crowd.

When Chuck stood down one night to play a one-off gig with Stevens, the club owner realized that he was the main attraction, and offered him a contract. As first he was billed as 'Chuck Berryn' – 'in an attempt to camouflage my worldly doings from the holy environment my father's name was associated with,' writes Berry in the curiously stilted style of his autobiography. For a while, it seems, he was running two bands, because a poster exists advertising Chuck Berryn at the other club. Since his face was smiling out of the poster one wonders how successful the subterfuge was – shades of 'John Lee Booker'.

Berry says that he became a songwriter to inject some fresh material and variety into his live repertoire. His earliest studio date seems to have been as a session guitarist behind Joe Alexander and his Cubans in 1954, at the Premier Studio in St Louis. He was still Chuck Berryn at this stage, and studio owner Oscar Washington has regretted ever since that he resisted Chuck's pleas to be recorded in his own right.

A trip to Chicago early in 1955 with a school friend introduced him to Elmore James, Howlin' Wolf and Muddy Waters. Chuck spoke to his hero Waters after a gig and was directed towards Chess, where Leonard Chess told him to come back with an audition tape. The song 'Ida Red', recalled by Chess as a 'country music take-off', was the number that struck him most, and a session was fixed for 21 May. He wasn't keen on the name of the song, however, and Chuck changed it to 'Maybelline' on the spur of the moment. For the session he and Johnny Johnson were joined by Jerome Green and Willie Dixon, as well as drummer Jasper Thomas – Ebby Hardy didn't make the trip.

Willie Dixon recalls that Leonard Chess was not in Chicago at the time of the session. 'When he came back "Maybelline" was playing on the air because we made a dub of it that quick... We had so much confidence in "Maybelline". Chess would never get over 1,000 or 2,000 records on anybody but when we first cut that Chuck Berry number, I think he put 10,000 on the floor at the first shot.'

As he gazed proudly at the label of his first record, Berry had a sharp lesson in the ways of the music business. He had been joined on the composer credits by two other names. Leonard Chess had given disc jockey Alan Freed a one-third share in return for heavy airplay, and another one-third went to his printer and stationery supplier Russ Fratto – presumably in return for a good deal on label printing. It took Berry many years to regain his sole rights to the song.

The story of 'Maybelline' is established in the first lyric couplet, in which Berry also coins a new word that perfectly establishes the mood: 'As I was motorvatin' over the hill I saw Maybelline in a Coupe de Ville.' A race develops between Maybelline and the singer in his V-8 Ford, and the song is the granddaddy of every car-cruising song and hot-rod number, the inspiration for the Beach Boys and Jan and Dean, and a stunning confirmation of a new direction for rock 'n' roll, interweaving teenage concerns with its blues base. It went to number one in the r&b chart and *Billboard* gave it an award for what was then a unique achievement, of featuring in its pop, r&b *and* country lists. The Berry band bolstered their sudden fame with a 101-date tour – in 101 days.

'He put on a beautiful show even in those days,' says Willie Dixon. 'Chuck was cooking because he insisted that everybody playing with him cook with him. He was very serious about his music.'

The follow-up, cut in September, was 'Thirty Days', another r&b top-tenner with the same studio line-up. In December a fruitful session included another car-fetish song (and his third hit), 'No Money Down', and a further indication of Berry's originality in 'You Can't Catch Me', with its complex lyric beautifully welded to the rhythm. But it took the next session, in April 1956 and with Fred Below now on drums, to confirm that Berry was more than an original talent, and that his work was touched by genius.

At any other time the pleasant 'Drifting Heart' might have constituted a satisfactory day's work. But Berry went on to cut 'Brown Eyed Handsome Man', 'Roll Over Beethoven' and 'Too Much Monkey Business'. Recorded a month after Carl Perkins hit with 'Blue Suede Shoes', 'Beethoven' was the second anthem for the rock 'n' roll era,

ANOTHER BIG ONE FROM-
Chuck Berry

"TOO MUCH MONKEY BUSINESS"
b/w
"BROWN EYED HANDSOME MAN"

CHESS # 1635

PROVEN HITS!!!!

and in June became the first of Berry's 26 pop hits. As an r&b chart success it was swiftly followed by a coupling of the other two numbers, between them more adventurous and lyrically ingenious than any pop songs before them. The theme of the boastful 'Handsome Man' is a plane flight across a surreal desert landscape, drawing on Biblical and mythological imagery, that starts with the satirical line, 'Arrested on charges of unemployment.' Berry had now perfected his trademark skill of marrying a choppy rock 'n' roll rhythm and his complex, allusive lyrics, in a manner that opened the doors for such willing students as Bob Dylan and John Lennon ('Subterranean Homesick Blues' and 'Come Together' are just two of the more nakedly Berry-inspired songs).

'Too Much Monkey Business' is a hilarious catalogue of frustration, again expressed as an intricate series of tongue-twisters.

'Blonde hair, good looking, trying to get me hooked, wants me to marry, settle down, get a home, write a book': there seems to be a world of suburban pretensions hinted at in adding 'write a book' to the predatory lady's ambitions for the singer. As with 'Maybelline', Berry coined a new word for the song, in this case 'botheration'.

In his live performances at this time Berry added another element to his legend, when he introduced his 'duck walk' during an Alan Freed show in New York. This squatting, guitar-toting strut was based on a childhood party piece, when he could walk underneath a table like a miniature limbo dancer.

In January 1957 Berry cut the next song to score in both charts, and the first to take his strategy of creating a specifically teenage music into the classroom: 'School Day' reached the top of the r&b list, and number five in the Hot Hundred. By this time he had cut a demo of his next classic anthem, and in

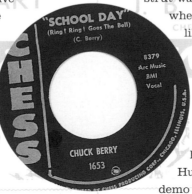

May he returned to it. The rhythmic changes and complexity of 'Rock 'n' Roll Music' took several takes to master, but the result was another top-tenner in both charts, preceded by a minor hit from the same session, 'Oh Baby Doll', another school song. Johnny Johnson didn't make the

Chuck beret:
a photo-studio pun that seemed a good idea at the time.

trip to Chicago for any of Berry's 1957 sessions, but Lafayette Leake was the perfect replacement, well able to match Johnson's bizarre flights of keyboard fancy that are such a background feature of Berry's records. Indeed, in the recollection of Willie Dixon, it was actually Leake on 'Maybelline'.

If Berry had decided to go back to hairdressing at this point he would have left behind a catalogue almost unmatched in rock 'n' roll. And yet he had hardly started. Just after Christmas 1957, with Leake, Below and Dixon, he cut seven new titles. They included 'Sweet Little Sixteen' (number one r&b, number two pop), 'Johnny B Goode' (five and eight, respectively) and 'Reelin' and Rockin' (a 1972 hit in a live version, when issued as the follow-up to the dreadful 'My Ding-a-Ling'). They are all classics of the genre, and 'Johnny B Goode' is perhaps the archetypal Berry song. It includes a stunning, perfectly executed guitar intro and solo, studied,

Already 46th on the charts
"SWEET LITTLE SIXTEEN"   CHUCK BERRY
Chess 1683

"THE WALK"   JIMMY McCRACKLIN
Checker 885

"THE SHAKE"   MARK IV
Cosmic 704

"BEEN SO LONG"   THE PASTELS
Argo 5287

"YEA YEA"   KENDALL SISTERS
Argo 5291

"THE BOOK OF LOVE"   THE MONOTONES
Argo 5290

CHESS CHECKER ARGO
2120 S. Michigan Avenue   Chicago 16, Illinois
All Phones: CAlumet 5-2770

DJ Alan Freed, king of the rock 'n' roll cinema quickies, casts himself as a drummer.

copied and recycled by every rock guitarist since, it has a strong storyline and its aspirational theme – 'Maybe some day your name will be in lights, saying "Johnny B Goode Tonite"' – is at the heart of the music's appeal.

In February 1958 Berry cut 'Around and Around', possibly as a demo dubbing all the

instruments himself. Johnny Johnson returned for the year's remaining sessions, and the first two also reunited Berry with the St Louis trio drummer Ebby Hardy.

The gems continued to be mined but they were not becoming too polished – however much Berry honed his lyrics his sound retained its inspirational, improvised sound. 'Beautiful Delilah', 'Carol', 'Jo Jo Gunne', 'Sweet Little Rock 'n' Roller', 'Memphis Tennessee', 'Run Rudolph Run' and 'Little Queenie' were the new 1958 masterworks, and the hits rolled on. In terms of commercial success, multi-racial appeal and international celebrity ('School Day' and 'Sweet Little Sixteen' hit in the UK at this time), Berry had probably become the most successful black entertainer of all time.

Things were to go seriously wrong in 1960,

Hold it right there: Chuck duckwalks into a classic publicity shot.

when the long legal process that ended with
Berry's imprisonment in February 1962 got
underway, following the arrest of one of his
waitresses, Janice Escalante, for
prostitution. What followed was not a great
advertisement for the American legal
system, enthusiastically pursuing a
successful black man on flimsy grounds.

Berry's creativity was undimmed in the
years preceding this trouble, however. The
rude blast of rock 'n' roll was being
tempered at the end of the decade by a
business that wanted instant, malleable
idols, the Frankies and the Bobbys, but
Berry's anthems still flowed. 'Back in the
USA' and further hits with the cute 'Almost
Grown' and the novelty 'Too Pooped to Pop'
(his last r&b hit), the wonderful 'Let It
Rock', the story of railroad workers too busy
playing dice to notice the approaching
danger ('Can't stop the train, gotta let it roll
on'), 'I Got to Find My Baby', 'Bye Bye
Johnny' (continuing the 'Johnny B Goode'
theme), 'The Jaguar and the Thunderbird',
cover versions of 'Down the Road Apiece'
and 'Route 66' that seemed to be reborn as
Berry originals, 'I'm Talking About You' and
'Come On' – delights all. In the US and
Britain, blues-besotted bands of the early 60s
borrowed from Berry's catalogue almost
before looking anywhere else. 'Come On'
provided the Rolling Stones with their first
hit, Berry tunes with half their repertoire.

But in February 1962 Berry was in
prison, remaining incarcerated until October
1963, first at the Federal Penal Institution
near Terre Haute, Indiana, hence to
Leavenworth in Kansas and finally to
Springfield, Missouri. The clutch of songs

Berry wrote at Springfield would, once again, constitute the finest fruits of a life's work to a lesser artist – 'No Particular Place to Go', 'Nadine', 'Tulane', 'You Never Can Tell' and 'Promised Land'. Berry recalls the difficulty of 'trying to secure a road atlas of the United States to verify the routing of the Po' Boy, from Norfolk, Virginia, to Los Angeles' for the last of these songs – prisoners requiring maps were naturally regarded with suspicion.

Berry emerged from jail embittered, at odds with the world, and it was a world beginning to hail his followers the Beatles and the Stones. He laid down his new material, beginning with 'Nadine', at sessions between November 1963 and the following March, and his creativity was undimmed by imprisonment. He resumed an occupation of the US charts that had been interrupted for four years, while 'Go Go Go', 'Let It Rock'/'Memphis Tennessee', 'Run Rudolph Run', 'Nadine', 'No Particular Place to Go', 'You Never Can Tell' and 'Promised Land' all scored in the UK. He also recorded contrasting cover versions at this time: the Ray Price country standard 'Crazy Arms' and the Robert Johnson/ Elmore James bottleneck belter 'Dust My Broom'.

Nineteen sixty-four saw Berry's first tour of Britain, on one of the greatest bills of the

Ready to rock:
Chuck Berry emerged from jail in 1963 to cut new classics like 'Nadine'.

decade, comparable to Bo Diddley's 1963 début.
His co-star (though advertised in much smaller
type) was Carl Perkins, just beginning the
recovery road after years of obscurity and
alcohol. Perkins was tearfully overwhelmed by
the reception he received, particularly from the
Teddy Boy contingent – at home this great
rockabilly bluesman had almost been forgotten.
Berry seemed happy and confident, strutting
through his peerless catalogue. The land of the
blues revival, of the Beatles and Stones, was
relishing a state visit from their heroes, their
musical models. At Bristol's Colston Hall I sat
entranced as cigarettes fizzed past my ears and,
from somewhere in the gloom, came the sound of
a seat being ritually knifed.

In 1959 Berry had been the token rocker in
the film record of that year's Newport Jazz
Festival, the elegant and pioneering festival
documentary *Jazz on a Summer's Day* – his other
film appearances had been in Alan Freed quickies
Rock, Rock, Rock, *Mr Rock 'n' Roll* and *Go
Johnny Go*. Incidentally, in the last of these he is
waiting in the wings when emcee Freed explains
that there is no money to pay the performers.
'Let's do this one for rock 'n' roll,' says Berry, in
hilarious reversal of his true nature. Ten years
later he was to withdraw from the Monterey
Festival, and hence from the hit movie *Monterey
Pop*, because the promoters couldn't come up with
payment in advance.

He returned to Newport in 1964, by which
time the folk and protest singers were providing
the commercial leavening to hard-core jazz,
among them Phil Ochs, a tortured political singer
with a rock 'n' roll heart. And so, as in 1959,
Newport enabled Berry to widen his constituency.
Meanwhile worthy studio additions to his song
list were the double-sided single 'Little Marie'/'Go

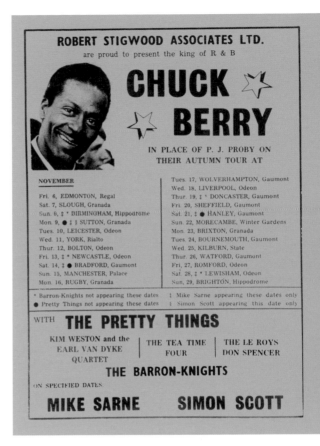

Little Bobby Soxer' and the wistful teenage angst
of 'Lonely Schooldays'.

In January 1965 Berry was back in London to
record a low-key album with a band called the
Five Dimensions, which was released as *Chuck
Berry in London*. As Adam Komorowski has
noted in a box-set booklet, this introduced Berry
to the red, slimline Gibson guitar that was to
become his familiar companion. After a further
album session in September, which resulted in a
so-so collection released as *Fresh Berrys*, Chuck
suddenly left his Chess home, having been
tempted by a $60,000 advance offered by Mercury.

'You'll be back in three years,' said Leonard Chess, and he was right.

An album called *Golden Hits*, consisting of recuts of many of the Chess masterpieces, hardly indicated fresh creative flow, though the next two Mercury albums were more imaginative and successful – a visit to Sam Phillips's new studio produced *Chuck Berry in Memphis*, while a gig at the western outpost of hippie rock in San Francisco, backed by the Steve Miller Band, came up with *Live at the Fillmore*.

Berry completed his Mercury obligations with two further albums, *From St Louis to Frisco* and *Concerto in B Goode*, before fulfilling Leonard Chess's prediction. In the meantime he had appeared at the Toronto festival that resulted in the film *Keep on Rockin'*, one of the key resuscitation points for ageing rock 'n' rollers.

Ironically, Berry returned to Chess at around the time of the two events that marked the start of the label's decline – Leonard's death and the sell-out to General Recorded Tape (GRT). But on the album front he seemed briefly rejuvenated – *Back Home* and above all 1971's masterly *San Francisco Dues* suggested what record reviewers call 'a return to form'. Purists might have regretted his discovery of the guitar gizmos that allowed a modish squelchy sound to invade some of the tracks, but the meditative 'Oh Louisiana' (engagingly pronounced 'Loozana'), a lively recut of 'Lonely Schooldays' (by a man in his mid-40s), the over-the-top 'My Dream' and a handful of bluesy new rockers suggested fresh inspiration.

However, this does not chime with Berry's memories, in his autobiography, of rejoining Chess. 'The recording sessions became more foreign than ever, full of red tape and requirements for permission from other departments of the company for any changes, as opposed to the family-type, small-business settings of the earlier sessions. Leonard was never there any more [not surprising, as he was dead] and his brother Phil was not a man who could replace Leonard's authority or humor. Nor did I feel Phil ever cared about how the songs turned out.'

Berry also had problems with the publishing side of the company, Arc, and noted that no royalties had been paid on sales of his Chess material during the period of his defection to Mercury. Also, by what the company described as a 'mistake', he had previously been receiving the same royalty for an album as for a single. Overseas royalties had become mysteriously log-jammed somewhere in the system. Berry began the process of unravelling his dues.

He was, of course, better placed as an articulate and suspicious man to do so than most bluesmen. In 22 years, he reckoned, he'd acquired '23 pieces of property' costing $677,000. And by 1972 he was just a little short of his target, to have a million dollars in savings. So a lot of earnings had in fact managed to squeeze through the clogged filter of the music business, and Berry had invested wisely or squirrelled it away.

On 3 February 1972 Berry played a gig at the Lanchester Arts Festival, near Coventry. Unknown to him, he says, this was recorded for inclusion in an album, *The London Chuck Berry Sessions*, together with the results of a geographically more accurate date at Phillips's studios. For some years he had been performing a version of an old double-entendre song, 'My Ding-a-Ling', which may have originated with Dave Bartholomew in 1950s New Orleans, or on the other hand in some Stone Age schoolyard, and now his student audience joined in lustily. Ironically, this piece of nonsense was Berry's first hit for seven years and his first-ever number one

Look into my eyes: what could have been a routine publicity snap hints at Chuck Berry's darker side.

– it topped both the US and UK charts. Armed with his new agreement with the company and its publishing arm, Berry noted that by December he had sold 1,295,075 'Ding-a-Ling' singles and 187,975 *London* albums. He immediately negotiated a better deal. But the company was now totally unrecognizable as the old family firm. Berry cut two further albums, the adequate *Bio* and then *Chuck Berry 75*, before resurfacing on Atco in 1979 with the defiant *Rockit*.

Meanwhile he had played the glorious Wembley festival, appeared in the Alan Freed

evasion and served a cocktail of imprisonment and community service. Ten years later came the humiliation of the discovery of those video cameras in the women's lavatories at his club.

All this seems a long way from the exhilaration, the sheer inventiveness, of 'Johnny B Goode'. But in the end it's only 'Johnny B Goode' that matters. That and another score of the finest rock 'n' roll songs ever written.

The Ding-a-Ling years: in the early 1970s Berry was back on top as a festival favourite.

bio-pic *American Hot Wax* (semi-fictional, but a warm and wonderful celebration of rock 'n' roll), and was now comfortably established as a rock 'n' roll legend, controller of his own song catalogue, real-estate investor, country-club owner – and jailbird once more. He was found guilty of tax

CHAPTER 5

NEW RHUMBA

Early 1955 was an auspicious time for Chess, because not only did the signings of Bo Diddley and Chuck Berry secure the prosperity of the company for the immediate future, but Leonard and Phil decided to branch out into jazz, launching the Argo label to accommodate this venture. This predated the more celebrated move by Atlantic into the jazz field in 1956 – rightly more celebrated, since Nesuhi Ertegun's early signings included the Modern Jazz Quartet, Ornette Coleman, John Coltrane, Charlie Mingus and Roland Kirk, making it an instant market leader in contemporary jazz.

Chess maintained a narrower vision, by and large sticking to local Chicago outfits, though they too were to enjoy periods of considerable commercial success at a time when jazz was undergoing one of its occasional boosts in popularity. Realizing the importance of the New York market, they found a valuable ally there in distributor Esmond Edwards, who could help to raise the jazz profile of the company outside its home town.

On 23 May 1955, two days after Chuck Berry's studio début, Chess recorded the Ahmad Jamal Trio for an album titled *Chamber Music of the New Jazz*, containing such titles as 'New Rhumba', 'A Foggy Day' and 'I Get a Kick out of You'. Pianist Jamal, who had changed his name from Fritz Jones when converting to the Islamic faith, was born in Pittsburgh in 1930 but made his name in the Chicago clubs of the early 50s, initially with guitarist Ray Crawford and bass player Eddie Calhoun. His deft, considered style, as impressive in what he elected to leave out as in his lightness of touch on the keyboard, was an influential one: 'Listen to the way Jamal uses space,' an admiring Miles Davis once advised.

In 1956 another pianist, the Chicago-born Ramsey Lewis, formed a trio with Eldee Young on bass and Red Holt on drums. Signed to Argo, their début album was delicately titled *Ramsey Lewis and his Gentlemen of Swing*. Lewis and Jamal were to prove the big sellers for the label, but other signings during the second half of the 1950s gave the label substance – they included James Moody, Zoot Sims, Johnny Griffin, Max Roach, Sonny Stitt, Yusef Lateef, Buddy Rich and Marian McPartland – while in 1959 on the parent

First Time I Met the Blues:
Buddy Guy was the last major signing in Chess's great blues decade.

label, Chess, a series of Benny Goodman sessions were released.

The first big commercial breakthrough on Argo came in 1958. After three steady sellers, Jamal decided to cut an album live at a Chicago club he had worked at throughout the decade, the Pershing Lounge. The idea, he said in his sleeve note, arose from a conversation with Leonard Chess, though brother Phil was to handle the production. By this time his trio was completed by bassist Israel Crosby and drummer Vernell Fournier. A total of 43 numbers were recorded on 16 January and eight of them – including his most-requested number 'But Not For Me' – became the album *Live at the Pershing*.

Its success was phenomenal – it reached number three in the pop album chart, staying in the Hot Hundred for more than two years. Later that year Jamal cut 'Secret Love' as a single, and it rose to 18 in the r&b chart. Even if the big-band crooning of Frank Sinatra in the 1940s is included under the jazz umbrella, the music had known nothing like this before, and rarely has since.

Live at the Pershing, Argo's first hit album, alerted the company to the potential of LP sales. They had always had a 'singles' mentality, and were expert at it. As Marshall Chess recalled in the Willie Dixon book: 'Many times my father would put out a record, always on a Friday, and he'd have the radio covered so it would be blasted. You could buy a blues record in Chicago Friday and Saturday night until two in the morning and we put 'em out just to make money on the weekends.' Jamal's sales broadened the company's scope – without it, it may be that such apparently obvious releases as the early-1960s compilations *The Blues, Volumes 1–4*, which introduced a whole generation to the label's riches, may not have occurred to them.

Nor was this a freak one-off success, though of course its scale could hardly be repeated. In September 1958 Jamal again recorded live, at the Spotlite Club in Washington DC. Tracks cut there appeared on the 1959 album *Ahmad Jamal, Volume 4*, which reached number 11 on the pop chart, and a February 1959 gig at Chicago's Penthouse Club, this time with a large string section, also produced a pop hit – *Jamal at the Penthouse* peaked at 32 in the album chart.

Jamal was still a mainstay of the Argo label in 1965, when as a result of a protest from the long-standing English folk-music label of the same name, Chess created a new imprint, Cadet, moving all its jazz output there. He remained with Cadet until lured away by ABC/Impulse in 1968, releasing at least an album a year, one of which – 1967's *Cry Young* – was a further modest pop-chart success.

Although Ramsey Lewis did not have an album to equal Jamal's *Live at the Pershing*, overall he was even more successful in commercial terms. His Argo releases like a 1962 Christmas album and 1964's *Bach to the Blues* and *Live at the Bohemian Caverns* were following Jamal into the lower reaches of the pop chart, but it was when in 1965 he hit on the idea of giving a jazz treatment to pop successes that he became the biggest-selling jazzman of the decade. To which purists would of course reply that he was no more a jazzman than was that later 'jazz' phenomenon George Benson – they both simply played a classy form of commercial pop music cloaked under a more dignified label.

Curiously, as a singles artist Lewis scored in the pop chart one record before he made the r&b list – in 1964 he produced a swift instrumental cover of Alvin Robinson's current soul success 'Something You Got', peaking at 63. But the follow-up brought the big breakthrough – he gave a staccato treatment to Dobie Gray's pop-soul hit 'The In Crowd', wrapped it in a party atmosphere, and went to number five in the pop chart and two in the r&b list. He marked the change to Cadet with a similar treatment of the McCoys' chart-topping 'Hang On Sloopy', and while the gospel number 'Wade in the Water' was the only other single to reach the Top Twenty he had clocked up 13 Hot Hundred singles by the end of the decade – the others being 'A Hard Day's Night', Tommy Tucker's Chess hit 'Hi Heel Sneakers', 'Up Tight', 'Day Tripper', 'One, Two, Three', 'Dancing in the Street', 'Soul Man', 'Since You've Been Gone' and 'Julia'. Lewis also supplied Chess with more than 30 albums during this time, most of them making the charts, before he moved to Columbia in 1972.

Lewis and Jamal between them accounted for most of Chess's involvement with jazz during the rest of the label's life, though other artists were still recorded. Saxophonists Budd Johnson, Illinois Jacquet and James Moody were cut in 1963, as was pianist Hank Jones, and Johnson returned to the studio on a number of subsequent occasions. In 1968 organist Jack McDuff and the veteran clarinettist Woody Herman had releases on Cadet, and probably the last jazz session cut during Chess's active life was by trumpeter Bobby Bryant with a big band, in 1971.

Since they were consistently aiming at the black population, the Chess brothers were naturally aware of the importance of serving the market for gospel music as well as r&b. The major project was a lengthy series of 78rpm sermons on Chess itself, each taking a particular Biblical text as its theme, and delivered by the Reverend CL Franklin, father of Aretha. Franklin was pastor at the New Bethel Baptist Church in Detroit, but was nationally known as a preacher. It was a local record-shop owner, Joe Von Battle, who hit upon the idea of cutting Franklin's stirring sermons on disc. He produced them for his own JVB label and then leased them to Chess for national distribution. Franklin also had a weekly radio show, and as a result of this and the success of the records became a star of the gospel-music world.

Aretha Franklin's musical apprenticeship was gained in the Detroit church and on her father's gospel tours, singing with her sisters Erma and Carolyn. Her precocious talent was soon apparent to Von Battle, who recorded her as a 14-year-old in 1956 singing a selection of gospel songs in her father's church. Again he leased the tapes, Aretha's first recordings, to Chess. Ironically, it was Chess's New York rival Atlantic – one of the founding partners, Jerry Wexler, in particular – who ten years later discovered the trick of turning Aretha's stunning voice into a commercial success as a soul singer.

One of the leading gospel groups, The Original Five Blind Boys of Mississippi, cut a Checker album in 1960. There were other regular signings like the Christland Singers in 1961 and, a year later, a choir consisting of one female and 34 male voices, the Kyok Koral-Aires, sang such devotional favourites as 'I'm on the Battlefield for My Lord'. Given that there has always been considerable demand among black record buyers, in particular, for gospel material, its comparative lack of promotion in the Chess catalogue – apart from the Franklin series, which of course simply arrived from Detroit ready-made – suggests that the hearts of the Chess brothers weren't really in the music, but that they felt the need to make a gesture towards this market while concentrating more on what they knew best.

And indeed those gestures remained a regular feature of the catalogue, and over the years it did add up – to a total of around 90 sacred albums. A Georgia choir named The Morning Stars of Savannah recorded for Checker in 1963, as did the Norfleet Brothers and preacher Reverend Barrett, declaiming such titles as 'I Have a Friend Above All Others', backed by piano, organ and a vocal chorus.

There was a sudden spate of gospel releases in the mid-60s, including some big names like the Soul Stirrers and Alex Bradford alongside the Violinaires, the Cleveland Golden Echoes and the Universal Kingdom of Christ Choir. In 1968 Chess recorded Ben Branch and the Operation Bread Basket, and in 1970 the Jordan Singers, but these forays – and even the extraordinary commercial success of two of their jazz artists – seem like diversions from the core development from blues to r&b to the Chuck and Bo revolution and onwards to 1960s soul, in which Chess played an important role.

SEE YOU LATER, ALLIGATOR

Chess's continuing licensing deals with southern labels, an important part of the company's activities ever since their early relationship with Sun, enabled them to build an impressive catalogue of bought-in rock 'n' roll material, including many classics of the genre. Along with licensed blues titles, this gave the catalogue greater depth and broadened the northern market for southern music.

An early oddity, no hit but an amusing novelty, was when Ike Turner's saxophone player Eugene Fox, seemingly after drink had been prescribed, declaimed his 'Sinner's Dream' in 1954 for release on Checker. Weird sound effects, shimmering reverb guitar by Turner and Fox's

In 1956 a further Charles session for Chess came up with 'Ain't Got No Home', swiftly covered by another New Orleans signing to the label, Clarence 'Frogman' Henry, with the song tailored to suit Henry's vocal gimmick of alternating between growling 'frog' noises and a feminine falsetto. Released on Argo, which the Chess brothers began to use for such out-of-town material as well as its jazz roster, the record reached number three in the r&b list.

over-the-top vocal contributed to this dialogue between a drunk and God.

Bobby Charles, born in Abbeville, Louisiana in 1938, was actually signed to Chess directly by the label's New Orleans agent Paul Gayten, but usually remained at home to record, uncompromisingly southern in his music. He was one of the first white men to be signed to the label – a brief experiment with country and early rockabilly material from such artists as Guy Blakeman, Harmonica Frank and Bob Price had already foundered – and as a 17-year-old he cut a demo of a song, 'Later Alligator', which borrowed heavily from local hero Guitar Slim's 'Later for You Baby'.

As he was to demonstrate with a peerless solo album recorded for Bearsville in 1972, the reclusive Charles was imbued with all the qualities of the musical melting pot of Louisiana – r&b, blues, country and cajun. Renamed 'See You Later, Alligator', his teenage classic was his first Chess release and was instantly covered by Bill Haley. In the same year, 1955, Chess leased a New Orleans knees-up, 'Mardi Gras Mambo' by the Hawketts, a group that included the young Art Neville.

From 1954 to 1957 Paul Gayten also cut tracks in New Orleans for submission to Chess, resulting in releases like 'I'm So Tired', 'Driving Home' and 'You Better Believe It', without ever matching his 1950 success on the Regal label when a duet with Annie Laurie, 'I'll Never Be Free', had reached number eight. But as an a&r man he was invaluable to Leonard Chess in maintaining the label's fertile southern outpost, and when he and Charles wrote the soaring rockaballad 'But I Do' and gave it to Henry, the result was a huge Argo hit – number four in the Hot Hundred, nine in the r&b chart and three in the UK, one of the biggest records of 1961.

Clarence 'Frogman' Henry then enjoyed a run in the pop charts which lasted into 1962 – 'You Always Hurt the One You Love', 'Lonely Street', an early Bobby Charles composition entitled 'On Bended Knee' and 'A Little Too Much', while Charles – who as an artist has recorded only sporadically – wrote such hits as Fats Domino's 'I'm Walking to New Orleans'.

TERRIFIC NEW SMASH!!!!

"SUSIE-Q"

by DALE HAWKINS

CHECKER #863

CHECKER RECORD COMPANY 4750 S. COTTAGE GROVE AVE. • CHICAGO 15, ILL.

Chess licensed material from another white Louisiana performer, the rockabilly singer Dale Hawkins, starting with 'See You Soon, Baboon' in 1956. The connection here was a tie-up with the Shreveport-based distributor Stan Lewis, later of Jewel/Ronn Records. Released on Checker, the following year's 'Suzie Q', one of the great rockabilly classics, reached number 29 in the Hot Hundred. Distinguished by a relentless cowbell and, above all, an irresistible riff by the great country-rock guitarist James Burton, the song became a standard of the genre, and was successfully revived by Creedence Clearwater Revival in 1968 when it gave John Fogerty's band their first hit. Meanwhile Hawkins reached the 30s in 1958 with 'La-Do-Dada' and had further Checker hits with 'A House, a Car and a Wedding Ring' and 'Class Cutter'. In 1957 a further Louisiana artist, TV Slim from Shreveport, gave Chess the rollicking 'Flat Foot Sam', licensed from the local Cliff label. Although it was not a big hit it too has lived on, and is, for example, in the repertoire of British revivalists the Blues Band.

When it comes to pure cajun (if such a kaleidoscopic music can ever be 'pure'), the best-known musician is undoubtedly the accordion player and singer Clifton Chenier, 'the king of zydeco'. Although not immediately associated with the Chess roster, he recorded for the label in Los Angeles a couple of times, producing such singles as 1956's 'Where Can My Baby Be'/'Squeeze Box Shuffle'.

The link with Louisiana stretched into the 1960s, when the swamp-rock ballad group Cookie and the Cupcakes leased their 'Got You On My Mind', recorded in Lake Charles for the local Goldband label, to Chess in 1963.

Two other Chess records also blurred the distinction between black r&b and white rockabilly – GL Crockett's driving 'Look Out Mabel' in 1957 and Eddie Fontaine's rocker 'Nothin' Shakin'' a year later. Other one-offs included a 1960 Argo release, Freddy Fender's 'A Man Can Cry'. Fender, a Chicano purveyor of soulful Tex-Mex ballads, has been recording since 1957 but had to wait until 1975 and the international hit 'Before the Next Teardrop Falls' to receive his due recognition. Although Chicago artists would always remain at the heart of the Chess catalogue, such slabs of southern rock lent the label extra breadth and distinction.

FIRST TIME I MET THE BLUES

The great decade of Chicago blues was drawing to a close, but Chess remained a forerunner in the field, in particular with three important signings. The catalogue had until then been based on the records of the great originals, first-generation electric bluesmen like Muddy and the Wolf. Buddy Guy, contracted to Chess in 1960, continued in their spirit, as indeed he does today, Otis Rush made his contribution to the label, and Little Milton arrived a year later to smooth the progression from blues to soul.

An artist who links the two decades, however, had signed to Chess as early as 1954. Lowell Fulson, born in Tulsa, Oklahoma on 31 March 1921, half Cherokee and from a family steeped in music, was already a seasoned bluesman based in California, a pioneer, along with T-Bone Walker, of exploiting the blues potential of the electric guitar, and he first recorded in 1946.

Fulson grew up in the era of the 'classic' blues, went electric after the Second World War, rode smoothly into the r&b era, made the transition into 60s soul and was still playing in the 1990s as an elder statesman of the blues, a living link with every development in the black musical mainstream. Early in his career, before wartime navy service, he even strayed outside that mainstream, singing hillbilly songs and playing in Oklahoma with a string band. He also teamed up with Texas Alexander for a while.

After the war Fulson settled in Oakland, California, where he recorded sides for local labels Big Town/Swingtime, Downtown/Trilon and Aladdin, usually accompanied by a trio or a small band – though a Los Angeles date in 1949, which produced songs associated with the blues 'shouters' like 'Ain't Nobody's Business' and 'Everyday I Have the Blues' (which reached the r&b top five) was with a big band that included pianist Jay McShann.

In September 1954 Fulson was in Dallas for a session that launched his Checker career, and the first song he cut was perhaps his masterpiece, one that became a blues standard to be covered many years later by Elvis Presley. 'Reconsider Baby' is a west-coast shuffle that gave him his only major hit on the Chicago label (number three), with a mellow, dark-brown guitar riff that contrasts with the acidic tone of Fulson's soloing, and an instantly memorable melody. When Chess began to recycle their material on 'best of' compilations, particularly in the UK in the 1960s, 'Reconsider Baby' seemed ever-present, a sophisticated contrast to the downhome blues from the Chicago Delta boys. 'Lovin' You (Is All I Crave)', from the follow-up session in January 1955, also scored well.

Fulson continued to cut singles for Checker well into the 1960s, once or twice in Chicago but usually in LA, until moving to the Kent label and further hits in the mid-60s. 'Black Nights' reintroduced him to the r&b list, but this was topped by Fulson's original version of 'Tramp', later turned into a hilarious southern-soul rap by Otis Redding and Carla Thomas that reached number two in the r&b chart and 26 in the Hot Hundred. In the 1970s Fulson moved on to the Jewel label.

Although Fulson had stayed on Checker for several years, there were other great bluesmen who had a more fleeting relationship with the label, being remembered more for work elsewhere. Indeed, of those at the very top of the blues pantheon at the time, only Jimmy Reed totally eluded Leonard Chess, a rare misjudgement.

In old age John Lee Hooker is probably the most celebrated bluesman who has ever lived,

establishes its own emotional logic, requiring in backing musicians an intuitive sympathy with Hooker's genius beyond the demands of conventional blues form.

After working at local parties with Moore as a very young man, Hooker ran away to Memphis in his early teens, played with Robert Nighthawk among others, moved on to Cincinnati and arrived in Detroit, the city most associated with him, in 1943. He first recorded for the Modern label in November 1948, cutting an eventual million-seller in the rhythmic drone 'Boogie Chillen', which shows that the elements of his style were already in place. This charted in January 1949, to be followed by 'Hobo Blues' and, in November, by the double-entendre 'Crawling King Snake Blues'.

Although contracted to Modern, he would happily moonlight for other labels as Texas Slim, John Lee Cooker (!), Delta John, Birmingham Sam, Johnny Williams, the Boogie Man or simply John Lee. In early 1951 a Detroit session for Modern also mysteriously arrived at Chess, and 'Louise'/ 'Ground Hog Blues' appeared as a single on both labels. For Chess he was now cloaking his identity beneath the impenetrable name John Lee Booker. The next hit, however, was destined for Modern – the sensuous 'I'm in the Mood', which climbed to the top late in 1951, has been in his repertoire ever since, and was revived in the 90s in a duet with Bonnie Raitt.

In 1952 Hooker was back on Chess for a session that included the gimmicky single

thanks to a remarkable revival in his career in the 1990s that has led to hit albums, on which superstar guests queue up for a duet with him, and numerous appearances on TV commercials. Born in Clarksdale, Mississippi on 22 August 1917 (though he claims it was 1920), he learned to play guitar from his stepfather Willie Moore. Since sharecropper Moore never recorded we cannot know how much of Hooker's distinctive style was inherited, though Hooker has always fully credited the older man.

The elements are an introspective, confessional voice in a rich baritone, a guitar that sets up a hypnotic rhythm that is reinforced, in Hooker's solo recordings, by a stamping shoe studded with a bottle-top, the use of the guitar as a stabbing punctuation to the lyric, and a disregard of rhyme, metre or the straitjacket of the 12-bar form. Whether it is a rollicking boogie or a dark-brown meditation, a Hooker song

'Walking the Boogie', with the tape played at double speed and a manic extra guitar part dubbed on, backed with another Hooker mainstay, 'Sugar Mama'. In the mid-50s, however, he moved officially from Modern to Chess's rival imprint, Vee-Jay, home of Jimmy Reed – who contributed harmonica to a 1955 session. In 1956 Hooker cut one of his finest numbers, 'Dimples', and in 1962 he even made the pop chart with 'Boom Boom'. When re-released in the UK in 1964, 'Dimples' was also a hit.

By this time he had become a hero of the blues bands emerging in Britain, first touring Europe in 1962 and returning frequently. Producer Ralph Bass supervised an outstanding 1966 album, *Real Folk Blues*, which included a recut 'I'm in the Mood' at slower tempo, and in 1967 his early sides were re-packaged in the UK as the album *House of the Blues*, which reached number 34. Hooker recorded for Bluesway in the late 60s and in 1971 cut a successful collaboration with white blues band Canned Heat, *Hooker 'n' Heat*.

Hooker has always been shrewder than most bluesmen businesswise, and by the mid-1970s was probably looking forward to a reasonably comfortable old age as a blues hero, touring or recording when he felt like it. His remarkable renaissance came when, under a new management, he cut the hit album *The Healer* in 1989 – and in its wake the follow-up collection, *Mr Lucky*, made number three in the UK album chart, making him the oldest performer to achieve such status. 'Boom Boom', re-recorded for a TV campaign, was a hit all over again in 1992, and the album *Chill Out* was another success in 1995. By now he was, even by his own reckoning, in his mid-70s, and he decided to take it a little easier once more. Hooker has written a large part

of the history of the blues single-handed, and for a while in the 1950s he became a footnote to the Chess story as well.

Elmore James first recorded his anthem, a version of Robert Johnson's 'Dust My Broom', for the Jackson label Trumpet in 1951, and for a decade and more cut some of the most impassioned and exciting of all blues. His resounding voice was seemingly almost overcome with emotion, and his slashing bottleneck guitar threatened to burst the loudspeakers. He was born in Richland, Mississippi on 27 January 1918 and as a young man teamed up with the 'second' Sonny Boy Williamson, Rice Miller, appearing on the radio show *King Biscuit Time*. Miller introduced him to Trumpet and played on that first session – 'Dust My Broom' put James into the r&b top ten.

In 1952 James turned up in Chicago, where he recorded his second hit, the equally powerful 'I Believe', for the Bihari brothers' Meteor imprint. In January 1953 he recorded an instrumental, 'Country Boogie', and a new 'Dust My Broom' variant called 'She Just Won't Do Right', for a Checker single. But he and his band the Broomdusters never settled on any label for long, and during the 1950s he also appeared on Flair, Kent, Chief and Fire among other imprints. In 1960 he scored with 'The Sky Is Crying', and then returned briefly to Chess for 'I Can't Hold Out' and 'The Sun Is Shining'.

Ironically, this most robust of performers had long struggled with a heart problem and in May 1963, at the Chicago home of his cousin Homesick James, he was taken ill, lay down for a rest and died. There was a posthumous hit – the marvellous 'It Hurts Me Too' in 1965 – but alas James could not have known of his crucial influence on the 1960s blues revival in such bands as Fleetwood Mac and the Rolling Stones. Like Hooker, this giant of the blues had touched base on Chess just briefly.

Among the other blues greats who had a passing relationship with Chess several were even more transient. The company picked up, for example, a 1958 Miami session by BB King, and a year later licensed some tracks by Albert King that had been cut for Parrot in 1953. A 1955 session by Louisiana bluesman Lightnin' Slim arrived at Chess, and ten years later the label leased a Nashville set by another Louisiana legend, Clarence 'Gatemouth' Brown. In both cases, however, the tracks were dusted down and released much later.

A St Louis bluesman based in San Francisco, Jimmy McCracklin, had been recording for more than ten years before his irresistible dance novelty 'The Walk', bolstered by repeated plays on the influential TV show *American Bandstand*, gave him an r&b top-tenner and a pop hit as well in 1958. Chess set up three sessions that year in an unsuccessful attempt to repeat the trick and McCracklin cut a few more tracks for the label in 1963, but his other singles successes, notably 'Just Got to Know' on Art-Tone in 1961, were all for other companies.

Harmonica player Buster Brown's rumbustious 'Fanny Mae' had been a 1959 r&b number one on the Fire label, and 1962's 'Sugar Babe' also scored. But he never managed a third success, and most of the tracks he cut for Checker in 1964–5 remained in the can. In the mid-60s Checker picked up on a 1962 album cut in Los Angeles by Johnny 'Guitar' Watson, including his version of 'Reconsider Baby', for re-release. The Arkansas-born guitarist Freddie Robinson, who had recorded with Little Walter in the 1950s, had a Checker single in 1966 with

'The Creeper', but again most of his limited Chess work was unreleased.

Lonnie Brooks, who had previously traded at home in Louisiana as Guitar Junior, notably with 'The Crawl', came up with a local hit for Chess in 1967's 'Let It All Hang Out', but proved to be another bird of passage, as did club favourite Hound Dog Taylor, whose Chess tracks remained on the shelf for years but who later made successful albums for Alligator. There was another one-off success on Checker in 1966, when Little Joe Blue's 'Dirty Work Going On' reached number 40 in the r&b list. Chess also put out Memphis Slim material dating from the 1940s, to capitalize on the piano player's huge concert and festival success in the 1960s.

Although Vee-Jay was Chess's main Chicago rival, a significant 'school' of bluesmen found a home on the West Side, where Eli Toscano briefly ran the Cobra label, and even more briefly a subsidiary imprint called Artistic. In particular, he recorded a triumvirate of guitarists who are associated with creating the 'West Side sound' on Cobra – Otis Rush, Magic Sam and Buddy Guy. The sound owed less to the Delta than that created at Chess, with a greater emphasis on acidic, treble-heavy guitar lines, use of tremolo and an impassioned vocal style. It was also a cruder sound – whereas Chess began at the professionally set-up Universal Studios before moving into a purpose-built place of their own, Cobra was situated in the back room of Toscano's record shop.

Since Dixon had no firm contract nor weekly wage guaranteed by Leonard Chess, he was happy to freelance for Toscano in 1956, and it was in fact at Cobra that for the first time he was given total control in the studio. He was also prompted by what he regarded as Chess's imperfect ear for blues talent. 'If it sounded close to someone the Chess brothers knew, they didn't want to record it. I found Otis Rush down on 47th Street and I knew he was a good artist but Leonard Chess thought he sounded too close to Muddy Waters. They couldn't see the difference.'

This is a serious charge – once Dixon had found a more enthusiastic reception at Cobra, and put Rush's sound through Toscano's back room, it is hard to hear any similarities with what Waters was doing then or indeed at any time. Rush, by contrast with the dignified, rural-sounding Muddy, was neurotic and desperate, creating a sound of the mean streets, not of the farm boy up in the big city.

Rush was born in Philadelphia, Mississippi, on 29 April 1934, and was 14 when his family moved to Chicago. After getting apprentice guitar gigs whenever he could, he formed his own group in 1955, styling himself as Little Otis, to play clubs like the Alibi and Jazzville. Dixon, spurned at Chess, hired pianist Lafayette Leake, a drummer, and harmonica player Walter Horton, played bass himself, and cut Rush's first single, the impassioned 'I Can't Quit You Baby'. According to Dixon, Toscano was not a blues aficionado, but when Rush finally hit upon the extraordinary chord that introduces the song, 'red pimples broke out on his face like he had smallpox or something. That must be the first time I ever saw anybody's hair stand straight up on their head.'

They took the dub straight over to local disc jockey Big Bill Hill, who at first was unwilling to play it because they hadn't brought the customary bribe with them. When finally persuaded, the switchboard lit up, and the race began to get pressings made while the demand was still hot. By the end of the year it had

reached the r&b top ten, giving Toscano his first hit, and Rush followed it with 'My Love Will Never Die'. His subsequent Cobra recordings maintained the standard, and 1958's 'Double Trouble' and 'All Your Love', with the Ike Turner Band backing him, also sold well.

Leonard Chess quickly revised his opinion of Rush, and the fact that the artist eventually signed to Chess was helped by Toscano's dubious character. 'Eli was trying to be a gambler and a con man – he was more interested in gambling than anything else,' recalls Dixon. 'He was a chronic liar, too.' Among those Toscano borrowed money from was Chess, which gave his rival an ever stronger hold on rights to the Cobra artists. By 1959 Cobra was effectively out of business, and when Toscano's body was fished out of Lake Michigan it was assumed that he had fallen foul of a money-lender who had been somewhat less patient than Chess.

Rush didn't linger at Chess for long, but his January 1960 session for them produced another significant hit, 'So Many Roads, So Many Trains', before he moved on to Duke. It is fitting, however, that Chess belatedly recognized his outstanding talent. Not so with Dixon's next great protégé, Sam Maghett, known as Magic Sam. Again he was taken to Leonard Chess, again rejected, again he gave Cobra a hit with 'All Your Love'. In Sam's case Chess had no second chance – he moved from Cobra to Chief, and had he not succumbed to a heart attack in 1969 would undoubtedly be recognized today in his rightful place with Rush and Buddy Guy. Indeed he was probably on the brink of breaking through to the white audience through a new deal with the Delmark label when he died.

Guy was born in Lettsworth, Louisiana on 30 July 1936 and gained his apprenticeship in the

Baton Rouge area, playing with local musicians, including the biggest stars among them, Lightnin' Slim, Slim Harpo and Lazy Lester. He made one unreleased single, 'The Way You Been Treating Me', before moving to Chicago at the age of 21 – 'You couldn't go into the clubs until then, so there was no point in going earlier,' he says. He was befriended by Muddy Waters and taken around the clubs, played with Otis Rush – whom Guy credits with giving him a vital break into the city's music scene – and inevitably came to the notice of Willie Dixon. Dixon thought at first that he sounded too much like BB King, but also noticed a promising element of showmanship in Guy's style, and decided to work on that.

Guy was already aware that, with Chicago blues still at its height, he had to do something special to get noticed in the clubs, where it was common to hold 'guitar battles' with a booking as the prize, and so he had taken to playing with a long lead that would let him move among the audience, and was developing tricks like playing the guitar behind his head. Dixon encouraged him to take this further. 'They got a guy round there in Florida called Guitar Shorty who used to do a lot of trick guitar playing. That was the guy Buddy Guy resembled because I was explaining to Buddy Guy about how to twist his guitar around, throw it up in the air, upside the wall, different little trickeration stuff just to excite the people.'

Guy himself was instantly intimidated by the standard of guitar playing in Chicago. 'I would just walk in the door and see these people and just say, "Shit, man, I might as well sell my guitar."... But I didn't have a choice. I couldn't find no labour work.'

Of course, his innate showmanship without skill would not, many years later, have elicited Eric Clapton's opinion that 'Buddy Guy is by far

and without doubt the best guitar player alive ... the way he plays is beyond anyone. Total freedom of spirit.' Indeed 40 years after his recording début, Buddy Guy remains the most exhilarating of all bluesmen, allying technical skill and imaginative use of light and shade, moving from pin-drop silence to a blistering single-note run, from a cry of anguish to confessional *sotto voce*, from passionate blues power to hilarious pantomime antics.

Soon after he arrived in town Guy left a tape at the Chess offices on 49th and Cottage Grove. He heard nothing, but through his friendship with Rush he was introduced to Dixon and Toscano. They cut Guy for the Artistic imprint in 1958 – two saxophones, pianist Harold Burrage, Rush himself on guitar, Dixon and drummer Odie Payne produced 'Sit and Cry (the Blues)' and 'Try to Quit You Baby' as his first single. Guy did meet the Chess brothers at Cobra because 'they used to come over and gamble a lot'. But after just one further session Toscano was dead and his company defunct (though Willie Dixon's collaborator on his autobiography, Donald Snowden, hints at a rumour that it wasn't Toscano in the lake at all, but that he had fled town). The result was the same – Buddy Guy, now a proven talent and a big local draw, was available to the brothers, who once again belatedly took notice.

Guy's first Chess session, on 2 March 1960, produced four tracks – his first two singles. 'First Time I Met the Blues' by Little Brother Montgomery, who played piano on the session, marries the freneticism of the West Side sound and the greater sophistication of the Chess studio. Guy reveals a precocious skill at combining naked emotion with telling guitar phrases. 'Slop Around' was ill-considered,

Smile please: Leonard Chess's faith in Buddy Guy never matched the guitarist's growing reputation.

Hello London:
Buddy Guy pitches
camp at the Marquee,
March 1965.

Guitar man:
a tow-truck driver by
day, Guy became one of
the most influential
bluesmen of the 1960s.

chart. He continued to record regularly for Chess, however, until 1967, as well as being frequently called upon as a session guitarist, for example on the sessions for the great *Muddy Waters – Folk Singer* album. Another particularly strong outing was on one of the 'Chess superstar' albums of the late 60s, *Folk Festival of the Blues*, also known as *Live at the Copacabana*, where Guy is included with Muddy Waters and Howlin' Wolf (and a dubbed-on Sonny Boy) and shines particularly on a version of 'Wee Wee Baby'.

It wasn't until 1967 that Guy, who was by now the biggest blues name of his generation in Chicago, decided to take his chances by becoming a full-time musician. 'Dick Waterman, who'd rediscovered Son House and so on, dropped by the garage. He wanted to team me up with the harmonica player Junior Wells, but I didn't want my family to go hungry. The boss

however – Guy does as good a job as the song deserves, and since he shares writer credits with Dixon and Montgomery it seems likely that they were trying to hedge their bets by coming up with a dance novelty to set against the unvarnished blues.

Guy, prudently keeping a day job in a garage as well as playing the clubs at night, went back into the studio in December, but it was another year, December 1961, before he cut his one and only hit record, another manic blues, 'Stone Crazy', which reached number 12 in the r&b

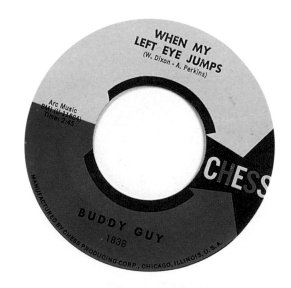

gave me a two-week vacation, to see how I got on. I went to Ann Arbor, Michigan – sold out. Toronto – they'd already had two Buddy Guys, now they got the real one. San Francisco the same. I never went back.'

The partnership lasted more than two decades, and Guy also recorded under his own name for Vanguard such impressive albums as *A Man and the Blues* and a live set, *This Is*. The duo's first album in terms of recording, though it was not

From Muddy to Stevie Ray: Buddy Guy has kept the blues alive throughout four decades.

dellahoussaye

Blues and soul:
Little Milton carried
Chess blues into the
soul era.

Chicago, partly out of determination to maintain a Chicago forum for the blues and give a new generation of bluesmen the same opportunity as he had, and in the 1990s, with such albums as 1991's *Damn Right I Got the Blues*, appearances with Clapton at the Royal Albert Hall and an autobiography in the shops, Guy's place in the blues pantheon is secure.

A recording session at Herb Abramson's A-1 Studio in New York City on 27 November 1963 produced a left-field international hit when leased to Checker, and one of the most delightful blues records of the decade. Tommy Tucker, real name Robert Higginbotham, born 5 March 1939 in Springfield, Ohio, was a jazz keyboard player who had played with Roland Kirk among others. Kirk's avant-garde music is almost as far away as can be imagined from that day's main piece of work, 'Hi-Heel Sneakers'. Inspired ad-lib playing conspires to turn just another 12-bar blues, albeit one with unusual and amusing lyrics, into a classic of the genre. Tucker's slurred, drawling, Jimmy-Reed styled vocals and stuttering organ were complemented by the beautiful, spiky little guitar lines of Dean Young, creating an instant dance-floor smash that surged out of the r&b list to reach 11 in the Hot Hundred and 23 in the UK. Its popularity as a blues standard has subsequently surpassed even this success. The irresistibly languid blues 'I Don't Want 'Cha' completed the package.

When it first charted in February Tucker was rushed back to the studio, and he saw no reason

issued until much later, was for Quicksilver in 1968, with Fred Below among the band, and included Wells's anthem 'Messin' with the Kid'. They returned to the song in 1970, with Eric Clapton and Dr John supporting them in Miami for an Atco album. Guy has long owned a club in to alter the formula – 'Long Tall Shorty' and its instrumental b-side 'Mo' Shorty' were sons of 'Sneakers', another modest pop hit, and a month later Tucker cut nine further tracks for a Checker album. After another impressive number the following year, 'Alimony', Tucker's star faded somewhat, but he remained a club hero in the UK. He died suddenly in 1982.

If Tucker flared brilliantly for a short time with an uncompromising, downhome music, it was left to Little Milton to burn a steady candle for a more sophisticated blues throughout the 1960s, though inevitably his work was inflected with soul rhythms and brassy arrangements as Chess attempted to keep abreast of changing taste. It worked – nine of his Checker singles charted in the Hot Hundred in the second half of the decade, and he also retained his appeal among those blacks who remained faithful to an updated version of the music.

James Milton Campbell Jr was born on 7 September 1934 in Inverness, Mississippi, began work as a guitarist in nearby Greenville in his early teens, recorded with pianist Willie Love and cut his first records under his own name as one of Ike Turner's signings to Sun, backed by Turner and the delightfully named Playmates of Rhythm. He worked throughout the 1950s in Memphis, Chicago and above all St Louis, and in 1958 signed to the Bobbin label. Recordings made for them in 1961 and 1962 were bought for release by Chess, and included his first Checker hit 'So Mean To Me' (number 14 in the r&b list), with Fontella Bass on piano.

After this he signed with Checker direct, breaking into the lower reaches of the Hot Hundred with 'Blind Man' in 1965, and the big breakthrough came with a February 1965 session that produced 'We're Gonna Make It' (number one

r&b, number 25 pop) and 'Who's Cheating Who' (four and 43, respectively) – a good evening's work. What distinguished Little Milton from many of the older bluesmen was that, like BB King (and, as it was to be proved when he signed to the Stax label, Albert King as well) he could add a contemporary soul feel to the blues discipline of his voice, thus appealing across the board, though his main constituency was among those blacks to whom contemporary blues still had an appeal.

Remaining on Checker until 1971, Milton gave them a roster of 16 r&b hits, bolstered by his Hot Hundred successes. Perhaps the finest and most distinctive of these was the 1969 song 'Grits Ain't Groceries', with its declaration: 'If I don't love you grits ain't groceries, chicken ain't poultry and Mona Lisa was a man.' He then moved to Stax, and the way he had managed to straddle the market is well illustrated by the fact that while his only r&b hit with the label was 1971's 'If That Ain't a Reason', his sole Hot Hundred entry was a different release, 'That's What Love Will Make You Do'. He appeared in the film *Wattstax*, and made funk records in the late 1970s before returning to blues form on the Malaco label. But his place in the Chess story is as the last of their male blues signings to maintain the company's profile in the charts.

CHAPTER 6

TOWARDS THE ENDGAME

SOULFUL DRESS

Leonard and Phil Chess were record men in the old-fashioned mould, cigar-chomping, shirt-sleeved, blue-mouthed and hands-on. They remained so as the company grew, as the offices became more sumptuous, as they diversified into local radio. But their musical talent, in spite of the blind spots, lay in getting the best out of their bluesmen. Whether it be Muddy Waters or Chuck Berry, Leonard or Phil would usually be there in the studio with Willie Dixon, listening for the sound that his intuition demanded.

Chess Records could surely not have continued to prosper in the 1960s to the extent that it did if it had remained dependent on the talents of its founders. The musical climate was changing, moving away from the hard-core blues. That would always remain the bedrock of the music, but its development into soul, the next step that gospel took away from the church, demanded new techniques, new ideas. 'Oh my God, is this going to be a symphony or something?' asked Leonard Chess when he once dropped in on an Etta James ballad session. But, of course, the reason that he was just looking in on the work in progress was that he had already had the sense to hire in fresh talent, with up-to-date ideas.

Fresh but seasoned talent, that is. When Ralph Bass, a white producer, joined the company in 1959 he was one of the most experienced a&r men in the business. Born in 1911, he had been a disc jockey in Los Angeles, produced T-Bone Walker for Black & White during the 1940s, and gave the label the biggest r&b hit of 1947 with Jack McVea's 'Open the Door Richard'. He worked with jazzmen like Charlie Parker and Erroll Garner, and in 1950 looked after West Coast talent for the Newark-based label Savoy, signing Johnny Otis and his protégée Little Esther Phillips. He founded the Federal label, which became an important wing of the Cincinnati independent King, and his most significant recruit there was James Brown.

Since the mid-1950s Chess had been having dealings with a Detroit record man, the singer, writer and producer Billy Davis, born in 1937. In 1956 he joined his cousin Lawrence Payton in the Four Tops, and hustled them a session at Chess. Their single, 'Kiss Me Baby' coupled with 'Could

Wang Dang Doodle: as Chess moved into soul during the 1960s, Koko Taylor kept the blues flame burning.

It Be You', did nothing, but the enterprising Davis also sold two songs which established his credentials – the Moonglows took his 'See Saw' to number 11, and 'A Kiss from Your Lips' did well for the Flamingos.

He was also writing for Jackie Wilson, and producing local artists, in partnership with Berry Gordy. In 1958 Davis set up Anna Records with Gordy's sister Gwen, signing distribution deals for the label first with End and then with Chess. In 1961 Chess invited him to move to Chicago and work for them, something he was already doing on a casual freelance basis, and when he accepted he sold out his interest in Anna to Berry Gordy, who turned it into Tamla Motown. Chess briefly set up an imprint specifically for Davis's projects, Checkmate, and Davis hired arranger Phil Wright as an integral part of the new team.

Other important players were saxophonist Gene Barge, signed by Phil Chess as a staff producer, and a pool of writers, musicians and producers whose skills usually covered at least two of these requirements, like keyboard players Leonard Caston Jr and the blind songwriter Raynard Miner, drummer Maurice White and bass player Louis Sattersfield. White became Ramsey Lewis's drummer in 1966, and four years later formed Earth, Wind and Fire.

Women performers had played little role in the growth of Chess during the 1950s blues decade, but now they seemed to dominate the output. The biggest star among them was Etta James, the first on to the label was her cousin Sugar Pie DeSanto, the closest to the blues was Koko Taylor, the greatest 'deep soul' stylist was Mitty Collier, Fontella Bass had the biggest international hit, and the pop-soul field was covered by artists like Jackie Ross, Jan Bradley and Jo Ann Garrett.

DeSanto, born of a black mother and a Filipino father and growing up in San Francisco (though she stopped growing up at four feet eleven inches), was one of the many artists who came within the orbit of the bandleader and talent-spotter Johnny Otis, who saw her in 1951 at a talent show. He nicknamed her Little Miss Sugar Pie, recorded her in Los Angeles and took 'I Love You (Boom Diddy Wawa)' to the Federal label. When she moved to Aladdin in 1958 she sang with guitarist Pee Wee Kingsley's band, and a year later producer Bob Geddins cut her and the band in Oakland, California, for his Veltone label, with 'I Want to Know'. When Chess picked up the song for wider distribution it gave DeSanto her only big hit, reaching number four in 1960.

As a result of this success, Chess brought her to Chicago, signed her to Checker, and in December 1960 recorded a marathon session of songs to add to three numbers she had cut for Veltone, to make up her début album. 'Can't Let You Go' was selected as the follow-up single, but it was on the strength of her hit that DeSanto toured for the following two years as part of the James Brown Revue.

In February 1964, produced by Davis and backed by his house band – Caston, Sattersfield, White and guitarist Gerald Sims – DeSanto cut her next classic song, a humorous, raunchy answer to Tommy Tucker's hit called 'Slip-In Mules'. In reached number 48 in the Hot Hundred in April, her only solo pop hit, but this seems poor reward for such a delightful track. A session in May produced the other song for which DeSanto will always be remembered, again beautifully tailored to her sassy, vibrant personality – the dance-floor strut 'Soulful Dress', backed by the same musicians. 'Don't you girls go gettin' jealous when I round up all of your fellas,' she rasps. An r&b number one and a big pop hit would have been just reward, but there was no justice whatsoever for DeSanto. Her dynamic stage presence, however, kept her successfully on the circuit, sharing the bill with such acts as Gladys Knight and the Miracles.

In September 1965 Davis teamed DeSanto and Etta James, with somewhat greater and much-deserved success. The sensuous groove of 'Do I Make Myself Clear?' was a minor pop hit, peaking at 96, but when they got back together in the following April they managed to crack the r&b chart as well with the big-lunged holler 'In the Basement', driven along by a pulsing bass beat and decorated with the kind of background party atmosphere that was working wonders for Ramsey Lewis at the time. Even

so, the chart rewards did not do the song justice: just 97 in the Hot Hundred, 37 in the r&b list. And, ominously, a DeSanto session that was recorded between these two collaborations stayed on the shelf.

There was one more single in July 1966, 'Go Go Power'/'Good Timin'', and DeSanto had also

They called it jazz:
and if they were right, Ramsey Lewis's 13 Hot Hundred entries make him the most successful jazzman ever.

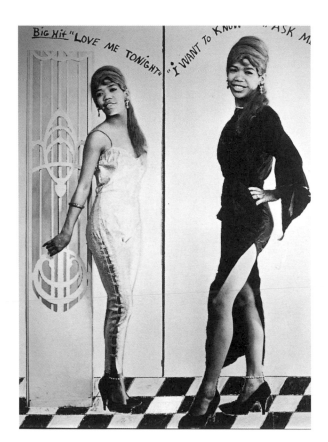

Sugar Pie DeSanto was the first of the Chess female stars of the 1960s.

discovered by Johnny Otis. She was living in San Francisco and performing in a high-school trio called the Peaches when, in 1954, Otis heard them and furnished them with an 'answer' to the lascivious Midnighters' hit 'Work with Me Annie'. This had reached number one earlier in the year, and the Peaches rejigged it as 'Roll With Me Henry', a precocious piece of work. Otis took them to the Modern label and the single was a big success locally, encouraging James to go solo.

She hit immediately with 'The Wallflower' and, later in the year, with 'Good Rockin' Daddy'. Mysteriously, a further four years of recording for Modern couldn't produce another hit, but her three successes ensured constant work on the r&b package shows touring throughout the country. On one of these in 1959, sharing a bill with the Moonglows, she got involved with the group's bass singer and leader, Harvey Fuqua. The Moonglows themselves hadn't had a hit since 1957, and Fuqua had shrewdly diversified into a&r work for Chess. He took James to Leonard Chess, who had no difficulty in picking up her contract from the Bihari brothers at Modern and moving her to Argo.

Chess cast her as a singer of big, soulful ballads, wrapped in Riley Hampton's lush arrangements, while Fuqua teamed up with her to cut a doo-wop single as Etta & Harvey. Though 'If I Can't Have You' reached number six on the r&b list it was almost a one-off ('Spoonful' scored for them six months later), while as a solo artist James's career suddenly rose to a new peak. Although the style of song was somewhat

been pitching songs to other Chess artists, including Little Milton and Fontella Bass. In 1967 she went back west and from then on has based herself in San Francisco. It remains a mystery why such a dynamic performer didn't have considerably more commercial success.

That was left to her older cousin Etta James. Born in Los Angeles in 1938, again to mixed parents – black and Italian – she too was

in Etta James, Chess had one of the greatest voices of the soul era.

conservative for a seasoned r&b artist, James did not object. As she told her biographer David Ritz: 'I figured I could sing anything. Besides, these were songs my mother had loved... I'd been a soloist in church as a little girl, I was doing gutbucket r&b when I was 15, but standards sung by Sinatra and Sarah and Billie, man, they were always part of my life.'

Chess's hopes for James are indicated by the fact that five big sessions were held in 1960 alone, and the faith was justified – a flow of big r&b hits were uncannily mirrored in the pop charts – 'All I Could Do Was Cry' (two and 33), 'My Dearest Darling' (five and 34), 'At Last' (two and 47), 'Trust In Me' (four and 30), 'Fool That I Am' (14 and 50), 'Don't Cry, Baby' (six and 39). The flip side of 'Fool', 'Dream', made the pop charts in its own right, while the last release of 1961, 'It's Too Soon to Know' and 'Seven Day Fool', was also a double-sided pop hit. Such precise 'crossover' success was rare indeed, and established James as one of the top black stars of the era.

In 1962 the tougher sound of 'Something's Got a Hold On Me' and the impassioned ballad 'Stop the Wedding' continued what must by now have seemed an automatic process of crossover hits, and the sessions were also producing a series of albums. The last of this remarkable sequence came in spring 1963, when the more brassy, poporiented 'Pushover', recorded in Nashville, climbed to seven in the r&b and 25 in the pop list.

However, the pace of touring and recording constantly had told on James, and by now she was a registered drug addict. Nevertheless, she cut a live album back in Nashville in September 1963, and the flow of singles continued. There were two pop hits in 1964, with the Jimmy Reed number 'Baby What You Want Me To Do', from the Nashville album, and 'Loving You More Every Day', although after 'Pushover' she faded from the r&b chart for almost four years. But clearly Leonard Chess was keeping a paternalistic eye on her. As James told journalist Bob Fukuyama in 1976: 'He always looked after me, even though I was the company's black sheep, always getting into trouble. When I was a junkie he set me up with the rehabilitation centre and made sure I was staying straight.' It was also during this difficult time that the two fruitful sessions with DeSanto were held, conceived perhaps as supportive, less taxing than the responsibilities of solo work, but commercially successful nonetheless.

The next stage of James's career began with a session in autumn 1966, when 'I Prefer You' – released on the renamed Cadet label – was a modest r&b success. And this final phase on Chess reached its peak with two dates a year later at producer Rick Hall's Fame studios in Muscle Shoals, Alabama, where James was surrounded by the house musicians who had helped to create the phenomenon of southern 'deep soul'. They included drummer Roger Hawkins, bass player David Hood, keyboard players Barry Beckett and Spooner Oldham.

Clearly seen primarily as album sessions, this inspired marriage produced a handful of James's finest singles. The driving, full-tilt funk of 'Tell Mama' gave her one of her biggest hits (which reached ten in the r&b and 23 in the pop list), while the aching, spacey blues ballad 'I'd Rather Go Blind', with James's soaring voice perfectly complemented by the restraint of the backing, is one of her finest performances – unluckily for her, it was the swiftly cut cover version by British blues band Chicken Shack, with Christine Perfect respectfully copying James's phrasing, that scored commercially. But 'Security' almost matched 'Tell Mama' in both charts, while 'Steal Away' was equally strong. And returning to Muscle Shoals for two sessions in 1968, the singer cut two further hits, 'I Got You Babe' and 'Almost Persuaded'.

After Leonard Chess's death there was to be one more modest hit for James, 'Losers Weepers Part 1' in 1970, before drugs took hold once again. She returned occasionally during the dog days of Chess for what proved largely to be album sessions. But her singles continued to find a market – there were five modest hits during this period, including one, 'Jump Into Love' in 1976, after the company's ownership had passed to All Platinum. James then moved on to a succession of labels – among them Warner Brothers in 1978, MCA for an Allen Toussaint-produced New Orleans set in 1980, and in the late 80s for a reunion with the Muscle Shoals musicians, by which time she was signed to Island. She was still active in the 1990s, when her records included a tribute to Billie Holiday. Indeed, the post-Chess years have produced some fine material from James, but it is as the Chicago label's most prolific and successful female star that she will be best remembered.

James was just one example of Leonard Chess's fruitful relationship with the Fame studio. The first Chess act to record there was the 1966 Checker signing Bobby Moore and the Rhythm Aces, an Alabama soul band destined to be remembered for three minutes of genius, their first Checker release 'Searching for My Love'. This soupy southern shuffle reached number seven in the r&b chart, and the group did enjoy two further minor hits, 'Try My Love Again' and 'Chained to You Heart', also Fame productions.

Maurice and Mac spent five years on Chess from 1966, and were also sent to Muscle Shoals for their sessions. Maurice McAlister and Green McLauren, fresh from the Radiants vocal group, didn't have any national hits, though their revival of Barbara Lynn's 'You Left the Water Running' was a big seller in the South. Most successful of the Fame stable was Laura Lee, Chess's last significant soul signing. Born in Chicago in 1945, Lee turned from sacred to secular music at the age of 20, and on joining Chess cut her first and biggest hit, 'Dirty Man', which peaked at number 13. This rootsy slab of r&b betrayed little of Lee's religious past, as the title suggests. The follow-up, 'Up Tight, Good Man', was almost as successful, and the singer rewarded Chess with three more lesser hits before transferring to Hot Wax in 1971.

While Etta James bridged r&b and soul, Koko Taylor continued to fly a flag for the blues in the 1960s, and helped to keep Willie Dixon's part of the operation busy. Both James and DeSanto had big, bluesy voices but Taylor out-lunged them both. Her style had roots in the 'classic' blues singers of the 1920s, above all her heroine, Bessie Smith. The genre got a harder edge in the 50s with shouters like Big Maybelle ('Whole Lotta Shakin' Goin' On') and Big Mama Thornton ('Hound Dog'), and ended with gravel-throated Janis Joplin taking it to the west-coast hippies in

the late 60s – indeed, Taylor was the last of
Joplin's prototype models.

Cora Walton was born in Memphis in 1935,
and followed a time-hallowed pattern as a
youngster – picking cotton in the week and
singing in church on Sundays. At 18 she and her
husband-to-be, Robert Taylor, headed for Chicago,
finding day jobs and hitting the blues clubs at
night. Whenever Taylor got the nod to sit in with
the band and sing a floor spot the talent behind
her rasping tonsils became obvious, and so she
got to know the biggest names around, Waters
and the Wolf among them.

It was the all-powerful local disc jockey Big
Bill Hill who introduced her to Willie Dixon. She
cut a record for the USA label with JB Lenoir on
guitar, 'Like Heaven To Me'/'Honky Tonky', and
then Dixon put an ad-libbed basement jam on an
album issued on Victoria Spivey's label, Spivey,
which he was helping to set up for the veteran
blues singer and pianist. 'What Kind of Man Is
This' and 'Which-a-Way To Go' were the titles.
Nothing happened for her at the time but the
talent was obvious, so Dixon took her to Chess.

One of the reasons Dixon was the greatest of
blues writers and arrangers is that he was
constantly looking for commercial tricks – a twist
in the lyric, an unexpected melody line, a
rhythmic surprise, a catchy chorus – to lift his
song out of the routine 12-bar mould, and he
then went further and either wrote or tailored his
material for a specific artist. After years of
dealing with crusty old die-hards like Howlin'
Wolf and the second Sonny Boy Williamson he

relished the challenge presented by the eager-to-
learn Koko Taylor.

He assembled a stunning cast for her début
session with Chess in June 1964 – Clifton James
on drums and Jack Meyers on bass, Lafayette
Leake on piano and Walter Horton on harmonica,
Buddy Guy and Robert Nighthawk on guitars –
and cut his 'I Got What It Takes', a tough, riffing
number on which Taylor sings like a seasoned
veteran and Horton is inspired to produce a
remarkable solo.

A session the following January produced
some more commanding material – 'Don't Mess
with the Messer', 'Whatever I Am, You Made Me'
and, with Gene Barge added on tenor sax, 'I'm a
Little Mixed Up' – destined for album release. The
commercial breakthrough had to wait until a
December 1965 session when Dixon, still perhaps
smarting from the Wolf's dislike of his 'Wang
Dang Doodle', refashioned this Runyonesque low-
life tale for Taylor. With Buddy Guy and Johnny
'Twist' Williams constructing a fluid, sensuous
guitar riff decorated with single-note chimes, the
song could have been made for her.

But her first reaction was, 'That ain't no song
for a woman to sing.' Dixon convinced her, just as
he had reassured her that a unique feature of her
voice, the heavy, rasping growl that appeared
naturally within a lyric line rather than being
added seemingly as an affectation, was a strength
rather than an off-putting eccentricity. Dixon
took a dub of the song to disc jockey Pervis
Spann at the radio station that Chess owned,
WVON, and the immediate favourable reaction of
listeners convinced Dixon that 'this tune is as hot
as July jam'.

With an r&b chart smash and an eventual
number 58 placing in the Hot Hundred, this was
clearly the case. And yet, as Dixon made clear in

his autobiography, the Chess brothers were up to their usual creative accounting – and it is striking that, after all his years of service to the company, Dixon was kept in the dark like everyone else. 'They made the contract with all artists that said after the expense had been paid, then you split the royalty. They make the expense whatever they want it to be, let the artist have a few dollars at a time, and it takes a million dollars for 'em to see the expenses paid as far as they're concerned. When "Wang Dang Doodle" started selling, Koko and her old man were saying, "Dixon, why don't you give us some money? We know they're paying you." They weren't paying me a damn thing. They were doing Koko like they were doing me, telling her I was getting the money and telling me she was getting the money.'

There were no more big hits for Taylor on Chess, but plenty of cuts to be relished. The strutting '(I Got) All You Need' dates from the 'Wang Dang Doodle' session, while a highlight of 1966 was a riffing duet with Dixon, '(What Came First) The Egg or the Hen'. There was only one session in 1967, but it produced two classics in the up-tempo 'Fire' and an over-the-top narrative that starts out like 'St James Infirmary', the snappily titled 'Insane Asylum'. A final studio session in 1972, cutting material for her album *Basic Soul*, showed that while the musical tide and the label itself might be slipping away from her, Taylor was still in prime form. The most stunning cut is yet another Dixon number, this time little more than a riff, 'Um Huh My Baby'. Louis Satterfield's bass and the guitars of Joe Young and Reggie Boyd set up a relentless rock 'n' roll groove, beautifully decorated by Lafayette Leake's piano. Chess recorded Taylor once more during an All Stars blues set at the Montreux

Festival in 1972, though only a duet with Muddy Waters made it on to the resulting album. Leake and Little Walter's reunited group The Aces – the Myers brothers and Fred Below – as well as Dixon were backing Chess's last blues star.

Happily, however, Koko Taylor's story did not end with the decline of Chess – far from it. She formed a band called Blues Machine, moved to the enterprising Alligator label, and when the music enjoyed yet another surge of popularity in the 1980s she rose to the top once more.

The connection with Bob Lyons's Bobbin label in St Louis that introduced Little Milton to Checker also brought two other artists under the Chess umbrella – Fontella Bass and Bobby McClure. Bass, born in St Louis in 1940, was steeped in music as a child – her mother Martha had been trained as a gospel singer by the renowned Willie May Ford Smith, joined the Clara Ward Singers and then became a solo gospel star – she was featured in Chess's gospel series, for example. Fontella learned to play piano very early, and as a five-year-old was freelancing at local funeral parlours!

Although her mother resisted the almost inevitable move from sacred to secular music, Bass persisted – talent shows while still at school, professional work from the time she left in 1958. She was spotted by Oliver Sain, a musical director working with Little Milton, and joined Milton's band on piano in 1961. When Milton and Sain parted company in 1963 Bass became part of the Oliver Sain Review as featured singer, soon to be joined by vocalist Bobby McClure. A year later Bass followed Milton to the Chess label, and Leonard Chess signed McClure as well. Sain was assigned to produce them, and as a duo they cut Sain's 'Don't Mess Up a Good Thing' at their first session in June 1964.

This stomping r&b duet was underpinned by the house band, Caston, Satterfield and White, with Pete Cosey on guitar and Sain himself among the brass line-up, and echoed the sound that Ike Turner was currently achieving with his revue – Sain and Turner had worked together at Sun. Far from being rushed to the radio station in dub form, the record was not released on Checker until January 1965, but it immediately began to climb the charts and peaked at number five r&b and 33 pop. The flip side was a sensuous version of Jimmy Reed's 'Baby What You Want Me To Do'.

The follow-up session for the duo in April came up with their second and last hit, 'You'll Miss Me (When I'm Gone)', using the same house band but now produced by Billy Davis, with another strong flip in the brassy 'Don't Jump': it reached 27 and 91, respectively. As a double act Bass and McClure then split up, because whereas she was contracted to Chess he was still under contract to Sain.

McClure was born in Chicago in 1942 but moved to St Louis as a child. Again he made the switch from gospel to r&b in his teens and became featured singer with a local outfit, the Big Daddy Jenkins Band, before being hired by Sain for his revue and so being teamed with Bass. After they split up he had one solo hit on Checker, 'Peak of Love' in 1966, an up-tempo number produced by Billy Davis and written by Davis with Sugar Pie DeSanto, which made number 16 in the r&b and 97 in the pop list.

After one other single failed to make the charts McClure left Chess.

Bass fared somewhat better. Part credited to pianist Raynard Miner, and led in by one of the most memorable bass lines in pop music courtesy of Louis Satterfield, 'Rescue Me' – for which Bass claims to have written the uncredited lyrics – was one of the all-conquering records of the mid-60s. Ironically it might have remained as a b-side – Billboard featured Sain's composition 'The Soul of a Man' as the 'plug' side, a tune that pre-dated Bass's signing with Checker, and indeed it is one of her finest soul performances.

But it was 'Rescue Me' that conquered the world: an r&b number one, number four in the

Don't mess up a good jacket: Fontella Bass's singing partner Bobby McClure.

Hot Hundred and – as the first big hit under Chess's deal with the London-based Pye label – number 11 in the UK. Bass has spoken of the sudden contrast she experienced, from the comparative security of performing as part of a duo backed by familiar musicians, to being out there on her own plugging one of the hottest records of 1965. And why does she hum her way into the fade-out rather than singing? Because the lyric sheet fell off the music stand.

Short of original material but with an urgent need to capitalize on this smash, Chess opted to cut an album, *The New Look*, consisting of Bass's versions of recent soul and r&b successes. And when it came to pay-day, as she told David Nathan of *Blues & Soul*, it was a familiar story. When she collected her first royalty cheque, 'I looked at it, saw how little it was, tore it up and threw it back across the desk. I'd had the first million-seller for Chess since Chuck Berry about ten years before... I bought them a new building ... it was the same old story...'

The follow-up record, 'Recovery', was in similar vein but performed well in the charts: 13 r&b, 37 pop, 32 UK. And there was a further handful of 1966 releases that made the thirties in the r&b chart, 'I Can't Rest', 'I Surrender' and 'You'll Never Ever Know'. But it would seem that Bass was too versatile and ambitious to be contentedly squeezed into a limited mould – for example, as Chess's nod towards the Motown sound – and certainly too intelligent and shrewd to be happy with Leonard Chess's paternalistic attitude and tiny royalty cheques. She left in 1968, moved to Paris to work with her husband, the distinguished jazz trumpeter Lester Bowie, and then returned to the States for brief and unfruitful relationships with the Paul/Jewel and Epic labels. Having raised a family, she returned

to her roots in sacred music, for example joining with her mother Martha and brother David Peaston for the 1990 album *Promises: a Family Portrait of Faith*. So Fontella Bass's mother got her way in the end!

Since 'I Had a Talk with My Man Last Night' is one of the most beautiful soul ballads ever recorded, it is a sad irony that Mitty Collier is hardly known beyond the world of die-hard soul freaks. It should go on an album, alongside other works of genius such as Linda Jones's terrifying reading of Jerry Butler's 'For Your Precious Love', with a title like 'The Greatest Records that Golden Oldies Radio Stations Have Never Heard Of'.

Straight from the church: Gospel singer Mitty Collier recorded some of the finest of the Chess soul singles.

Collier made the same musical journey as Fontella Bass – from the church out into the naughty world and back again. She was born in Alabama in 1941, and her church singing led to her joining a travelling group, the Hayes Ensemble, while still at school. A visit to Chicago when she was 18 resulted in appearances on talent shows, and at one of them Ralph Bass was in the audience scouting for talent. She signed to Chess in 1960, but it took three years to find a suitable song to do the trick. In August 1963 Little Johnny Taylor entered the Top Twenty of the pop charts, and reached the top of the r&b list, with his driving r&b number 'Part Time Love'. Collier was furnished with an answer song, 'I'm Your Part Time Love', which reached 20 in the r&b chart.

A year later 'I Had a Talk With My Man' proved the breakthrough into the pop chart. As frequently happens in soul music, the song was a secular rewrite of a gospel song, in this case James Cleveland's 'I Had a Talk with God Last Night'. Leonard Caston was playing a Cleveland album in the studio, and this particular song caught the attention of Billy Davis. The arrangement is classically pure, with subtle string patterns overlaid with a French horn, and whereas the strength of soul singing is often in its display of emotion, Collier's rendition gains strength from its control and precision. The record was a huge r&b hit and reached 41 in the Hot Hundred.

Cleveland's 'No Cross, No Crown' was the source of the masterly follow-up, 'No Faith, No Love', which did well in the r&b list and edged into the pop charts too, and in 1966 Collier had her third and last hit with the soulful 'Sharing You'. But five further Chess releases sold less well, and in 1969 Collier signed with Peachtree, based in Atlanta. But there were to be no more hits, and in 1972 she returned to gospel music.

The Chess women didn't have it all their own way in the 1960s. Steve Alaimo, a white medical student from New York, based in Miami, had three hits on Checker – notably the one that became an r&b standard, 'Every Day I Have to Cry', in 1963. Songwriter Tony Clarke, who had worked with Billy Davis in Detroit, had a big 1965 hit with his own 'The Entertainer' before moving to Hollywood in search of a movie career. However, it didn't last long – Clarke's wife killed him defending herself from one of his beatings. But the company's most successful male solo artist of the decade was Billy Stewart, who had made his début back in 1956 with the instrumental 'Billy's Blues'.

Stewart was born in Washington DC in 1937, and sang with the family group the Stewart Gospel Singers. He moved on to form a secular high-school group, the Rainbows, and was 'discovered' in Washington by Bo Diddley, who hired him as his pianist. But his uniqueness did not lie in his keyboard playing, and it was not until 1962, after a couple of unsuccessful singles on Okeh, that he was re-signed to Chess and unveiled the vocal gimmick that was to prove his successful trademark.

'Reap What You Sow', which, like most of his subsequent hits, was self-penned, introduced his habit of stuttering and repeating the words in a big-voiced, lung-bursting style, as if he had been driven to expressing emotion by twisting and spitting out his words. The technique lay somewhere between jazz scat singing and soul 'testifying', but it was Stewart's own. It reached the 70s in the pop chart, as did his next hit a year later, the more restrained but even more affecting 'Strange Feeling'.

Although his next single, 'Count Me Out', only sold within earshot of Chess's radio station, February 1965 saw the release of his biggest hit to date, and arguably the finest demonstration of his curious way with a big ballad, 'I Do Love You', which manages to be uplifting even though it is an expression of insecurity. It made 26 in the Hot Hundred. The follow-up, which edged two places higher, was equally strong, and became his best-known song when successfully covered by Georgie Fame. 'Sitting in the Park' is an atmospheric piece of work, with the structure of a doo-wop ballad overlaid with Stewart's extraordinary vocal gymnastics.

In his detailed study *Chicago Soul*, Robert Pruter notes that Stewart gave Chess, and his producer Billy Davis in particular, something of a hard time. He found touring more lucrative than making records – not surprising, given the Chess method of calculating royalties – and so entered the studio only reluctantly, and when he did the songs he brought with him tended to be unfinished, requiring time-consuming work to polish into a finished article.

The next three singles were perhaps not polished enough, and only limped into the bottom of the charts, and Stewart's fortunes were revived by giving a standard, George Gershwin's 'Summertime', a thorough going-over. His stuttering is way over the top, trampling all over a poignant lyric with relish, and the result is a hilarious classic of musical hyperbole, which gave Stewart his only Top Ten hit. As a follow-up, he gave Doris Day's 'Secret Love' a good seeing-to.

These demolition jobs on two hallowed standards ripe for destruction proved to be the peak of Stewart's career. After three further minor hits he and three of his band were killed in a car crash in 1970.

Chess also turned to Washington in its search for other performers during the 1960s. The Knight Brothers, Richard Dunbar and Jimmy Diggs, had one moment of greatness, 'Temptation 'Bout to Get Me', in 1965, with Billy Davis once again using French horn behind the duo's exquisite harmonizing.

As well as signing female singers in the 1960s who covered the blues, r&b and soul field, Chess also tried to exploit the lighter, more pop-oriented sound that was gaining in popularity, both with 'girl groups' and solo singers, black and white. The finest result of this policy was 'Selfish One' by Jackie Ross, from St Louis, who got her break singing with the Syl Johnson band. The record peaked just short of the Top Ten in 1964, and Ross had a couple of further minor hits before she covered Evie Sands's ballad 'Take Me For a Little While'. Unfortunately for both singers the versions tended to cancel each other out, neither selling enough to score a substantial hit.

Chicago girl group the Gems made a number of impressive sides for Chess in the mid-60s but achieved only local success. They are notable chiefly as the starting point for Minnie Riperton, who was working as the Chess receptionist when she joined the Gems. After leaving the group she remained with Chess and sang lead with the company's one attempt to tap into the progressive rock market with the band Rotary Connection, who had a couple of reasonably successful albums in the late 60s, but it was when she moved to Epic in the early 70s that she made her name as a solo singer. The remarkable range of her soprano voice was best displayed on her international hit 'Lovin' You' in 1974, but tragically she died five years later of a brain tumour.

Jan Bradley, born in Mississippi in 1943, cut a Curtis Mayfield song, 'Mama Didn't Lie', for the

Formal label in 1962. Chess picked it up for national promotion, and in the following January it became a Top Twenty hit. Two years later, now signed directly to Chess, Bradley had a minor success with 'I'm Over You'. Subsequent releases only sold locally and Bradley retired from the music business in 1969. Jo Ann Garrett, a Chicagoan born in 1949, made a couple of pleasant records backed by Chess's star vocal group, the Dells – 'You Can't Come In' and a revival of the Heartbeats' 1956 doo-wop hit 'A Thousand Miles Away', but these likewise enjoyed no more than local success and she too eventually left the business.

The Radiants, referred to earlier, were a five-piece male harmony group who began as a secular offshoot of the Greater Harvest Baptist Church choir, assembled by lead singer Maurice McAlister. Chess signed them in 1962 and their first release, 'Father Knows Best', sold reasonably well locally, and subsequent singles also failed to establish the group beyond their own constituency. In 1964 they were re-organized as a three-piece, with original members McAlister and Wallace Sampson being joined by Leonard Caston. During this time they managed the national breakthrough, charting with two Impressions-styled numbers, 'Voice Your Choice' and 'It Ain't No Big Thing'. The group survived several further changes of personnel before calling it a day in 1972, and provided Chess with a brace of further r&b chart successes in 'Feel Kind of Bad' and 'Hold On'.

But the Chess label's chief contribution to the vocal group sound of the 1960s was the Dells, a group whose long career spanned the doo-wop era and 70s funk, who virtually kept Chess going as an active company during its last years, and who then moved on into the 1980s on first Mercury and then Chi-Sound, a longevity perhaps matched only by the Four Tops.

The Dells were formed in 1953 in Illinois. The original five-piece comprised baritone lead Marvin Junior and tenor Johnny Funches, second tenor Verne Allison, Mickey McGill (baritone) and Chuck Barksdale (bass). Signed to Vee-Jay, they had a huge r&b hit in 1956 with 'Oh What a Nite' and toured successfully on the back of it for a couple of years. But in 1958 a car crash put the Dells on hold until 1960, with Junior now taking the sole lead and ex-Flamingo Johnny Carter replacing Funches.

They now went to Chess instead of Vee-Jay, and four singles appeared on the Argo imprint. One, 1962's 'The (Bossa Nova) Bird', crept into the Hot Hundred and charted modestly in *Cashbox*'s r&b list, though not *Billboard*'s – it sold in pockets including, of course, Chicago, but not nationally. So the group was still heavily dependent on live work in and around Chicago.

In 1964 the Dells went back down the street to Vee-Jay, which by now was ailing financially, and in June 1965 returned to the r&b list with their original version of one of their finest numbers, the lilting 'Stay in My Corner'. But the demise of Vee-Jay in May 1966 meant that they were back in the street, *en route* to Chess, who signed them to the renamed Cadet. The group's wanderings were over for a while but Billy Davis couldn't conjure up a hit for them, and so they were reassigned to the team of producer Bobby Miller and arranger Charles Stepney. This did the trick at last – the magnificent 1967 album *There Is* provided a sequence of hit singles as well, and from then until leaving the label the Dells were to chart 24 times. The ballad 'O-o I Love You' reintroduced the Dells to both r&b and pop lists (22 and 61) late in the year, swiftly followed early in 1968 by the title track (11 and 20), and 'Wear It On Our Face' (27 and 44). But the surprise smash of the album was their recut of 'Stay in My Corner', all six minutes of it, that reached the top of the r&b chart in June and broke the Dells into the Top Ten for the first time.

Taken as a suite of soft-soul harmonizing, the consistent quality of the writing, production ideas and performance makes *There Is* the creative peak of the Dells' career, and one of the great albums from what was at heart a singles-orientated company. Its follow-up, *Always Together*, continued the run – the title track made three and 18 in the two lists, and the album also spawned three more modest hits, 'Does Anybody Know I'm Here', 'Hallways of My Mind' and 'I Can't Do Enough'.

Remarkably, the Miller and Stepney team did the trick a third time, confirming the Dells as one of the most consistent vocal groups of the era. 1969's *Love Is Blue* showed a change of tactic – just one original number amid a series of confident (and in the case of Otis Redding's 'Sitting on the Dock of the Bay' surely misjudged) versions of existing material. One of the mysteries of the Dells is why the UK, where the Four Tops and the Tamla groups sold consistently well, remained resistant to them.

The one exception was their next release, an energetic, welded-together medley of 'I Can Sing a Rainbow'/'Love Is Blue', which having raced to number five and 22 in the American charts also reached 19 in Britain during July 1969. It typified the style of the album, far less subtle than previously, more shouting than crooning.

The oldies covered on *Love Is Blue* included a remake of their 1950s doo-wop hit 'Oh What a Night' (now, strangely, with the Anglicized spelling), which exactly matched the remade 'Stay in My Corner' in the charts, reaching the top of the r&b list and the pop Top Ten. If the Dells' distinctive sound had been somewhat coarsened for this album, it was clearly an experiment rather than a firm change of direction, because the suppleness returned for their last album of the decade, and last with Bobby Miller, *Like It Is, Like It Was*. This gave the group three mid-table hits in the vibrant 'Oh What a Day', the double-sided 'Open Up My Heart'/'Nadine' (disc-jockey preference varied across the country) and 'Long Lonely Nights'.

The Dells remained on Chess throughout its decline during the 1970s, and the last listed Cadet single is, in fact, by them – 'We Got To Get Our Thing Together'/'The Power of Love' – but with the demise of the company they moved to Mercury, who tried to fit them into the currently successful Philadelphia mould, and then to another Chicago company, Chi-Sound, where they became label-mates of the Chi-Lites, and where they remained until Chi-Sound also went under, in 1984 – an event which Robert Pruter identifies in *Chicago Soul* as the death of the genre of music that gave his book its title, and of which the Dells were the finest and most consistent example.

Thirty years of harmony: the Dells carried the vocal group sound from the rock 'n' roll era through to the disco days.

FEEL LIKE GOIN' HOME

In 1966 Chess seemed to be booming, ensconced at 320 East 21st Street with two fully equipped studios, a demo studio, and office space for everyone. In 1967 a further imprint was added to the Chess umbrella, Cadet Concept – an attempt by Marshall Chess to update the company's image by setting up a home for contemporary material. Marshall launched it with an album by Chess's entry into the progressive rock market, Rotary Connection, and it was deemed a success – more than a quarter of a million units were sold.

He was also involved in the controversial attempts to find a new young audience for his ageing blues stars by cutting them in up-to-date style, and the next release was *Electric Mud*. In fact the record sold quite well, and did indeed broaden awareness of Muddy Waters, but inevitably it annoyed the long-time fans. 'I was always very upset back then,' Marshall Chess told writer Mark Humphrey at the time the set was re-released in 1997, 'because the blues purists really hated this record. But it was never an attempt to make Muddy Waters a psychedelic artist – it was a concept album, like David Bowie being Ziggy Stardust... It was just, "Take a shot," and it sold. None of these albums were trying to change these guys...'

Cadet Concept was also the place to put product licensed in from the UK – Status Quo's first hit, 'Pictures of Matchstick Men', was an early example – and Chess continued to be an active distributor of smaller labels, which brought them the O'Jays on Neptune, for instance.

But Chess as a distinctive label was always going to be associated with the Chess brothers, Leonard in particular, and could only survive creatively as a family concern. Soon after the launch of Cadet Concept the first cracks in the organization began to appear. In 1980 Marshall Chess recalled that he had wanted to keep the company in the family, even if Leonard was ready to withdraw from the front line. 'I was outvoted by my father and my uncle and their wives, who desperately wanted them to get out of the business. They thought they would see more of their husbands, you know?... My father had already left the record business at the time we sold it. He was in the radio business...'

On 4 January 1969 *Billboard* reported the imminent sale of Chess, headed 'GRT Wrap-Up Near of Chess Purchase'. 'The Chess group – 19 corporations – will be acquired for $6.5 million cash and 20,000 shares of General Recorded Tape general stock... The cash transaction includes Chess Producing Corp., Mid-West and Midsouth Record Pressing companies and Aristocrat Records... The companies to be acquired for GRT stock are Chess, Checker and Cadet Record companies, Heavy Music Inc and III C Tape Corp ... Chess's L&P Broadcasting interests are not included... The group is based in Chicago with Midsouth Record Pressing Inc in Nashville. III C Tape Corp holds tape rights to all Chess recordings, and licenses those rights to pre-recorded tape companies...'

The week's r&b chart shows how the black music focus had by now switched from Chicago to Detroit, with Tamla holding the top three slots with 'I Heard It Through the Grapevine' (Marvin Gaye), 'Cloud Nine' (The Temptations) and 'For Once in My Life' (Stevie Wonder). The Dells 'Always Together' was at 22 and on its way down, while Laura Lee's 'Hang It Up' was stuck at 49. In the following week Etta James came in at 32 with 'Almost Persuaded'.

And so, while Leonard and Phil looked forward to a less stressful future as radio station proprietors, GRT started asset-stripping. Marshall Chess again: 'They made me President. They wanted my uncle out of there, and then they started to really manipulate me and piece by piece dismantle this organisation. And I became very frustrated and decided to quit. And they then came to me, with a whole team of organisational experts – they were going to reorganise Chess Records, not even knowing what it was to begin with, so I quit on the spot.'

Marshall set up a production deal with Boz Scaggs and negotiated it with 'the same assholes who were going to reorganise Chess and ruin it.' When this fell through and Chess was paid off from the company a timely opportunity came up to work for the Rolling Stones as their label manager – a nice irony, joining the band who had based their career on his father's records. But before he left, in *Billboard* of 18 October 1969, he was talking of launching a 'new vintage blues series' and of selling it by mail order to those who could not find specialist service in regular record stores. He announced an initial slew of releases by Muddy Waters, Howlin' Wolf, Albert King and Otis Rush, Elmore James and John Brim, Sonny Boy Williamson and Little Walter.

Leonard, of course, didn't live long enough either to run his radio station, WVON, or to retire. Just seven days after Marshall's announcement of the blues reissues, *Billboard* of 25 October 1969 carried the

sad news on page three, under the heading 'Leonard Chess Dies, Co-Founder of Chess'.

'One of the founders and co-chairman of the Chess-Checker-Cadet group, Leonard Chess, died of a heart attack here Oct. 16. He was 52 years old.

'With his brother Phil, Chess was a pioneer in the independent record field and was one of the outstanding executives who developed the speciality field of r&b in the 1950s. The Chess brothers, immigrants from Poland who came to the US on Columbus Day 1928, formed the Chess label in 1948 with a recording by tenor saxophonist Gene Ammons, a soul version of "My

Back where it all began: Gene Ammons, the first artist on Chess.

Foolish Heart". This led to national distribution of the Chicago-based label.

'Chess was not the first excursion into the record business for the Chess brothers. Two years earlier they formed the Aristocrat label, also in Chicago. On this label Muddy Waters made his first singles and went on to become one of Chess's longest lasting and biggest selling blues artists.

'Another Chess artist was Chuck Berry. Leonard Chess recalled once: "Berry came in with a wire recorder and played a country music take-off called 'Ida Red'. It had been turned down by Capitol and Mercury. We recut it in our little studio behind the office with two sidemen. Phil and I were the engineers. We called it 'Maybelline'."

'Via Alan Freed plugging, this emerged as a major hit and was an example of the way that the Chess label contributed to the development of rock music in the 1950s with Atlantic, Imperial and other leaders.

'Beside Berry and Waters, the Chess label also recorded Willie Dixon, Willie Mabon, Bo Diddley, Sonny Boy Crudup [sic], Otis Spann, and Jimmy Rogers. Groups recording for the Chess-Checker-Cadet combine included the Flamingos (they recorded "I'll Be Home" which was a hit also for Pat Boone using the original Chess arrangement), the Moonglows and the Cornets.

'Leonard Chess was a complete record man. In the early Chess days, the two brothers would distribute their product by car to their Chicago South Side accounts. He also went on the road during the 1950s in the south, where he discovered artists like Howlin' Wolf. He even did field recordings – Crudup was recorded in this way.

'The Chess brothers were also studio experimenters. They used tape echo effects and distortion new at the time and even improvised with a 10ft sewer pipe to obtain a 1/10th of a second delay in one of their singles.

'Throughout the 1950s and 1960s the labels continued to grow and were acquired early this year by the GRT organisation. In addition Leonard and Phil owned two radio stations, WVON, Chicago and WNOV, Milwaukee.

'Surviving Chess are wife Revetta, two daughters, Susan Chess and Elaine Chait, son Marshall – a vice-president of the company – and mother and father, Mr and Mrs Joseph Chess.

'Paul Ackerman, *Billboard*'s music editor, said that throughout the rock 'n' roll era Chess continued to produce fine basic blues, despite the fact that much of the general rock product at that time represented a watered down version of the blues idiom. Chess, through its association with blues artists who were also writers, such as Muddy Waters, Willie Dixon and many others, developed a vast body of copyrights in the field. These are held by Arc and Regent. And, of course, one of the major contributions by Leonard Chess and the Chess company was the vital part they played in the development of Chicago as a music centre.'

Although Leonard Chess had already withdrawn from active involvement in the company, his death surely symbolized that of the label as well. Recording sessions and new releases continued during the 1970s, but no new stars, no new energy were discovered. At around the time of the fateful sale to GRT the successful team that had revived the company's fortunes in the 1960s was drifting away. Billy Davis and Phil Wright left in 1968, and Leonard Caston and Raynard Miner transferred to Motown a year later, to be followed by Bobby Miller. Now only Ralph Bass and Gene Barge remained.

When Marshall Chess baled out his replacement ensured the death of the company. Record executive Len Levy, formerly of Epic Records, was appointed in his place – and moved Chess's centre of operations to New York! The Chicago office of the company that had lived and breathed the city's music for quarter of a century was now just an outpost of yet another New York marketing organization. Said Gene Barge: 'GRT gave you a good example of how to dismantle an excellent record company.'

Artists like Little Milton and Ramsey Lewis took the opportunity to jump ship.

The founder of the Janus label, Marvin Schlacter, was brought in as Chess president in 1971, and attempted to stop the rot by combining Chess, Janus and GRT's own label as one operation. In commercial terms this did have the effect of stabilizing the company for a while, helped by the continuing popularity of the Dells, but in 1975 all pretence that Chess remained an active record company ceased, and Ralph Bass, who died on 5 March 1997, having worked at the heart of the entire postwar blues scene, was charged with shipping all the company's master tapes to a storage warehouse in Nashville.

In Britain the slow death of Chess had been masked because the label was being licensed by Phonogram during the 1970s, who did an enthusiastic reissue job on the catalogue. Three lavish boxed sets, *Genesis*, traced the development of the blues on the label from its earliest days, a handsome series of *Chess Golden Decade* compilations reflected the company's commercial successes of the 1950s, and individual artists, notably Chuck Berry, were treated to comprehensive repackages. This was all in marked contrast to the slow strangulation taking place back in America.

In August 1975 the New Jersey company All Platinum, owned by Sylvia and Joe Robinson, paid GRT $950,000 for Chess, but they could not afford to reactivate it as a going concern and so, suddenly, the label was finally transformed into a back catalogue. All Platinum itself went bust and parts of the bankrupt company were acquired by Sugar Hill. From there, rights to exploit the riches of the Chess catalogue passed to MCA, though not without a long, bitter and bloody fight in the UK, where the independent reissue label Charly also felt they had legal title to the catalogue. In 1996 MCA established their rights, and in 1997 the company celebrated the half-century since Leonard Chess decided to quit the nightclub business and set up a record label, with a series of remastered reissues.

In the 1970s Phil Chess sold his radio stations, moved to Arizona and became a rancher, though he retained his interest in Arc Music, the publishing side of Chess. On 29 January 1992 the 76-year-old Willie Dixon, the heart and soul of Chess's greatest years, died in California. In the last decade of his life he gradually regained the rights to his compositions, he set up the Blues Heaven Foundation designed to perpetuate awareness and appreciation of the blues, and in 1988 he cut his last album, the delightful *Hidden Charms*, which won a Grammy award as the Best Traditional Blues Recording. But his chief legacy is shared with Leonard and Phil Chess, and we too share in it when ever we take down a record or CD by Muddy Waters or Buddy Guy from the shelf. It takes me a little longer to enjoy one of my all-time idols, Bo Diddley. After 40 years, I can still never remember whether he is filed under 'B' or 'D'.

I've just checked. In this house he is known as Mr Diddley.

POSTSCRIPT
BUDDY GUY REMEMBERS CHESS RECORDS

I first came to Chicago in 1957 with a note from a disc-jockey out of Baton Rouge, saying Leonard Chess should listen to me. At that time he and his brother Phil would go from city to city in the south and they knew every disc-jockey who played the kind of music that the Chess people had, like Muddy Waters, Jimmy Rogers, Little Walter. I handed the note in but I never did see them, because they were in a session. I came out a little disappointed. I went back out on the street and I was looking for work. That's when I ran into Muddy. He fed me – I guess you've heard the story. And then I met Magic Sam, and he took me over to Cobra Records.

Then when the owner of Cobra Records accidentally drowned and the business went broke, Otis Rush came to my house and said that Chess wanted to see me. I went down there and signed up with them. I think the first record was 'First Time I Met The Blues'. By that time I'd had a couple of singles on Cobra, so Leonard Chess knew about me by then. He had known the guy at Cobra Records, of course. Otis Rush had had a pretty big record there with 'I Can't Quit You Baby'.

I met Willie Dixon at Cobra. He was affiliated with anybody who would cut his songs. As far as Leonard Chess is concerned, you have to give credit where credit's due. He created that sound with Muddy Waters, Jimmy Rogers, Sonny Boy Williamson. The amplified guitars and harmonica. But when I first arrived in Chicago my first thought was to turn round and go straight back. It was so cold, I thought how could people live in a place that cold? But then I met Muddy Waters and I was never cold again!

I didn't feel that Leonard Chess dealt fairly with me, though. He didn't release much on me, and the first time I sat down and talked to him was after Cream and Hendrix came out. That's when he called me in. Before that Muddy and all those guys would bring me in when they wanted me on a session. But Leonard would say that the shit I was playing was too loud, just noise. But then when he heard how Eric Clapton and Hendrix were playing he called me in and said he should let me kick his ass. He said, 'That shit you've been trying to sell me is selling like hot shit and I've been fucking dumb.' So at least he was big enough to admit that.

As far as Leonard Chess's dealings were concerned, well, people like Willie Mabon and Eddie Boyd were my friends, and they gave me some bitter answers about him. If you look back to those times every black blues player got screwed. It wasn't just Chess. Don Robey was the same. And they had you under their thumb, because if you wanted to go somewhere else they'd refuse you. They were working together, in league like that.

Of course, Buddy Guy didn't sell enough records for me to complain! I just didn't get to know the Chess brothers that well. But I have seen a little money lately for those things that I did for them. See, I'd go in with a song that I'd written and they'd be sitting there, with Willie Dixon, and they'd say this song is all right but it's not strong enough, you know? So if I wrote in a song, say, 'She left me last night,' they'd change it to 'She left me this morning'. And then I'd see the record come out and it would be their song! And I couldn't do anything about it, otherwise they wouldn't even put the record out.

So they had you under control. Really my only contact, like I said, would be when I was

called into a session, and Muddy would say, 'Sit over there,' and there'd be Freddie Below and those guys there, and then you'd hear Leonard Chess say, 'You're playing it wrong, motherfucker,' and you'd have to look up to see who he was pointing at, who the motherfucker was! My wife tells me I learned bad language from him!

Around 1967 I found out that there were these white musicians who said they'd learned a lot from me. Like Mike Bloomfield. And they'd start coming in the clubs. Now, I'd assumed they were cops, because you wouldn't see a white face in those clubs unless they were a cop. So I'd look around and think, I'm old enough to be in here, who are they trying to catch, you know? Paul Butterfield, Steve Miller, all these guys were coming in. I didn't know what was going on out there because I was still working days. And then Willie Dixon said Leonard wanted to see me and I thought I'd finally got my release. But he sat me in the big chair, and that's the time he put on those Cream and Hendrix records and told me to kick his ass.

But in spite of all this, I still think you've got to give him credit. If it wasn't for him maybe we wouldn't know who Muddy Waters was. I saw a chart from the early days and he had Muddy, Jimmy Rogers, Howlin' Wolf, about four records in the Top Ten, you know? He made their names, but he was the one making the money.

BIBLIOGRAPHY

The Chess Labels: A Discography, Michel Ruppli. Greenwood Press, 1983
Blues Who's Who, Sheldon Harris. Arlington House, 1979
The History of the Blues: The Roots, the Music, the People from Charley Patton to Robert Cray, Francis Davis. Hyperion, 1995
The Story of the Blues, Paul Oliver. Penguin Books, 1972
Blues Records 1943–1966, Mike Leadbitter and Neil Slaven. Hanover Books, 1968
Chicago Blues, Mike Rowe. Eddison Press, 1973
Chess Blues, Les Fancourt (discography), 1989
Chess R&B, Les Fancourt (discography), 1991
Feel Like Going Home, Peter Guralnick. Omnibus Press, 1978
Chicago Soul, Robert Pruter. Illini Books, 1992
Nowhere to Run, Gerri Hirshey. Macmillan, 1984
Urban Blues, Charles Keil. University of Chicago Press, 1966
The Devil's Music, Giles Oakley. BBC Books, 1976
Black Chicago, Allan H Spear. University of Chicago Press, 1967
I Am the Blues, Willie Dixon with Don Snowden. Quartet, 1989
Bo Diddley, Living Legend, George R White. Castle Communications, 1995
The Rhythm and the Blues: A Life in American Music, Jerry Wexler and David Ritz. Jonathan Cape, 1994
The Arrival of BB King, Charles Sawyer. Da Capo, 1982
Sun Records: The Brief History of the Legendary Record Label, Colin Escott and Martin Hawkins. Quick Fox, 1980
Damn Right I've Got the Blues: Buddy Guy and the Blues Roots of Rock 'n' Roll, Donald E. Wilcock with Buddy Guy. Woodford Press, 1993
Genesis: The Beginnings of Rock, Mike Leadbitter. Chess Records booklet, 1973
The Mercury Blues 'n' Rhythm Story, Dick Shurman, Billy Vera, Jim O'Neal and Mary Katherine Aldin. Mercury Records booklet, 1996

Muddy Waters: The Complete Plantation Recordings, Mary Katherine Aldin. Chess Records booklet, 1997
Muddy Waters, Les Fancourt. Chess Records booklet, 1992
Little Walter, Les Fancourt. Chess Records booklet, 1992
Sonny Boy Williamson, Neil Slaven. Chess Records booklet, date unknown
Chuck Berry, Adam Komorowski. Chess Records booklet, 1991
Sugar Pie DeSanto: Down in the Basement, David Nathan. Chess Records booklet, 1997
Koko Taylor: What It Takes, Don Snowden. Chess Records booklet, 1997
Fontella Bass: Rescued, David Nathan. Chess Records booklet, 1997
The Dells: On Their Corner, Robert Pruter. Chess Records booklet, 1997
Muddy Waters: Electric Mud, Mark Humphrey. Chess Records booklet, 1997
The Guinness Who's Who of Blues, Colin Larkin (ed.). Guinness Publishing, 1993
The Faber Companion to 20th Century Popular Music, Phil Hardy and Dave Laing. Faber and Faber, 1990
Billboard magazine (various)
'Confessin' the Blues: The Story of Little Walter', Neil Slaven. *Blues Unlimited*, 1975
'Blacks, Whites and Blues: The Story of Chess Records', Pete Golkin. *Living Blues*, 1988
'Jimmy Rogers', David Walters, Laurence Garman and John Matthews. *Blues Unlimited*, 1973
'Deep Blue', Paul Trynka. *Mojo*, 1996
This Is Hip, Joel Selvin. RCD, 1989
Bo Diddley interview with Bill Dwyer. *Blues Unlimited*, 1970
'Bo Diddley, the *Rolling Stone* Interview', Kurt Loder. *Rolling Stone*, 1987
'Young Fashioned Ways'. *Blues Access*, 1996
'Marshall Shoots the Breeze', Ray Topping. *Blues Unlimited*, 1982
'Howling Wolf: An Appreciation', Bez Turner. *Blues Unlimted*, 1976
'I Was Really Dedicated: Billy Boy Arnold', Mike Rowe and Bill Greensmith. *Blues Unlimited*, 1978

'Below's the Name, Drumming's the Game', Bez Turner. *Blues Unlimited*, 1978
'Going to Chicago', Alex Cramer. *Jazz & Blues*, 1972
'Buddy Guy: His Time Is Now', Scott Spencer. *Rolling Stone*, 1991
The Rock Primer, John Collis (ed.). Penguin, 1980
The Blues: Roots and Inspiration, John Collis. Salamander, 1997
'Buddy Who Owes It All to Muddy', John Collis. *Independent on Sunday*, 1991
'Comin' Home to the Recorded Blues', John Collis. *Independent*, 1997

ACKNOWLEDGEMENTS

My first vote of thanks must go to Les Fancourt, diligent discographer and blues expert, who gave me much encouragement and was kind enough to read this work in progress, on a floppy disk, shuttling between London and Faversham in Kent. Of course, any errors remain my responsibility, much as I might wish otherwise.

I was also grateful at the outset for the good wishes of George R White, Bo Diddley's biographer, particularly as he may well have his own tale of Chess to tell in due course. Thanks also to my editor at Bloomsbury, Penny Phillips, for keeping me hunched over the computer and CD player throughout the summer of 1997. Most of the window in my work room is covered in hardboard – a temporary measure adopted some years ago after a slight accident – but I hear that the weather was pretty bad anyway. The manuscript was edited by Richard Dawes, whose enthusiasm and knowledge of the subject provided a valuable safety net.

Andrew Lauder lent me some rare records from his marvellous collection, showing a generosity and trust rare among vinyl junkies. The examples of Chess trade advertisements are taken from Gart Galen's fascinating series of scrapbook annuals *First Pressings: The History of Rhythm & Blues* (Big Nickel Publications, PO Box 157, Milford, New Hampshire 03055, USA). These can be bought in the UK from mail-order specialists A&R Bookscarch (tel: 01503-220246).

I found the National Sound Archive, then in South Kensington but now within the British Library complcx, an invaluable source of reference. I had not used this institution previously, simply because I took its name too literally, assuming that this was the place to hear those rare out-takes of Ernest Luff singing 'O for the Wings of a Dove' (the ones sung in a butch baritone) or the cry of the corncrake. In fact, of course, it holds a wealth of printed matter as well, and humping bound copies of *Billboard* around the room also has its place in an integrated fitness programme.

The first lengthy account of Chess could not have moved far from first base without recourse to every relevant nugget of information that I could track down. For this reason I have listed in the bibliography, with immense gratitude, every significant reference down to the briefest magazine piece. There was a huge temptation to quote screeds of Willie Dixon's *I Am the Blues*, written with Don Snowden, which is recommended as a revealing insider's story.

Finally, I dedicate this book with respectful thanks to Buddy Guy, for countless hours of enjoyment, whether in tiny clubs or the Albert Hall, on ancient vinyl or crisp new CDs. He is the joyous embodiment of blues power, and will no doubt escort the music triumphantly into the 21st century.

John Collis
London, December 1997